SECRET SCIENCE OF BLACK MALE & FEMALE SEX

TC Carrier

About the Cover

I designed the cover myself which was inspired by a vision I had during sexual intercourse. It represents the esoteric or sacred, the science of sex. The ancient and occult symbol for the feminine principle is the upside-down triangle always descending from the heavens. The right-side-up triangle, underneath the feminine principle, always represented coming from the earth; it is the occult symbol for the masculine principle. The point where the two triangles meet signifies the Sun with six sun rays. This six-pointed Sun represents the electro-magnetic "Gateway" that is open when the feminine and masculine principles of Inner G join together as one. The "Gateway" brings the spiritual realm into the physical dimension. The deep purple color in the background of the cover symbolizes higher consciousness of the Crown Chakra and the metallic gold color of the triangles represents the "spark" of divine manifestation.

The diagram on the following page is very similar to my cover design. I did not come across this illustration until after I came up with the design for my cover. It is basically a formula for the possibility of time travel based on the theory of relativity. This concept and illustration supports my theory of infinite possibilities and manifestation when one has an orgasm during sexual intercourse under the pretense of higher, spiritual consciousness.

The Minkowski diagram was developed in 1908 by <u>Hermann Minkowski</u> and provides an illustration of the properties of space and time in the <u>special theory of relativity</u>. It allows a quantitative understanding of the corresponding phenomena like <u>time dilation</u> and <u>length contraction</u> without mathematical equations: http://en.wikipedia.org/wiki/Minkowski_diagram-

FIG. 1. Minkowski diagram of the four solutions of the electromagnetic wave equation which are represented by Eq. (1). Here the wave number k is taken to be along the x axis and the emitting source is located at the origin (t=0, x=0):

<u>http://mist.npl.washington.edu/npl/int_rep/tiqm/TI_fig_02.html</u>

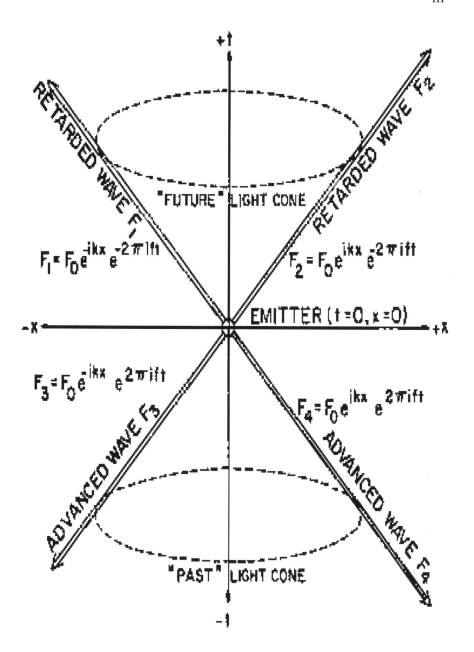

$$F_1 = F_0 e^{-ikx} e^{-2\pi ift}$$

$$F_2 = F_0 e^{ikx} e^{-2\pi ift}$$

$$F_3 = F_0 e^{-ikx} e^{2\pi ift}$$

$$F_4 = F_0 e^{ikx} e^{2\pi ift}$$

EMITTER (t = 0, x = 0)

RETARDED WAVE F1

RETARDED WAVE F2

ADVANCED WAVE F3

ADVANCED WAVE F4

"FUTURE" LIGHT CONE

"PAST" LIGHT CONE

+t

-t

-x

+x

SECRET SCIENCE OF BLACK MALE & FEMALE SEX

Table of Contents

About the Cover   i

Dedication   iv

Acknowledgements   1

Preface   6

Introduction   11

Chapter One: Lose Your Mind to Find the Truth   15

Chapter Two: Return to Your Past in Order to Move Forward.   23

Chapter Three: The Bible: The Blueprint of Universal Law & Higher Consciousness   40

Chapter Four: Melanin: The Khem-Mystery of Sex   64

Chapter Five: Pineal Gland: Was Blind but Now I See   79

Chapter Six: Man vs. Mankind (kind of a man)   96

Chapter Seven: Seen & Unseen Sexual Inner "G."   119

Chapter Eight: Big Sexual Organ Between Your Ears Not your Legs.   176

Chapter Nine: As Above, So Below   198

Chapter Ten: Chakras: Levels of Sexual Consciousness   212

Chapter Eleven: Science of the Heart   230

Chapter Twelve: The Orgasm: The Gateway to Heaven   250

Chapter Thirteen: Black Power: The Sexual Revolution   278

Black Love Topics & Issues   301

Epilogue   335

Notes   340

"Dedicated to the ancient, Afrikan goddess Nekhebet, who sent me here to prepare a place for her and her queendom. In my journey to serve her, I found my destiny." –T.C.

ACKNOWLEDGEMENTS

Our hearts are pounding and racing in unison, intermingling and vibrating at a rate where shared Inner G infuses into one divine song. My heart is pressed against her chest, trying to get as close as possible to my reflection, which yearns to be acknowledged. Similar to a child pressing his hands and face against a toy store window, yearning and dreaming of possessing the toy that he has always wanted, so my heart lies upon hers as I make my intentions known. With all my heart and soul, I hold this as my center from which I make my every move. She locks her feet around the outside of my ankles so that I cannot escape her blissful bond. She opens up her mind, heart, soul and legs to give me full access to the feminine gateway where all life begins. She has turned herself completely inside out in the ritual of divine manifestation. She has courageously exposed to me the depths of her life force. She has shown me the most sacred place that the universe has ever known. And to do this phenomenal feat, takes the courage, strength and trust that only a woman can possess.

The opening to all that is, is now awaiting my entrance. With full awareness of the depths that lie before me, I plunge further into the sacred, with every last drop of my being. My head starts to prepare for the initiation into the gateway of infinite possibilities. My thoughts start to sway to and fro from this dimension to the next, from the seen to the unseen, as our souls dance, play and swirl, above our heads. I get an intense, cold sensation, moving like a wave submerging my body, which must obey its rhythm. It begins at the bottom of my feet and steadily climbs up my ankles, then my inner thighs. She sighs in my ear. It feels like a butterfly has gently landed on my earlobe to tell me its secrets. This is her way of giving me permission to emancipate my masculine spark, whose main purpose is to give life at the expense of its own. As the feeling of inevitably involuntarily possesses my body, I convert my essence into liquid sunshine that flows into the gateway, leaving behind this human shell that imprisoned my soul.

As I swirl inside the dark matter, I am tossed wildly about but find bliss and purpose in the chaos that bombards my new definition of reality. I finally let go and relinquish my ego to a power greater than myself. I succumb to her will completely. I am her servant to do as she wishes. She guides me like a leaf on a rushing river, going downstream. I am helpless in her grasp, so I do not even try to fight or escape. I am defeated, but somehow joyous in my acceptance of being conquered. My journey has a purpose that I cannot comprehend, so I continue the process without any preconceived notions of where I will finally arrive.

Suddenly, I am in a tunnel with a blinding white light at the end. The light warms me and comforts me, in my liquid blanket of ecstasy. As I near, I feel the intrigue and power of a presence that demands my complete allegiance and respect. I am struck by the brilliance and overwhelmed by the entity who I am about to come face to face with. I see a figure on a golden throne on top of a hill, with lush green grass, and the scent of jasmine and honey is in the air. The figure is surrounded by light so I can only see the silhouette, which seems to be thirteen feet tall, in the sitting position. The only thing I can make out is the length and regality of her neck. Suddenly, I am instantly delivered at her feet in a fetal position. I dare not gaze into her eyes as I fear I will perish from the intensity of her light and her beauty. I try to clear my eyes, which have been blinded, by focusing on other objects around the temple. I see blue-greens, purple, teal, indigo, periwinkle and turquoise. I see gold and lapis lazuli that sparkle like a reflection off a full moon.

Without warning, she grabs me by one hand and throws me up in the air like a rag doll. I am no longer the 6 foot, 2 inches tall and 215 lb. man I used to be in the physical realm. I have somehow transformed into a being that is irrelevant in the presence of a goddess. Maybe I am of the same stature, but bearing witness to my insignificance in the unseen realm. I am petrified and honored all at the same time. She finally puts me down, after playing with me for what seems like an eternity. I fully understand how weak I really am and how powerful she is. I am humbled in my humiliation, but for some reason I feel empowered. She tells me that she has sent me to the physical dimension to pave the way for her return. She informs me that I have served her for thousands of years and have never failed her. She tells me that although I am not worthy to sit with her on her throne, I have earned her favor in my courage and commitment to serve her in eternity. Because of this, I shall always be favored.

She explains that she represents the feminine principle of higher consciousness found in the activation of one's Melanin produced by the "First Eye" or Pineal gland. She reveals to me that there has been a 130,000-year war to suppress her power. She further explains that when the world was dominated and embraced by her spirit and consciousness, the Black man was able to achieve the greatest feats that man has ever accomplished in the history of the world. She told me that the wonders and mysteries of the world can only be deciphered when one internalizes her vibration. Until then, these great wonders will never be fully known or understood. It was through her worship that Black people ruled the world and walked hand-in-hand as kings and queens. She states that the rise of the Caucasian race, coming out of the caves of Europe, signified her downfall. These recessive people could not decipher or embrace her higher consciousness because of their lack of Melanin, which was needed to open the door to her temple in the spiritual realm. Because they could not communicate with her, they understood that the only way they could compete with the Afrikan gods and goddesses was to change the playing field in their favor. That meant that these people must get the masses to embrace her opposite consciousness, which was the inferior, masculine principle. The world is now dominated by this white man and he has infected the globe by his lower level consciousness, otherwise known as the masculine principle. Now the world believes that strength and power lies in the person giving the punch and not in the ability of the one who can withstand it.

She tells me that my purpose is to internalize her consciousness and walk the path of the feminine principle. She says, "If you walk the path with me, they will emulate the principle." She states that the Black woman holds the key to her power, for all Black women reflect her Inner G and spirit. But through sexism, slavery and the domination of the masculine principle, the Black woman has been duped into embracing her masculine principle as a means to defining herself, her purpose and her environment. It is my purpose to prepare a place for the coming of the Afrikan goddess, Nekhebet, which is the epiphany for the resurrection of the Black man and woman!

She further states that when she decides to return to the physical dimension, she will lose all memory of who she is in the unseen or spiritual world. She tells me that it will be up to me to remind her. She tells me that it is not my mission to force her to accept her true identity. She says, "I am sending you to prepare a place for my queendom in the physical realm." It will be her duty to find her way back. All she wants me to do is have the place ready for her return. If she so happens to get sidetracked or forgets who she is, she will send me back yet again in another life, until she truly recognizes the goddess she is. She sends me because I won't let her fail. All she has to do is look in my eyes and she will remember her purpose. She tells me that she will place her truth in my eyes for safekeeping. I will hold the key to remembrance, just as the reflection of the Sun on still waters radiates back into the skies. This energy immediately reflects off of the surface waters, but always penetrates further into the depths of the water's soul, unlocking the life force of creation that's not readily seen.

She says it is in the interests of both of us that I succeed in my mission. She informs me that she is tired of reincarnating because she never recognized herself as a goddess. She tells me that if she has to come back, then I will have to come back as well. She tells me, "Do not fail me, for my patience is growing weak." I asked her how I would know it is her. She tells me, "I have been called many names on many dimensions throughout eternity. You will call me Nekhebet. You will see me when you make yourself blind. You will feel me when you are alone. And I will speak to you when you can no longer hear." I responded by saying that I didn't understand. So she further states to me, "Look in my eyes and it will be revealed, for the eyes possess the throne where I reside."

Instantaneously, I am dismissed. She pushes me off to return to the physical dimension. I try to fight the concept of returning to the physical world. I want to stay here with her, but I dare not go against her commands. So I wallow in the "in between" space of the seen and unseen worlds. I moan but cannot hear my own pleas. I travel on the edges of both worlds like a high-wire performer at the circus, walking ten thousand feet above the ground. I feel pity for myself. Not because of my mission, but because I must return to my human shell in the material world. I fight. I kick. I scream. It is time. It is inevitable. I dejectedly accept my fate. I finally succumb and return to this world with all my energy spent. I find my limp body on top of the woman, who opened her gateway, so that my destiny can be revealed. For this, I am eternally grateful.

Preface

I have fond memories in my childhood of a 1,000-piece puzzle sprawled out on my grandmother's kitchen table. It seems like she was always working on a puzzle throughout my entire childhood. I do not believe I ever ate a meal at her dining room table. In fact, I didn't even know dining room tables were for meals; I just assumed they were made for puzzles. We would have to eat our meals on the coffee table in the living room until she completed her prized puzzle, sprawled out in all its glory on the dining room table. Later, it was revealed to me that she was actually showing me the one lesson I would need to internalize in order to reach fulfillment in my life's journey. My grandmother's procedure for solving the puzzle gave me the blueprint for reaching my life's purpose and destiny. She would start the puzzle by finding the corners and edges of the puzzle pieces, first to create the border or template from which to fill in the remaining pieces. In life, one must come up with a basic foundation, philosophy or worldview from which to base their reality on how they interpret themselves and the environment around them. One must innately build the parameters and framework in their minds from which to create a paradigm in a three-dimensional form. This produces a four-sided cube that one interprets as their reality of space and time.

My grandmother would then meticulously categorize and separate the remaining puzzle pieces according to their size, shape and color. In life, one must also compare and contrast people, places, concepts and things in order to further decipher and define their meanings and purpose in relation to one another. We constantly and instinctively define our surroundings and prioritize what people, places, concepts and things we want to invest our time and Inner G. This is the basis for coming up with our priorities in life and what we deem as important. The things we feel are important to us we keep close and spend the most time on, whereas the things that are least important to us we keep farther away.

Next, my grandmother, through trial and error, would try to fit the pieces of the puzzle in their proper places. More times than not, she would have to try many times, through trial and error to fit the piece into its proper place. She found joy in not only finding the right spot on the very first time, on those rare occasions, but also in the task of her countless trials and errors for the majority of the other pieces. The more difficult it was, the more rewarding the experience when she eventually found the right spot. This taught me that life was a journey to be experienced and appreciated, and not a destination. One may never complete their life's puzzle. In fact, I now know that one is not supposed to. My grandmother taught me to focus on life's experiences and how to embrace those times, whether they bring me joy or pain. She taught me to work hard and never give up my dreams and goals. The harder I work and the more difficult the task of accomplishing my goals, the greater my reward will be when they were accomplished. I have learned to fall in love with the struggle that comes with achieving my dreams, as much as the accomplishment of attaining them.

When my grandmother was almost finished completing the puzzle, it would inevitably seem like there were always pieces that were missing. Sometimes, she would go for days without finding the missing pieces. Just when she wanted to give up completing the puzzle and clear off the dining room table, the missing pieces would miraculously appear in places around the house that they had no business being in. She would find them under the couch or on top of a cupboard, of all places. Somehow, no matter where they were hiding, she would always find some way to claim them back. I now know to never question incidents and experiences that happen in my life. It is in those experiences and those incidences that I am not comfortable in or familiar with that hold a missing piece of my life puzzle. For example, if I am brought to my knees through hardship, unfortunate circumstances or pain, I realize that there is a piece of my puzzle in that low place that I would never have found unless I was forced on my knees or any other "compromising" position. On the other hand, when I reach that "high" place in my life where everything is going right, I must be humble. I must not define myself by the place I find myself in, but instead, I must look on the "top shelf "for the missing piece to my life puzzle. I must embrace both high and low places in my life and search for the missing pieces I may find in either circumstance, for both pieces are equally valuable to completing my life's puzzle.

This book is about one man's journey to collect all the "pieces" to the one puzzle of his life. I have come to realize that my personal journey in life is to seek truth by achieving a higher consciousness. Through my own unique experiences of religion, philosophy, spirituality, physics, mathematics, art, astrology & astronomy, biology, nutrition, chemistry, music, language, culture, etc… I realized that they all contain pieces of the one source of truth. My life's journey was to collect as many pieces as I could and complete my own puzzle. I have discovered that this one source we call "truth" is constantly changing and evolving. "Truth" has different meanings for different individuals, according to their own initiation into consciousness. Consciousness can be defined as that which one pays closest attention to and invests their time and energy into fully internalizing and understanding their reality. Truth has many levels and they all are sufficient unto themselves. My purpose is to know 360 degrees of truth. When one discovers 360 degrees of truth, one has come "full circle." That person will wind up back where they began, but they will understand, overstand, backwards and forwards, the unveiling of the one source of truth. This is my destiny. This is why man should never become an expert too soon on any subject, because truth cannot be separated or isolated. Truth cannot be put in a box and contained. Truth must be expressed in its natural state to be fully known. In order for truth to be truth, it must always be in motion, or truth will wither away and resurrect itself into another form. Truth is in constant motion. Everything in the Universe is in motion. According to the laws of the Universe, if one is not "moving" they are considered dead or in the process of dying. So when man thinks that he knows truth and rests on his knowledge of what he knows in the present, then man retards his growth in manifesting the 360 degrees that truth holds. In essence, man limits himself by defining his truth through the eyes of his ego, which has tricked him into believing that he has "arrived" at the "one" truth. Understanding truth is a constant journey of self-discovery; it is not a destination. This is why I am here at this particular place in this particular time. I am here to chase "truth" with a passion and humble dedication, but always knowing that my constant unveiling of "truth" will reveal how little I actually know and understand.

I have discovered that one must show humility and humble themselves for truth to open its doors. Otherwise, one cannot enter. This is the threshold that keeps people from knowing truth. We get in our own way by taking ourselves too seriously, thus blocking the entrance. To know truth, one must kill the ego!   The character of Jesus says in the Bible, "Suffer the little children to come unto me." Jesus, symbolizing the concept of truth, can only be attained or understood if we become childlike in our quest for wisdom, understanding, enlightenment and knowledge. A child has no preconceived notions as to what is right, wrong, good or bad, possible or impossible. A child is conditioned later on in life to accept these attributes as reality. A child believes that he can become anything he sets his mind on. A child has no concept of failure or a reality that is meant to hold him hostage and enslave him with responsibilities called bills, jobs, religion and rent. A child is free of the chains that society and his environment forces upon him as he matures. A child has not fed his ego to the point where he defines himself through his ego and not his true self. A child's strength is in his innocence and not his sophistication. So I have learned to approach each day seeking truth as if the bell just rang in our kindergarten class and it's time for recess. So don't be afraid to yell out at the top of your lungs while running full speed down the hallway, with your arms and legs flailing wildly about. Start each day of your journey called life, as if the bell for kindergarten recess just rang!

This book is a glimpse of my playground. It is my own personal sandbox. I invite all of you to come and play with me as I convert each granule of sand into molecules and rearrange them in order to create my own reality. Do not be fearful or close-minded in terms of the concepts I present to you. Once your brain is close-minded and locked into a particular belief, this initiates the process that we call aging, which leads to death. Be like a child and open your mind and play with concepts and ideologies in your head. Remember, the best way to learn and decipher information is to embrace it, with the innocence of a child with your mind and eyes ready to receive infinite definitions of reality. A child's strength lies in their imagination. Therein lays infinite possibilities. Let's explore the meaning of life and our place in this vast universe that the Creator has allowed us to have recess in. The universe is our playground. Find strength and solace not in your cunningness, logic and sophistication, but in your innocence and naiveté. My recess yearns for me to play kickball with the planets while I pluck the stars from the heavens and store them in my back pocket in my marble pouch. Join me in my lifetime adventure, otherwise known as, "The Secret Science behind Black Male & Female Sex." I invite you to take my hand and come play with me. Tag! You're it!

Introduction

In today's society, sex has so many lower level connotations when one thinks of the concept. When we come up with words to describe the concept of sex, they are usually laden with derogatory inclinations. Terms such as: breaking her off, hitting it, doing the nasty, bumping uglies, doing the wild thang, pounding it, blowing her back out, killing it, taming it, serving it, smacking it, tearing it up, putting it down, flipping it, wearing it out, knocking the lining out of it, digging her out, and many others. Sex has always been something we do in the dark, behind closed doors, under the covers and with the doors securely locked. We can't be too loud for the neighbors to hear; the children have to be asleep; we have to creep in the middle of the night, on the weekends with the shades pulled down. Sex cannot be spoken of, thought of, or expressed in public or among children or the elderly. Sex is dirty. Sex is a sin. Sex is forbidden. Sex is degrading. Sex is taboo. Sex is a vice. Sex is nasty. Sex has its own film rating. Sex can only be used for procreation. Sex can only be partaken amongst your husband or wife.

People have sex for many different reasons. They include: love, lust, anger, fear, hate, revenge, manipulation, comfort, satisfaction, control, self-esteem, grudge, low self-esteem, financial gain, financial loss, fun, reproduction, power, seduction, exercise, oppression, freedom, healing, inflicting, brainwashing, consoling, mourning, as an escape and out of curiosity. Sex is the number one manipulator as well as the number one liberator for people. It is addictive. It is therapeutic. Sex can destroy life as well as create it. Sex can be used to make you rich as well as keep you in the poor house. Sex has a million different definitions to a million different individuals. All concepts are correct according to the conscience of the individual interpreting the act of sex.

I had planned to write several books on many different topics, but that all changed with one sexual encounter that enlightened my consciousness. As I alluded to in the Acknowledgment section of the book, while I was engaged in the act of sexual intercourse, I was transported to another realm located in the space between time and space by a Black goddess named Nekhebet. This porthole opened right at the inevitable moment before my ejaculation. Although this moment is only a fraction of a second long, time seemed to stand still as I was presented to this Black goddess sitting on her throne in her temple on the other side of this porthole. She enlightened me to a dimension which she ruled and gave me a blueprint from which to interpret and define the physical dimension from which I just came from. Once I internalized the lessons and concepts that she revealed to me, deciphering and understanding the mysteries of my life seemed to be simplified and exposed. She showed me that the more I researched individual subjects that seem to stand on their own, the more I realized they all had one thing in common.

The main foundation or blueprint that each one of these subject matters shared was the basic principle or the science of sex that Nekhebet revealed to me. I did not start my journey to write about sex, as I am far from an expert on this subject, but the more I researched other subjects, the more Nekhebet led me to research and explore the concept of sex. Nekhebet defined sex as the foundation or blueprint of life itself. The very act of sex is the proof that one is alive. Nekhebet explained to me that sex is a sacred, scientific formula that keeps the universe and everything in it in a delicate and balanced state of harmony. Sex is literally what keeps the atoms, molecules, elements, plants, humans, the Earth and the universe moving in synchrony. She defined sex as the engagement and synergy of the feminine and masculine Inner "G" that permeates all life. We will fully understand and overstand in this book, that the feminine principle is the act of "receiving"

Inner G and the masculine principle is the act of "giving out" Inner G. So life as we know it, from the smallest sub-atomic particle to the largest universe, has to be engaged in sex to exist! The very act of breathing is partaking in sex. Inhaling of air is the feminine principle of "receiving" Inner G. Exhaling that same air is the masculine principle of "giving" out Inner G. The digestive system practices sex. The act of consuming food is a feminine principle of "receiving" Inner G and the act of getting rid of waste is the masculine principle of "giving" out Inner G. The circulatory system practices sex. Blood flows to the heart to "receive" oxygen; this is feminine Inner G. Blood leaving the heart to "give" the body that oxygen is masculine Inner G. The nervous system practices sex. Neurons "receive" information from the body and relay them to the brain so that it can give the appropriate response, so they are engaged in the feminine principle of Inner G. The brain "giving" out directions and information back through the neurons to the body is engaged in the masculine principle of Inner G. Economics is also engaged in sex. The consumer buying the goods is practicing the feminine principle of "receiving", whereas the seller who produces and sells the goods is practicing the masculine principle of "giving" out Inner G. The same holds true for politics (voters/masculine and candidates/feminine); judicial system (defendant/feminine vs. the prosecution/masculine); sports (offense/masculine vs. defense/feminine); education (teacher/masculine vs. student/feminine); healthcare (doctor/masculine vs. patient/feminine) and all other facets of life that you can think of.

If one was to dissect everything that one does to be considered a living, breathing entity, they would be enlightened that life is sex and sex is life! Now, what would happen if one mastered the sacred and scientific relationship between masculine and feminine Inner G? One would be able to communicate with nature at a molecular level through the concept of the sexual principles of Inner G. What if one was able to manipulate nature by mastering its universal laws that everything in existence must abide by and adhere to? One could perceivably unlock the mysteries to life as we know it. This is what Nekhebet has revealed to me. This is what we are about to explore. This is the concept where dreams and miracles are manifested. If one could somehow harness the underlying power that is life or the concept of sex, they could manifest their thoughts and ideas into the material world and create their own reality. One would be able to see God face-to-face and recognize the divinity in all things. This is the science that has been kept from us so that the "powers that be" can manipulate and control the masses, and in particular, Black people around the world. Sex is where life begins and ends. Let this book be the first step in taking that journey towards self-fulfillment and self-actualization. Take the sacred and scientific journey with me and my divine guide, Nekhebet, who I vowed to serve in this dimension, as we unlock the secrets behind Black male and female sex!

Chapter One:
Lose Your Mind to Find the Truth

"In order to serve me properly, you must lose the mind you were given in the physical dimension and embrace the unseen. Understand that your physical world is the dream and my unseen world is your reality." —*Nekhebet*

In this day and age, people are always looking for a quick solution to their problems. We, as a society, want the rewards of change, but are too cowardly to look within ourselves subjectively, in order for true change to occur. In other words, we crave the concept of manifesting our goals and dreams, but to dig too deeply within our own fragile psyche is too painful a price to pay for the change or results we yearn for. Society has taught us that we can stay in our comfort zones and never challenge our deepest, strongest fears and weaknesses, and still have the ability to overcome our shortcomings. We have been brainwashed into believing that we can take a simple pill and never change our behavior and we will be cured of our illnesses. We have been taught that we can lose weight with a simple diet or even surgery, without changing our attitude, our lifestyle, discipline and nutritional habits. For some reason, we refuse to acknowledge the universal law that says real reward can only happen after great sacrifice.

"The definition of insanity is doing the same thing over and over and expecting a different result." — *Albert Einstein*

We have become comfortable with dying a thousand times every day. We succumb to our lowest expectations and fears, and we have such low self-esteem that we internalize our shortcomings as permanent fixtures in our DNA. We accept defeat without even trying to fight the good fight. We have learned that ignorance is bliss. If all behavior is learned, we have become scholars in the school of cowardice and fear. From the one-year-old baby to the ninety-year-old great-grandparent, we have voluntarily given up our personal definition and understanding of reality and adopted the reality of the same system that has never had our best interests as its goal. Do you wonder why you can't stay on your diet? Do you wonder why your children are rebelling? Do you wonder why you can never get ahead of paying your bills? Do you wonder why you can't seem to save money? Do you wonder why you vote for different politicians of different political parties but nothing ever changes? Do you wonder why you can't seem to stay physically fit? Do you wonder why your job does not fulfill you, but you stay in it? Do you wonder why your church is not satisfying your spirituality? Do you wonder why there are not enough hours in the day to do "you"? Do you wonder why your relationships are not satisfying? The system, or your indoctrinated thought process, was purposely designed and maintained to produce these above results! So what do we do to get better? We run back to the same system that inhibits our quality of life as human beings with inalienable rights and ask them to help fix us despite ourselves. We try to tweak the system. We try to justify and rationalize our participation in the system by accepting its flaws as a normal occurrence of life. In other words, because we have such low self-esteem and no concept of what it means to be free, we put up with the hurt, pain, disappointment, lack of fulfillment, strife, stress and anguish. This is not why we chose to be physical beings in this particular place and time. We all had a life purpose in the spiritual realm, before we agreed to participate in this physical body. Somewhere, along the way, somebody hijacked that purpose and replaced it with their own agenda.

"Cowards die many times before their death; the valiant never taste death but once." — *William Shakespeare's Julius Caesar.*

The advertisement industry understands that sex sells and we consume it with a passion. We believe that if I use this deodorant, people will find me more attractive. If I drive this car or wear a certain garment, people will fall in love with me. If I smoke this cigarette or drink this liquor, people will see me as a success. So on and so on. We are the people who think we are free, but in actuality, we are enslaved to a system of thought that keeps us in perpetual bondage. This is the worst type of slavery. The slave who really believes he is free. We are the slave who is comfortable in his oppression because he doesn't want to pay the price for his freedom. We have become too frightened to want to experience the depths of what true freedom represents, so we wallow in our own self-pity and continue to live and believe in a lie.

"Whoever controls the image and information of the past will determine what and how future generations will think; and, whoever controls the information and images of the present, will also determine how these same people will view the past." — *George Orwell, 1984.*

So you may ask yourself, "What does this have to do with Black male & female sex?" Everything. It is time to break free from the solutions that your slave master gave you to address your own problems that he created for you in the first place! When will we learn that the system thrives because of our pain, suffering, agony, hopelessness and lower level behavior, which are produced from our community? Do you actually think the system would give us anything beneficial to reach our higher selves and be free? That would undermine the whole agenda and why the system was set up in the first place. So what do they give us? "Half-truths." These "half-truth" capsules that we swallow contain enough truth to resonate in our hearts and minds, but the toxins that are attached to it promote our demise and perpetual destruction. It is like ingesting a chocolate-covered cyanide pill. It may look and taste good going down, but its purpose is to kill you or keep you in a weak and vulnerable state. This is the system or mindset that is forced upon us and we participate in it willingly every day. Through our conspiracy of silence, we validate the destruction of our community on a daily basis.

"Fear is expressed on two levels. You are either afraid to die or afraid to live. But to truly live, your initiation is death." — Nekhebet

To fix the Black male and female relationship problem, one must look outside the system that created the problem in the first place. This is where I hope to guide you. This is where the solution lies. Please be strong in your journey to free yourself and your mate through this book. Be humble and courageous. Do not be afraid to break through old paradigms of thought and behavior. Please leave your heart open and practice humility, for this is the only way to get to the root of our problems and reach a final solution. I am going to literally turn your world right side up because the system has turned the world upside down. From this vantage point, the picture will be clearer and your solutions will be attainable. Don't be afraid to define up as down and down is now up. I promise you, if you open your mind to a new way of looking at things, based on this ancient, Afrikan science from our ancestors, then the solution will be that much closer to your grasp. You will come to realize that the solution always existed within you, while we were too busy looking outside of yourselves for the answers.

Let us break down the word "Conscience":

Conscience:

1. A moral sense of right and wrong especially as felt by a person and affecting behavior.

2. An inner feeling as to the goodness or otherwise of a person's behavior.

This is how the system manipulates us into embracing our lower selves and feeds our ego which interprets our reality in relation to defining ourselves and our environment. The system has created an environment that is similar to an aquarium which houses a fish. We are subjected to its influences while we are under the illusion of having freewill. If one can manipulate another person's conscience, then they can control their behavior. The person who controls the subject's definition of what is right and wrong controls their behavior and their reaction to the environment that they expose them to. This is how you make a slave without the person knowing that he is being oppressed and manipulated.

Let's break down the word "Conscience" into the two root words of "Con" and "Science":

Con:

1. To swindle; deceive

2. A reason against.

3. A convict.

4. With; together, jointly, altogether.

Science

1. A branch of knowledge or study dealing with a body of facts or truths systematically arranged and showing the operation of general laws: the mathematical sciences.

2. Systematic knowledge of the physical or material world gained through observation and experimentation.

When we take these two individual words into consideration, we get an entirely different definition:

Con-Science: To swindle or to deceive a person's understanding of a systematic knowledge and science showing the operation of general laws.

We have not been taught the truth about ourselves and the world we live in. We have been deceived into participating in a system that enslaves us so that it can take advantage of us without us even knowing it.

Oprah cannot help you. Dr. Phil has his own agenda. Dr. Oz will give you half-truths. Donald Trump won't make you rich and Kramer does not have your best financial interests in mind. Tyra Banks, The View, The Fitness Club, Judge Mathis or Barack Obama cannot make you a better person and set you free. In fact, these institutions thrive on you being simple, weak-minded, impotent, financially insecure, egotistical, overweight, low self-esteemed and gullible, to name a few. Their industries are designed not to help you out of your present condition, but to make more people like you! You will find acceptance in your condition if you see others in the same boat as you. Anything of value that seems to help you will always be short-lived. It was designed that way to keep you in an eternal state of dependency. Don't get me wrong, there are people who benefit as "individuals" from the advice or product they get, but these people are exceptions to the rule, not the norm. For instance, one person may lose 100 lbs. on Jenny Craig, but they never show the millions who didn't lose anything or actually gained weight. The system will prop up the "exception to the rule" as its spokesperson and tell you, the norm, that this can be you. So the end result is you getting frustrated because you internalize your failure to lose weight as something you did wrong. So you fall further into depression which causes you to gain even more weight. You will eventually get your will power back and start a "new and improved" diet that will give you the same results. We have become the horse drawing the cart with the carrot dangling in front of us, which represents the system of empty promises that is the American Dream. The system uses our energy and ignorance to push their agenda, while we chase the carrot that we can never attain.

1 Hear the word of the LORD, you children of Israel: for the LORD has a controversy with the inhabitants of the land, because there is no truth, nor mercy, nor knowledge of God in the land6 My people are destroyed for lack of knowledge: because you have rejected knowledge, I will also reject you, that you shall be no priest to me: seeing you have forgotten the law of your God, I will also forget your children. — HOSEA 4:1 & 6 (King James Version)

The same can be said with our relationships. In this book, we will cross the boundaries and limits of sex, race, religion, politics, consciousness, freedom, education, spirituality and philosophy. Please be patient in your understanding and comprehension of this book. Please do not shut down or write off a concept just because you are not comfortable with it or it goes against your indoctrination of reality. Let truth take time to resonate in your heart before you dismiss it. Do not become an expert on any subject too soon! This mindset limits your ability to transcend into higher consciousness.

"You must learn to embrace all lessons in life, whether they cause you joy or pain, because you will be graded on how well you take the test, not the place you wind up in." — Nekhebet

We cannot talk about sex and relationships as a single subject. We must incorporate all facets of life as one structural archetype, if we want to build a strong foundation from which to stand on. We will get to the "good part" soon enough. But our mindset should be that there is only one "whole part" that is good. Don't be afraid to, not just cross these barriers, but smash through them as if your life depended on it! I promise that if you do, you will be that much closer to finding the relationship and life you have always dreamed about. I am honored to be your guide, like Harriet Tubman going to the Promised Land to free the slaves. When asked how this feeble-looking woman ever freed 1,000 slaves, she responded, "I could have freed 1,000 more, if they only knew they were slaves." The first step to breaking the thought process, which leads to behavior, is admitting that we are not in our right minds. Once we are able to "kill the ego," we can begin to free ourselves from it. Let us all admit that we have a problem and that we all need help. It is the first step on the road to recovery.

We are all searching for the solutions to our collective problems. Quest comes from the word question. That is where our journey begins. We must first pose the right questions, the answers to which will free us. If we never question our reality, we will never be able to change it. Thank you for trusting me. I am honored and humbled to be your guide on your quest for answers that will ultimately lead to your freedom.

Chapter Two:
Return to Your Past, in Order to Move Forward

"You have become the Lion that has been captured by the mouse. In order to break your chains, you must embrace the characteristics that make you a Lion and not apologize, shun or despise them." — Nekhebet

One thing that has been kept from people of Afrikan descent, throughout the Diaspora, is the contribution that our ancestors have made in the upliftment of humanity. Afrika is the indisputable cradle of civilization! Afrika is where the first man and woman were located to start humanity. Thus, we are the first human beings to define male and female and the roles we play together in regards to how we relate to one another. The Black man and woman are the standard of humanity, period! We are the original concept of man and woman and the standard for divine union and how we relate to one another. This is your legacy. You are the Creator's original recipe. Afrika is where the first civilization was created for the world to emulate. Afrikans were the original teachers of the world. We taught the world the concepts of culture, spirituality, philosophy, mathematics, language, nutrition, history, art, sciences, music, biology, chemistry and any other subjects you can think of. There is no better place to observe humankind's epitome of the aforementioned sciences than in ancient Kemet, which is located in the modern day country known as Egypt. Europeans have continuously, throughout history, tried to take Kemet, present day Egypt, out of Afrika. Kemet means "The Black land." Egyptologists have debated that this description is related to the land being fertile and not the complexion of the people. Many of our scholars have refuted their attempts to take Afrikans out of the greatest civilization in the history of man. We will further delve into this subject later on in the book. But the last time I checked, Egypt was, is and always will be in Afrika, no matter who occupies it at the present moment!

"What a subject for meditation, just to think that the race of Black men today our slaves and the object of our scorn, is the very race to which we owe our arts, science and even the use of our speech." — Anthropologist Count Constainde Volney (1727-1820)

The European conqueror, Napoleon Bonaparte, once said, "History is a set of lies agreed upon." For over 500 years, Europeans have been subjecting their will and oppression on the darker peoples of the world. Because of this, they have controlled the history books. There is an Afrikan proverb that says, "In the battle between the lion and the gazelle, history will always be told by the lion's point of view." In other words, throughout history, we only hear the winner's version of what took place in history. History from the conquered or the defeated nation never gets told. *"History is going to be kind to us because I'm going to rewrite it."- Winston Churchill.* This is the European's mentality. This is how he stays in power. He takes credit for all the great accomplishments of the Black man, while at the same time, convinces us that we are inferior to him. It is up to us to uncover the truth if we ever want to reclaim our illustrious history that has been usurped from us. It is in this truth that the answers to our freedom lie.

Every foundation or concept needs a starting point. Kemet, the foundation of Afrikan ideology or spirituality, will be our base. I will be referring back to Kemet throughout the entire book because this civilization had us operating at the highest point in the history of the world. It is only logical to try to go back and comprehend and internalize their philosophies and understanding of the universe, so as to recapture the brilliance and divine nature of our Black ancestors.

One will find out that many of modern society's concepts and behaviors are directly related to our Kemetic ancestors and culture. The concepts of our school system, although our school system falls pathetically short of our ancestors' vision of education, it still retains their levels or initiation titles otherwise known as grades. Our school system can be divided under the following levels or schools: Elementary School, Middle School, High School & University or College. This system was in place thousands of years before there was even the mention of the name "Christ", just to give you an understanding of how ancient our Afrikan philosophy goes back. In Kemet, to be considered a scholar or master, one went to school until the age of 40 years old. This is why today, when someone reaches forty years of age, we say that they are "Over the hill." But instead of having a derogatory meaning, as it does today, in ancient Kemet, they viewed it as an accomplishment and a badge of honor. Now that a mature, wise man or woman was "over the hill," their life lessons and hardships were easy to master because they had the knowledge to deal with any adversity that life threw at them. So now, they view every life lesson as a "downhill" journey. Thus, their education was viewed as the "hill" that they needed to climb, but once it was attained, life was not a mystery anymore. One's vantage point on "top of the hill" allowed the person to see life from a different perspective. One's consciousness was now elevated to a point where one saw life from all angles, so life was now mastered. Life was no longer a mystery. The secrets of the Universe were unlocked and mastered at the discretion of the master teacher. This process was completed when he reached the age of forty years.

Unlike today, their school system was based on obtaining and acquiring 360 degrees of knowledge. A student went to school for forty years to become a master. Today, we go to school for about twenty-one years to receive one degree. Another two years after that and one receives another

Master's degree. Another two to four years and one receives another degree called a PhD. This process accounts for three degrees by the time one reaches thirty years of age. If one joins a secret society like Freemasonry, one can achieve another 32 or 33 degrees. This is still just a few degrees above freezing. Also, this knowledge is not accessible to the masses, but only a select few. In any case, we are still missing between 327 to 357 degrees of knowledge. This should let us know that true education has been hidden from the masses in order for a select few to manipulate and control the world's population. Remember that in ancient Kemet, man had reached his highest level in medicine, sciences, the arts, philosophy, government, engineering, law and many others. In fact, today's scholars still have not figured out how and why this ancient Afrikan civilization built the pyramids!

So what and how did these ancient Black people study to achieve the greatest civilization on the face of the Earth and how does it pertain to sex? Let us break it down: the first six grades in our school system, we call Elementary. This name comes directly from this ancient Afrikan civilization. The root word in "Elementary" is, of course, "Element". So in their school system, for the first six years or grades, the student mastered and learned all the elements and how they related to each other on Earth and in the Universe.

Six is the number of the beast or man at his lowest level, according to Biblical numerology, which we will address in greater detail later in the book. Being spiritual beings, we agreed to come down to have a physical experience. The physical dimension is the lowest existence of the spirit because it is trapped in a physical body that must adhere to the physics and laws of the physical realm. The spirit is imprisoned in the physical realm. Thus, we fell from the spiritual world to the denser physical world to participate in this dimension. So it is by no coincidence that we studied the properties of the physical world for six years in Elementary school. Our ancestors realized that everything in the Universe was subject to the same laws, whether it was in the form of a solid, liquid or gas. From the biggest

Sun in the galaxy, to the smallest sub-atomic particle, the same universal laws prevail. Understand that people knew about protons, electrons and neutrons thousands of years before the invention of the microscope! Once this knowledge of the elements was mastered, one could conceivably communicate with the rock, the plant, the star and even water. One just had to decipher what frequency or channel that particular object vibrated on. They did this by knowing how matter expressed itself. If you know how something expresses itself, you can conceivably communicate with that said entity.

"In their complex and many of the complexions and in physical peculiarities the Egyptian were an African race." — James C. Prichard's The Natural History of Man

Dr. Gabriel Oyibo suggests that there is only one element on Earth. That element is Hydrogen. Dr. Oyibo's theory is that all other elements are just different expressions of the one element called Hydrogen. Go through your junior high Elemental Chart and see for yourself. Hydrogen is made up of one electron and one proton. You can change Hydrogen into another element by simply adding more Electrons, Protons or Neutrons. For example, the next element on the Periodic Table is Helium. To make Helium, you need 2 Electrons, 2 Protons and 2 Neutrons. So the basic building block is Hydrogen. It just expresses different characteristics when you add Protons, Electrons and Neutrons to its structure. We call those unique expressions or personalities of Hydrogen elements, such as Helium, Carbon, Oxygen and any other element on the Periodic Table.

After the student learns how to communicate with the elements in "Elementary" school, the student gets promoted to "Middle School." The word "Middle" is in reference to what's between the Earth and the heavens. The answer is Man. This coincides with the same time our bodies are going through puberty. We attend middle school between the ages of 12 to 15 years old. This seems like the perfect time to understand and master the biology of man. Man is a composite of all the elements. In order to have knowledge of self, you must master the inner workings of the elements that make up man and his surroundings. The basic elements are Fire, Air, Water and Earth. Man needs fire or electricity in order for the spirit to function inside the body. That is why they shock the heart with a defibrillator to revive the patient from death. This act brings the spirit back inside the body. Air — man uses the air through his lungs to separate the oxygen he needs to feed his body through the bloodstream. Without oxygen, the body starves or suffocates. Water — we are made up of over 80% water. Water is the keeper and surveyor of life. We can survive without food, but take away water and we will perish in a matter of days. Earth — we are made up of the same composition as the earth. We will soon return to earth when we leave our physical bodies and make our transition to the spiritual world.

For the next two to three years in middle school, we study and master all the systems that regulate and govern the body.

According to Ali Muhammad, this is why the U.S. government has three branches that regulate its "governing body."

It is based on this ancient Kemetic system of universal law. The three glands that regulate the human body are the Pituitary, Hypothalamus and Pineal Glands. These three glands regulate the human body by functioning in different areas, with the goal of working in a synergistic relationship, to create a perfect balance of the body. So does the three branches of government in the United States of America. The United States government is comprised of the Legislative Branch, the Judicial Branch and the head or Executive Branch of government. These three branches work in conjunction with one another to regulate the one governmental body. This is why the President, who represents the Executive branch or "head" of the government, sits in the "oval office." He represents the brain of the governmental body.

The job of the president is to oversee the other two branches and make sure everything is running smoothly. The president also has the power to make the final decision in important matters relating to the body or nation, just like our brains. The Legislative branch of the government is the part that creates laws to help regulate and maintain the body or nation. It will introduce new laws or amend previous laws for the betterment of the body or nation. The Judicial branch is responsible for the interpretation of the laws in order to have clarity and balance in the body. The Judicial branch is the "law of the land" and there is no higher court that can overrule it. It is no coincidence that there are nine Supreme Court justices. In Biblical numerology, the number nine represents judgment. The number nine (9) is the number of man or beast (six) turned upside down (6). When man is placed in a position outside of his comfort zone, how he responds is a true test of his character. So the number nine equals man turned on his head. He will be judged on how he responds to this uncomfortable position.

It is hard for us to imagine that our ancestors mastered their bodies between the ages of 12 and 15 years. Society today gives excuses for our teenagers' behavior during puberty instead of holding them up to their highest standards of self-control. What better time in our lives to master our carnal urges, wants, desires and needs than the exact time we experience them for the first time? Our ancestors took complete control of their hormones before they had a chance to spiral out of control and lead them to lower levels consciousness and behavior.

"The dignity is so ancient that the insignia of the pharaoh evidently belonged to the time when Egyptians wore nothing but the girdle of the Negro. — Gerald Massey, author of "Egypt, Light of the World." Pg. 251

Once we mastered the body in "Middle School," we graduated to "High School." In high school, we study "higher" consciousness associated with the brain. The body below the neck was considered your "lower self," and the head above the neck was your higher self. This is one of the interpretations as to why the Harmaket, or what is known today as the Sphinx, has the body of an animal and the head of an Afrikan woman. It represents man's ability to transcend to god in human form. This is where we get the phrase, "As a man thinketh." Once man has mastered his "lower self," represented by the body, he can now achieve a higher self or consciousness, which is housed in the brain. This is the reason why all religions fast, go into solitude and practice celibacy in one form or another. Man must master his lower, primal urges, such as hunger, thirst, cravings, addictions and sexual desires. If he masters his lower body, he passes through the threshold to reach a higher consciousness. In other words, one must be able to tell their body what to do and not let their carnal urges control and dictate their life. One must master the body in order to enter the realm of higher consciousness that is found in the brain.

www.elevatedloc.com/.../Sphinx.jpg

This process is the initiation into higher or "god" consciousness. Now that the student operates from above the neck, they can dissect the functions of the brain. The brain is the focus in high school. The word "high" is associated with "higher" consciousness. The student will learn the functions of the right and left hemispheres of the brain. He will master the ego and the reptilian brain located in the brain stem. The student will now have the ability to manifest his thoughts into the material world at will. It is a shame that we only use a small percentage of our brains today. But, of course, this is by design to keep us from achieving and activating our higher selves. If we ever reached our potential, there will be no reason for us to participate in a system that does not have our best interests in mind. In other words, we would not look outside of ourselves for the solutions to our problems. This type of mindset is very dangerous to the system.

Cheikh Anta Diop, historian, anthropologist and physicist, studied the mummies in Egypt. He discovered a process to measure the concentration of Melanin found in the mummies' remains. He concluded that the Melanin content of the people who are referred to as Afrikan or Black today was the same as the mummies in ancient Kemet.

Once they mastered the elements under their feet, and mastered their lower selves (their body) in Middle School, and mastered their higher selves (functions of the brain) in High School, they went on to study the Universe (at the University.) Now we have arrived at our final school. This is the last stop on our 40-year journey of education to becoming masters. There was a saying in ancient Kemet, "As above, so below." These masters of Universal Law discovered that the more they understood and studied the realm above them — i.e. the stars, planets, moon, sun and cosmos — the more they understood themselves. They found that the Universe is nothing but a macrocosm to the microcosm of their existence. They studied the movement of the stars. They studied how the Sun, at certain stages of its movement, affected the seasons and consciousness on Earth. They studied the configuration of the planets and each individual property of the planets, and related it to the functioning of their own universal bodies. They realized their bodies were actually universes in themselves and behaved with the same predictable cycles of the stars and their relationship to one another out in the cosmos. They believed that man could attain "God consciousness" if he or she was willing and able to devote and commit himself and do the work to master the 360 degrees of knowledge. God consciousness could be defined as the "state of knowing." Man could become one with the Universe, and thus communicate and master the laws and principles of nature. God and nature were viewed as the same concept. There was no separation of God, man and nature. This is why the Pharaohs and Queens of Kemet were considered "godlike" or representatives of God in human form. It wasn't so much that they were considered Gods or had big egos. On the contrary, they were seen as reflections or representatives of God consciousness through their commitment to righteousness or the concept of Maat. They were the conceptualization of divinity manifested in the physical form. Our ancestors learned how to master energy, instead of being mastered by it. Now, I want you to see how their relationships reflected their culture. If you and your partner's lifelong ambition were to practice righteousness, one can see how their relationship must have been phenomenal. Everything was considered sacred. There was no separation from God. So let's take heed of these concepts and realize that when we raise ourselves, we raise the environment around us. In doing so, we attract better people to have better quality relationships with. In other words, we set ourselves up to succeed!

The ancient Greek philosopher, Herodotus, visited Egypt in the 5th century BCE. He described the Egyptians as "Black skinned with wooly hair."

The ancient Kemetic concept of MAAT, pronounced (Mah-aught), can simply be described as justice, truth, order, propriety, reciprocity, balance & reverence. If you are not familiar with these terms, then please take the time to learn their meanings. Our ancestors believed in Universal Law, meaning that everything in the Universe, no matter how big or small, is bound to the same rules. If these rules are violated, it creates an imbalance in the Universe. The Universe is always in the process of correcting itself. Put simply, "Whatever goes around comes around." Our ancient Afrikan or Kemetic ancestors internalized this concept in order to achieve the highest civilization that the world has ever known. MAAT was symbolized as a goddess in the hieroglyphs or what our ancestors called the Metu Neter, which means, God's word. Our ancestors believed God and nature meant the same thing. So whenever you hear them referring to nature, understand that they are talking about the one Creator and vice-versa. So whenever one goes against nature, they are actually going against God. This is the main factor that prevents Black people from having healthy relationships and overall health and well-being. The goddess MAAT was symbolized by the one feather in her headband; this is where the Native Americans got their feathered headdress from. This was a symbol that the person wearing the headdress was dedicated to becoming as close to God as possible here on Earth. For the Native American, the more feathers one had, the closer to God that person was. Thus, the chiefs or elders had the most respect, so they wore the most feathers. Also, the feather in MAAT symbolizes the bird. The hawk, in Afrika, flies the highest in the sky. Our ancestors believed the Sun symbolizes God's intelligence or higher consciousness. That's why today, if someone is considered intelligent, then they are labeled bright, enlightened, brilliant, etc... Also, in the comic books, when someone is thinking of a smart idea, they show a light bulb turning on above their head. Since the hawk was the animal closest to the Sun, it symbolized God coming down to Earth. In other words, they believed that man's goal was to become God here on Earth, and the way to achieve that was to practice and dedicate your life to the principles of MAAT. The feather of MAAT also represents the ostrich. The ostrich can turn its head 360 degrees without moving, so it can see all things at all times. Real knowledge or intelligence has 360 degrees that must be accountable. This characteristic also symbolizes God's omnipotence to be everywhere at all times. Also, the ostrich's eye is bigger than its brain. This means that we must place more value on the intuitive perception of things and not rely so much on logic. It is the unseen world we must see or be conscious of and not the seen world. Our reality should be based on the unseen, spiritual world and not the seen, physical dimension. The physical dimension has rules that must be obeyed, while the spiritual world has infinite possibilities from which one can make their own rules.

Our ancestors believed that when a person dies, the feather of a goddess named MAAT is weighed on a scale against your heart. This is where you get the image of justice here in America. Justice is represented by a woman wearing a blindfold holding up a scale. If your heart is lighter than the feather (this is where you get the term "light hearted"), then you can move on in the afterlife or what Christians call Heaven. The term "light hearted" refers to overcoming the ego. When one does not define him or herself through their ego, then one can achieve higher consciousness or become closer to God. When a person does not take "him or herself seriously", then true self is revealed. So the goal in ancient Kemet was to overcome the "Ego" in order to be closer to God. The ego is defined as carrying a "heavy heart". Think about it: it's our egos that get in the way of our growth. The ego has convinced your true self to switch places with you. So your true self is lost or forgotten and hides behind the "Ego" for a false perception of protection. The only true way to overcome the "Ego" is to show humility, self-sacrifice, truth and patience. This is very hard in a system today where we are encouraged to celebrate the ego through materialism, vanity, boldness, selfishness, fear, brashness, false pride, self-serving, kindness for weakness, survival of the fittest and individualistic behavior. The American system encourages and rewards this type of lower level behavior. Just look at our communities today. It is this mindset that is destroying our people.

***The Kemetic goddess Maat. She judges each individual in the afterlife
to see if they will transcend into heaven.***

This reaffirms the practice of MAAT. At the end of the day, our
ancestors recited what is known as the 42 Principles of Maat, which the
Europeans called the 42 Negative Confessions. This is where Christianity
got the concept of the Ten Commandments. All religions throughout the
world have taken our Afrikan concepts of spirituality and adopted them into
their religious doctrines and beliefs. In Christianity, the European believes
that he has fallen from God, and thus is separated from Him. Europeans
believe that God and man are separate beings. So the Ten Commandments
are written in a way where God is looking down at man, wagging His finger
and scolding man not to partake in these activities. So they start out with,
"THOU SHALT NOT....!!!!!" However, our ancestors believe they are the
manifestation of God in the physical realm. It is man's duty to remember
who he or she is. So man must reaffirm his divinity by repeating the 42

Principle Laws of MAAT to remind him or her that he or she is the manifestation of the Creator here on Earth. This was the goal of every man and woman:

1) **I have not committed sin.**
2) **I have not committed robbery with violence.**
3) **I have not stolen.**
4) **I have not slain men or women.**
5) **I have not stolen food.**
6) **I have not swindled offerings.**
7) **I have not stolen from God/Goddess.**
8) **I have not told lies.**
9) **I have not carried away food.**
10) **I have not cursed.**
11) **I have not closed my ears to truth.**
12) **I have not committed adultery.**
13) **I have not made anyone cry.**
14) **I have not felt sorrow without reason.**
15) **I have not assaulted anyone.**
16) **I am not deceitful.**
17) **I have not stolen anyone's land.**
18) **I have not been an eavesdropper.**
19) **I have not falsely accused anyone.**
20) **I have not been angry without reason.**
21) **I have not seduced anyone's wife.**
22) **I have not polluted myself.**
23) **I have not terrorized anyone.**
24) **I have not disobeyed the Law.**
25) **I have not been exclusively angry.**
26) **I have not cursed God/Goddess.**

27) I have not behaved with violence.

28) I have not caused disruption of peace.

29) I have not acted hastily or without thought.

30) I have not overstepped my boundaries of concern.

31) I have not exaggerated my words when speaking.

32) I have not worked evil.

33) I have not used evil thoughts, words or deeds.

34) I have not polluted the water.

35) I have not spoken angrily or arrogantly.

36) I have not cursed anyone in thought, word or deeds.

37) I have not placed myself on a pedestal.

38) I have not stolen what belongs to God/Goddess.

39) I have not stolen from or disrespected the deceased.

40) I have not taken food from a child.

41) I have not acted with insolence.

42) I have not destroyed property belonging to God/Goddess.

These 42 declarations were pronounced by the deceased after the god Anpu took the deceased in the presence of the Goddess Maat and the Divine Judge named Tehuti. If the principles of Maat were respected, then the heart of the deceased would have nothing weighing it down, so it would be lighter than the feather and everlasting life would be given, due to respect of these laws that balance the Universe.

***The weighing of the heart ceremony performed by Maat in the afterlife:
The deceased's heart is on the scale on the left. It is weighed against the
feather of the goddess Maat on the scale on the right. If the deceased's heart
is not "heavier" than the feather or burdened with guilt, shame or ego, then
the individual can move on to experience heaven in the hereafter.***

Our ancestors had a saying, "As above, so below." This means that
everything in nature must abide by the same Universal Laws. There is a
cause and effect to everything in the Universe! No one or thing is above the
law. Christianity refers to this concept in their Lord's Prayer, which says,
"On Earth as it is in Heaven." In Islam, the word "Muslim" means one who
submits to the will of God. This was the goal of our ancestors. They built a
society that was Heaven here on Earth. Can you imagine a country that had
no word or concept for jails or police, because they didn't exist? They did
not need them. Every man, woman, and child was held accountable for their
own behavior. They internalized their imbalance with nature and did the
work to correct it.   If you did not correct your behavior, you could not
communicate with the general population. So in a sense those people

basically ostracized themselves. They could not participate in everyday functions of society because they could not communicate with the people who were operating at a higher frequency or vibration. They had to raise their consciousness or vibration in order to function in the culture that had no room for lower level behavior. This is how far we have fallen as a people. This should be our collective goal. Thousands of years ago, our ancestors put it on the walls in Kemet as a blueprint for us to follow. It's as if they knew we were going to be lost and needed a road map to get back to our true selves. MAAT is that map. Now that you have the map, there is no excuse for any of us to be lost in any facets of our lives, let alone our relationships. Be the master of self that you were meant to be. Understand that you are the answer to all of your problems. Let us navigate wisely!

Chapter Three:

The Bible: the Blueprint to Universal Law & Higher Consciousness

"Use the 'Book' to decipher the codes of Universal Law. You cannot unlock the true mysteries of the 'Book' until you raise your consciousness. The Book has many meanings according to the conscience level of the individual deciphering it. Do not get complacent in your understanding. The 'Book' must be looked upon as a journey, not a final destination. Travel well and far." — Nekhebet

Those of you who believe that the Bible came directly from God into the hearts and minds of exclusively sacred men, who wrote down the information word for word, sent it to the scribes and the printing presses that printed millions of copies of over 125 different versions of the same text, in several different languages, without one word being changed or tampered with — you are foolish! The Bible was written 300 years **AFTER** anything in the Bible supposedly took place. So to put that concept in perspective, if we were to write about Jesus in the present, He would have come in the year 1710. The year 2010 is the first year that anyone could have begun writing about this great character who lived 300 years ago. Also, understand that there were no radios, TVs, computers or newspapers at the time! I am not here to discredit the Bible; that is not my focus. My goal is to loosen the stranglehold that religion has on the Bible, which is used to oppress the masses. We must use the Bible to uplift our consciousness, not to validate our religious beliefs. There are no "get into heaven free" cards in the Bible.

There are no magical words to recite to be "saved" from hell's eternal fire. Simply unlock the mysteries of our ancient Kemetic ancestors that are hidden within the pages of the Bible and you will discover the one life force that permeates the All.

Master Teacher, Dr. Phil Valentine, states that the Bible is actually:
"Fables — Factualized
Allegories — Literalized
Symbols — Personalized
Drama — Historicalized
Cosmic Forces – Anthropomorphized."

The Bible consists of ancient texts collected and inspired from Kemet, dating back thousands of years before there was even a figure named Christ. These Kemetic mystery systems have been fused into the Bible as parables and stories for the initiate to decode, in order to unlock the secrets of the laws of the universe and the mystery of man's life purpose. The Bible is coded with symbols, meanings and characters that represent a blueprint for acquiring a higher consciousness called KRST. We will get into KRST consciousness later in this chapter. For those who have been initiated, you have known, for quite some time that the Bible was never intended to be taken literally. The reader of the Bible is supposed to internalize "the meat" or "the fruit" of the life lessons in the Bible, not to be led astray by focusing on the peculiars and characters of the stories. That is why Christ always talks in parables and rarely explains events that are happening in His present time. Christ is a concept, not an actual person! The Bible is like the shell of a nut. We are supposed to digest the meat inside the shell that we must crack open and not focus on the outside package it comes in. The reader is supposed to "crack the shell" first, so that the real knowledge can be ingested. Too many religions and versions of the Bible keep the masses from uniting by focusing on the different characteristics that this nutshell has on the outside. When we get down to it, all religions believe in the same "fruit" that is located inside the shell. This fruit can be defined in one statement called the Golden Rule: "Do unto others as you would have them do unto you." So if all major religions have this ideology at their foundation, why are we so divided to the point where most wars seem to be waged because of religious beliefs? The powers that be use this ancient strategy of divide and conquer to control. Do you wonder why each side that is at war with each other, claims that God is on their side? This propaganda is implemented so the masses will be blind to the destruction, bloodshed and the infantile, animalistic level of behavior that war must promote, in order to get two strangers, who are probably good men, to pick up weapons and try to kill each other for a cause they deem bigger than themselves. Religion is for the benefit of the beast in man (lower self); spirituality is reserved for the God in man (higher self). These ancient, inspired Kemetic texts contain the blueprint in order for man to attain god or higher consciousness here on Earth. So you see why this concept would be a very dangerous threat to the powers that be, who want to manipulate and control you through lower level thoughts and behaviors. They need man to seek a God or power outside of himself, for if man was to look internally for the God inside himself, then he would not look towards another man for the answers to his problems. Thus, man could not be controlled or manipulated according to another man's agenda, which does not have his best interest at heart.

"The knowledge of the secrets of the kingdom of God has been given to you, but to others I speak in parables, so that, "though seeing, they may not see: though hearing, they may not understand." — Luke 8:10 (King James Version)

The Council of Nicea 325 AD

In 325 AD, the ruler of the Roman Empire was named Emperor
Constantine. There was a new Coptic or Gnostic-inspired religion that came
out of Kemet that was on the rise from region to region. The Roman
emperor, fearing this newfound religion would one day reach the gates of his
empire and threaten his rule over his people, decided to have a meeting with
all the religious leaders, nobles and head politicians of his time. In order to
ward off this inevitable religious threat, the Council of Nicea was called into
action. Its main purpose was to "high jack" this upstart religion from its
grassroots beginnings and somehow infiltrate and control its ideologies to fit
the needs of the people who wanted to keep their power over the masses.
The momentum of this new religion was too strong to quell its influence, so
the powers that be had no alternative but to take it over, before it consumed
them. You see, this Gnostic, Afrikan religion believed that every individual
had the power to achieve "God consciousness" within themselves. The
religion believed that man did not have to look outside of himself in order to
know and honor God. This ideology was dangerous because its followers
would have no need to look to authority figures in order to tell them how to
live their lives or how to define themselves or their reality. Constantine and
his fellow conspirators went through their written teachings called the Bible
word for word. These teachings were written in code and were not supposed
to be taken in the literal sense. The first thing the Council did was to
interpret these lessons in a literal sense. Any teachings that were deemed a
threat to the Council's power, they got rid of. Any concepts that empowered
the individual, they edited out. They included only images that promoted
them as having absolute power. Any symbolism that was allowed
represented the likeness of the emperor, the all-powerful state, the political
system and the accepted economic, business model as the only
unquestionable authority. Once these safeguards, principles and ideologies

were firmly in place and agreed upon by all who held power at the time, the authorities implemented or "allowed" this religion that they renamed Christianity, and unleashed it on the masses.

Over two thousand years later, the Bible is still being used to suppress information and the ideology that may save the people. It indoctrinates the masses with a mindset that takes the concept of God, or our higher selves, out of our physical bodies and places God in a place that we cannot attain until after we die.

Matthew 2:13-23 (English Standard Version)

The Flight to Egypt

¹³Now when they had departed, behold,⁽ᴬ⁾ an angel of the Lord appeared to Joseph in a dream and said, "Rise, take the child and his mother, and flee to Egypt, and remain there until I tell you, for Herod is about to search for the child, to destroy him." ¹⁴And he rose and took the child and his mother by night and departed to Egypt ¹⁵and remained there until the death of Herod.⁽ᴮ⁾ This was to fulfill what the Lord had spoken by the prophet,⁽ᶜ⁾ "Out of Egypt I called my son."

I believe this scripture is a clue to the true source for the knowledge that is in the Bible and the blueprint to Black people's reawakening. In order to escape death (lower consciousness), the character of Jesus needs to reconnect with the ancient wisdom of his ancestors in Kemet (modern day Egypt,) in order to survive the onslaught of the system that was designed to destroy him (keep him at a lower consciousness level.) King Herod represents the European system of its time that oppressed our ancestors. King Herod represents the state. He was the slave master. He represented the institution of white supremacy that subjected and oppressed the darker people of his time to the same racial discrimination we suffer under today. Just like in those biblical times, our young Black men are still being targeted by the state, for fear of a savior rising up in our midst to lead our people to the Promised Land, which is Kemet. Instead of the ancient weapons of biblical times, now King Herod uses miseducation, lower vibration through rap music, drugs, guns, toxic foods, self-hate, greed, broken homes, disunity, the church and the legal system to kill off young, Black boys. Kemet represents the universal mystery system that holds the key to our freedom, in the form of higher consciousness. So it is no wonder that the young baby Jesus would find refuge and safety in the very place that holds the key for him to become God (higher consciousness) here on Earth: the Afrikan advanced civilization known as Kemet.

"Your enemy manipulates you to fear God. I tell you that God is the absence of fear." — Nekhebet

For our ancestors, KRST, God consciousness or our higher selves was not only attainable in our lifetime, but was required and mandatory duty for all individuals to dedicate their lives to accomplishing. This is the main focus of the book. This is the foundation of the author's knowledge, from which to define the principles in this book.

Kerast is a "Chaldean" (Iraqi) Word for "oil"...as in "anoint or caress with oil". It is also the basis of the Chaldean word "Chris" which means "sun". The connection between "oil" (as in fuel) and the burning "sun" as its symbol is unmistakable By zorroz *— Posted on March 9th, 2008* Home *::* Zorroz's Blog http://memes.org

So Kerast is the "oil" that has been infused by the Sun or "Christ." The sun represents higher consciousness. The oil is the chemical Melanin that Black people have an abundance of in their bodies. This "oil" receives consciousness from the sun when exposed to the sun's rays. The Melanin translates to the body this higher consciousness so that the body can manifest miracles in the physical dimension. This is the meaning of the term "to be anointed". The god Heru in Kemetic mythology represents a man who operates according to higher consciousness. This is who the character of Jesus Christ in the Bible represents: Heru the KRST. Heru is also where we get the word "hero" from. KRST simply means the highest state of mind, body and soul that a man could become in the physical dimension. He is the "enlightened one", such as the Buddha and other higher conscious religious figures in all other religions. What they don't explain is that all men have the ability to achieve KRST or Christ consciousness, if they are willing to put in the work to master the self. To prove that Kemet was the foundation for Christianity and all other religions, we will examine the story of Heru and see how it is almost the exact story of Jesus Christ in the Bible. Remember, the story of Heru is 3,200 years older than the Biblical story of Jesus!

Kemetic God Heru the KRST vs. Christianity's Jesus

Event	Heru (Horus) circa 3200 BCE (before christian era)	Jesus of Nazareth circa 1 ACE (after christian era)
Conception:	By a virgin.	By a virgin
Father:	Only begotten son of Ausar	Only begotten son of God (in the form of the Holy Spirit)
Mother:	Heru had 2 motherz: Aset (Isis) who gave birth and Nephthys, who nursed him	Jesus had 2 motherz: Mary (aka Miriam) the Virgin who gave birth and Mary the wife of Cleophas raised him
Foster father:	Seb, (Jo-Seph)	Joseph
Foster father's ancestry:	Of royal descent	Of royal descent
Birth location:	In a cave	In a cave or stable

Annunciation:	By an angel to Aset	By an angel to Mary
Birth heralded by:	The star Sirius, the morning star	An unidentified *"star in the East"*
Birth date:	Ancient people of Kemet (Egyptianz) paraded a manger and child representing Heru through the streets at the time of the winter solstice (typically Dec. 21)	Celebrated on Dec. 25. The date was chosen to occur on the same date as the birth of Mithra, Dionysus and the Sol Invictus (unconquerable Sun), etc
Birth announcement:	By angelz	By angelz
Birth witnesses:	Shepherdz	Shepherdz
Later witnesses to birth:	Three solar deities	Three wise men
Death threat during infancy:	Seth tried to have Heru murdered	Herod tried to have Jesus murdered
Handling the threat:	The God *That* tells Heru's mother *"Come, thou goddess Isis, hide thyself with thy child."*	An angel tells Jesus' father to: *"Arise and take the young child and his mother and flee into Egypt."*
Rite of passage ritual:	Heru came of age with a special ritual, when his eye was restored	Taken by parents to the temple for what is today called a bar mitzvah ritual
Age at the ritual:	12	12
Break in life history:	No data between ages of 12 & 30	No data between ages of 12 & 30

Baptism location:	In the river Eridanus	In the river Jordan
Age at baptism:	30	30
Baptized by:	Anup the Baptiser	John the Baptist
Subsequent fate of the baptiser:	Beheaded	Beheaded
Temptation:	Taken from the desert of Amenta up a high mountain by his arch-rival Sut. Sut (a.k.a. Set) was a precursor for the Hebrew Satan	Taken from the desert in Palestine up a high mountain by his arch-rival Satan
Result of temptation:	Heru resists temptation	Jesus resists temptation
Close followers:	Twelve disciples. There is some doubt about this matter as well	Twelve disciples
Activities:	Walked on water, cast out demons, healed the sick, restored sight to the blind. He *"stilled the sea by his power."*	Walked on water, cast out demons, healed the sick, restored sight to the blind. He ordered the sea with a *"Peace, be still"* command
Raising of the dead:	Heru raised Ausar, his dead father, from the grave	Jesus raised Lazarus from the grave
Location where the resurrection	Anu, an Egyptian city where the rites of the	Hebrews added their prefix for house (*'beth'*) to "*Anu*" to

| miracle occurred: | death, burial and resurrection of Heru were enacted annually | produce *"Beth-Anu"* or the *"House of Anu."* Since "u" and "y" were interchangeable in antiquity, *"Bethanu"* became *"Bethany,"* the location mentioned in John 11 |
| Origin of Lazarus' name in the Gospel of John: | | |

— taken from the website <u>www.daghettotymes.com</u>

The Biblical story of Jesus Christ (KRST) and his crucifixion is the blueprint or procedure to overcoming the ego or one's lower consciousness. It is nothing more and nothing less. Overcoming the ego is the initiation or threshold that one must pass in order to enter the door of enlightenment. One cannot transcend to a higher realm of consciousness unless they can master their lower self. Let us break down the story in the Bible. Remember, all characters in the Bible, like the gods in Kemetic mythology, represent an ideal or principle of universal law and not an actual person in the flesh. The characters are anthropomorphic. This simply means a fictional character representing a principle of universal law that has the attributes or personality of said law. We are supposed to be aware and conscious of the personality of the character and how it relates to a given environment, and not the fictionalized person. So if the character in the Bible named Peter, which means rock, exhibits behavior that is unbecoming of his name, like denying Jesus three times, then one should understand that rocks can have cracks in them. Thus, all men should never stop working towards righteousness. Men should never rest on their accomplishments of the past, no matter how great they may have been. Jesus also called him Peter because he represented the principles of the foundation from which to build the church. As we know, a structure is only as strong as the foundation it is built upon. So the Bible is not supposed to be taken literally. The Bible and its characters represent the laws of the universe that one must adhere to in order to overstand oneself and the mental, physical and spiritual dimensions we reside in. Once we are conscious of ourselves and how we relate to the world around us, then we can be resurrected from the dead to a higher state of existence, where life truly begins.

Let's go over points in the Bible and examine the crucifixion scenario of Jesus the KRST.

1) KRST, or Jesus Christ, was accused of something he was not guilty of and accepted his fate.

    LESSON: *Show humility. Submit to the will of universal law. Be willing to carry another man's burden without complaining about your misfortunes. Don't question why things always happen to you. Look within yourself as to why you are creating this reality in your life. What type of vibration or energy are you sending out which comes back and hits you in the face in the form of discomfort or stress? What we put out in the universe is what we get back. Are you depositing good deeds into the karmic bank of the universe or are you withdrawing lower level energy that will return and hit you with a higher interest rate. It is better to give than receive. The universe will always reward higher consciousness and always seek to raise lower consciousness. One must be willing to accept what the universe is reflecting and receive the necessary lessons it gives to transcend to a better place.*

2) KRST or Jesus Christ was stripped down naked for all to see.

    LESSON: *Reveal all your insecurities and shortcomings. When man feels he is defeated and dwells at his lowest level, then it is there that he will come face-to-face with his true self. This is why people who are addicted to drugs need to "bottom out" before they can start to recover. Your ego will always justify your lower level behavior with rationality through fear and vanity. To kill the ego, one must be put into a position where all their defects, fears and insecurities are exposed. It is only after this that man can raise his consciousness. It is in this place where man will meet his true self, which his ego has kept hostage from him.*

3) KRST or Jesus Christ was tortured, spat on, ridiculed and slandered.

   LESSON: *Overcome your physical body; display humility, humility, humility! Accept the fate of universal law and be willing to let go completely. Do not interfere or question said fate. Keep the faith and be optimistic at all times, no matter what adversity you are experiencing. Display no fear, for fear is the opposite of love, not hate. Embrace all experiences in life, for they all have a lesson for you to learn and you will be better off going through them. The body, the mind and the spirit must be tested in order for them to get stronger. You must embrace adversity and figuratively die, with a smile on your face.*

4) KRST or Jesus Christ had to carry the very same cross that they were going to crucify him on.

   LESSON: *Accept without question; carry another man's burden; put your own life aside to carry the burden of another. Show courage and humility in difficult times. Never question why things happened to you. Learn to embrace all experiences in life whether they are perceived as miracles or predicaments. Put other people's feelings ahead of your own. Learn to sacrifice your own personal livelihood for the benefit of another. This is achieved even when that person doesn't appreciate or acknowledge what you have done for them. Your reward will be greater than any accolades a person can give you.*

5) KRST or Jesus Christ had to mentally, physically and spiritually test himself to the limits, in order to reach his full potential.

   LESSON: *Man must strip himself down to his barest essential in order to know and reach his full potential. One needs to know their lowest point in order to reach their highest potential. In order to resurrect and know one's true self, one must eliminate their perceived self. You must kill the ego in an effort to free your true self from its clutches. Your true self has been kidnapped by the ego. The only way to rescue it is to test oneself to one's limits, because true self lives outside of the box that your perceived self has trapped your perception in. The only way to go outside of the box is to face adversity and hard times with an undying spirit, so that your true self can be set free.*

6) KRST or Jesus Christ had to embrace the cards that were dealt to him and not throw a "pity party."

   LESSON: *We need to embrace all of life's ups and downs, for they are all beneficial lessons in our growth. We cannot pick and choose the lessons we want to learn. All of life's experiences are valuable lessons. Every adversity we face, every hard time we have overcome have made us better if we learned the lessons in those difficult times. The only way to raise your consciousness is to put it to the test. You cannot turn a lump of coal into a diamond without tremendous amounts of pressure over a significant amount of time. Believe that you are that diamond in the rough and you shall become one. Embrace the struggle.*

7) When KRST or Jesus Christ, completed his journey, he was ready to be resurrected to unlock the door to his higher self. Resurrection can be defined as the transformation from the lower self or consciousness to the higher self. It is putting to death a lower level existence and transcending to a higher or enlightened state of mind. This should be

the goal of all human kind. We are all here to learn the hard lessons of life in order to transcend to a higher existence. This is why all men must die. Death of lower level concepts, ideas and behavior give the spirit the ability to transform into a higher spiritual awakening. The symbol of death is the threshold that must be crossed in order to transcend. Everyone must die but not everyone will be resurrected.

When KRST or Jesus Christ completed his life lessons, he responded by saying, "It is done." Then the Father "raised" him up to heaven. Heaven is symbolized by higher consciousness. It is the mastering of the lower self and the ability to recognize one's true self. This is why heaven is blissful. This is why heaven is located above our physical selves. We are the heaven that we aspire to go to and we are also the hell that we fear we will end up in. It is all related to man's state of mind and consciousness. Hell is eternal because one refuses to do the work and change their behavior that will raise their consciousness. So one repeats the same lower level behavior and they suffer the consequences.

Man was born with "free will." This is God's gift to man. Man has a choice to live in hell or to reside in heaven. The choice is individually ours to make. Unfortunately, this system of white supremacy keeps you from recognizing and understanding your reason for living. This is an "ego driven" society that he has created for us. We are motivated and live for things that are not real, things such as: money, materialism, fame, acceptance, vanity, greed, pride, hate, stubbornness, conceit and FEAR.

"Fear feeds the ego and the ego creates more fear." — Nekhebet

I am not here to discredit the Bible. I am here to look at its pages according to the upliftment and resurrection of the Black man and woman. How can we address the secret science of Black male and female sex if we are not in our right state of mind? My objective is to resurrect our Black minds so that we may interpret our own definitions of reality, in order to raise our consciousness. Remember, we were given the Bible through Christianity, as a way and a means to control and manipulate our behavior as slaves. The white man gave the Afrikan the Bible and left with the Afrikan's land, resources and people. The Afrikan was stuck with only the Bible in his possession. Remember, the white man forced the Afrikan to give up his own religion as a means to enslave him. The Caucasians forced their interpretation of the Bible on their slaves. This is how Christianity was given to you. It was forced on you by the gun and the whip! They threatened to rape your woman and kill your children if you did not fully convert and commit to their version of the religion. The Bible was never given to the Afrikan as a means to free and uplift him. There were always controlling and cunningness behind the Caucasians' behavior and actions towards Black people. First, he made God or Jesus white in his own image. If God is the opposite of what you look like in a mirror, then how are you going to feel about yourself? Secondly, who are you going to look up to and trust with your life? In every other country in the world, the God they worship always looks like the people of that particular region, except when it comes to the people of Afrikan descent. What does this tell you? The following passages in the Bible were used by our Caucasian slave masters to oppress us in their ongoing strategy of psychological warfare. The Bible was their primary weapon of mass destruction.

Matthew 10:24: A student is not greater than the teacher. A slave is not greater than the master.

Genesis 9:25-27: Cursed be Canaan! The lowest of slaves will he be to his brothers. He also said, 'Blessed be the Lord, the God of Shem! May Canaan be the slave of Shem. May God extend the territory of Japheth; may Japeth live in the tents of Shem and may Canaan be his slave.'

Psalm 123:2 (New International Version (NIV)): As the eyes of slaves look to the hand of their master, as the eyes of a maid look to the hand of her mistress, so our eyes look to the LORD our God, till he shows us his mercy.

Ephesians 6:4-6: Fathers, do not exasperate your children; instead, bring them up in the training and instruction of the Lord. Slaves, obey your earthly masters with respect and fear, and with sincerity of heart, just as you would obey Christ. Obey them not only to win their favor when their eye is on you, but like slaves of Christ, doing the will of God from your heart.

Ephesians 6:5: Slaves, obey your earthly masters with respect and fear, and with sincerity of heart, just as you would obey Christ.

Ephesians 6:9: And masters, treat your slaves in the same way. Do not threaten them, since you know that he who is both their Master and yours is in heaven, and there is no favoritism with him.

Colossians 3:22: Slaves, obey your earthly masters in everything; and do it, not only when their eye is on you and to win their favor, but with sincerity of heart and reverence for the Lord.

Colossians 4:1: Masters, provide your slaves with what is right and fair, because you know that you also have a Master in heaven.

Titus 2:9: Teach slaves to be subject to their masters in everything, to try to please them, not to talk back to them.

1 Peter 2:18: Slaves, submit yourselves to your masters with all respect, not only to those who are good and considerate, but also to those who are harsh. —**King James Version**

My objective is to interpret the Bible according to the ancient Afrikan texts, which were its hidden inspiration. To resurrect our minds so that we can emancipate the secret science that lays dormant in our Afrikan DNA. Search the Bible's pages for your freedom and not your demise. Put down the interpretation that your master has given you, and decipher the codes for your freedom, upliftment and resurrection. Look to your Afrikan ancestors for the answers to the mysteries of the Bible. Do not trust your oppressor's version, for he only means to enslave you. Return to Afrika to retrieve your beautiful, Afrikan worldview and use it as a blueprint when you study the Bible. You will find in its pages your true salvation. Study the Bible again, for the first time.

KNOW THYSELF is written on the top of doorways and entrances of the temples in Kemet, so the person has to look up to read it. The act of looking up activates the part of the brain that the individual needs to define himself through his higher self or consciousness. Western religion has man look or bow down to pay homage to the spirit; this activates man's lower consciousness. Our ancestors looked up. The inscription "Know Thyself" was a Kemetic term that they put above all the temple doorways in ancient Kemet. They believed the answers to all the mysteries of the universe were contained inside oneself. It directly correlates to a person reaching their higher self or spiritual consciousness. If one was to transcend into their higher self, then the secrets of the universe would be revealed. This is why they put the sign above the doorways. This meant that a person had to look up in order to read the sign. The act of looking up would reinforce the ideology of pursuing and identifying himself through a higher self or spiritual consciousness. This is why the eyes roll to the back of your head while you are sleeping or experiencing extreme pleasure during sexual intercourse. It is this eye movement that triggers the spirit to travel to higher planes of consciousness.

This goes against Western or European philosophy and religion, which has placed the idea of God outside of man and not reachable, whereas in ancient Kemet, God was attainable from within, if one was willing to raise their consciousness and master their lower, physical self. This theory is promoted by having the individual bow down to pay homage to the God, instead of looking up. This act encourages a person to define themselves through their lower selves or consciousness. This is the act of someone who is ashamed of their lower level behavior and reaffirms the principle that they are not worthy of higher consciousness or spirituality.

"And be not conformed to this world: but be ye transformed by the renewing of your mind, that ye may prove what is that good, and acceptable, and perfect, will of God." — Romans 12:2

Biblical Numerology

Numbers are the highest form of communication in the physical and unseen realms. Numbers are the one universal language. Math is the same in any language and in any country. Its properties and principles are constant anywhere in the world, at any given time. Within the concept of numbers comes the art of communicating and expressing an ideology on numerous planes or levels. Numbers have the ability to tell the story within a story, for all people to decipher no matter what language they speak. According to the level of the initiate, the higher degree of communication can be deciphered by studying the mathematical blueprint that is expressed as an idea. This is the power of numbers. Numbers contain the key to decoding universal law and ancient Kemetic mystery systems. Numbers are nothing more than symbols. Symbols are used as a form of communication and control. Symbolism is the best form of communication on a subconscious level. Symbols or numbers hold subliminal messages that relay a message to our brains, whether or not we acknowledge them. Symbols and numbers speak directly to the part of the brain which is responsible for your behavior. So behavior can be predicted, controlled and manipulated through numbers, without that person being aware of its power over themselves.

"Symbols are an object, picture, written word, sound or a particular mark that represents or stands for something else by association, resemblance or convention, especially a material object used to represent something invisible."

So numbers hold within themselves meanings that are otherwise invisible to the naked eye. Numbers are the most effective way to communicate if one wants to keep information hidden from the unsuspecting masses.

"Convention – a gathering of individuals who meet at a designated location and time, in order to engage or discuss a common interest."

So if numbers can represent a convention's particular common interests, and those interests may not have your best interest in mind, then numbers can be used to empower or enslave the individual who is being subjected to this higher math. Free masons call it sacred geometry. There, God is called "The Great Architect." An architect's skills at building and creating things in the physical plane rely on math. This is where we get the term "numbers don't lie" or "things don't seem to add up." When one has access to decoding numbers, all intentions, lies and truth can be revealed. Although there are many numerology systems out there, the main focus of this book is Biblical numerology. I have included a generic code to understanding the numbers in an effort to free the reader from the reality that our oppressors have forced us to accept. When you read the Bible, or witness and experience anything for that matter, pay attention and understand the numbers. You will get a better understanding and clarity as to what is actually being communicated to you and on what level the communication is taking place. Pay attention to the month and day. Pay attention to addresses, phone numbers, receipts and numbered signs. Anything that displays a numerical value holds within it a piece of the puzzle to your past, present and future. Be aware of TV and radio channels, for these hold certain frequencies to enhance or suppress certain behaviors. Pay attention to the time. You will see patterns that you thought were irrelevant because you never paid attention to them. This is the science of our ancestors. This is another key to unlocking the mystery that we call life. This is where our freedom dwells. Numbers can be used to control and manipulate behavior, as well as help one understand the past, present and future. Use the science of numerology for your best interests, instead of the science being used against you.

ONE: Symbol of unity of the one life force that permeates all things, the state of being first and foremost. It represents the beginning. It represents the one, hidden life force that flows through all things. It is the energy that always was and always will be.

TWO: The number of division. It is the first number that can be divided unto itself. Man has two natures: human & divine. This number represents separation and division. It represents male and female, or the Yin and the Yang. It represents the opposite ends of the same thing: Hot & cold, high & low, or good vs. evil.

THREE: Divine perfection represented by the Holy Trinity of the father, the mother (Holy Spirit) & the Son. It is the necessary three dimensions for physicality. It represents the mind, body & soul; the past, present & future; or time, space and matter. The three qualities of the universe are solid, liquid and gas. It represents the length, width and depth of the third dimensional plane. To exist in the physical realm, all three states are required. This number promotes the idea that everything is made up of three parts when you dissect it down to its basic core. Jesus rose on the third day. Resurrection or new life needs to incorporate the three in order to manifest in the physical dimension.

FOUR: The number of creation represented by the North, South, East & West, and the four winds. It is represented by the four seasons of winter, spring, summer and fall. In the Bible, the fourth commandment refers to the Earth. The fourth clause of the Lord's Prayer also mentions the Earth: "One Earth as it is in heaven."

FIVE: The number of grace. It represents redemption. It is Creation (4), plus a new beginning (1). David picked 5 stones to slay Goliath. This concept represents that God was on his side. Five represents that God is pleased with your undertaking. Man has 5 fingers, five toes and five senses. This is proof that God is with man in his physical body. A five-pointed star represents man's highest nature, or "God" consciousness.

SIX: The number of imperfection. It represents the number of lower man or the beast or animal instincts in man. Man was created on the sixth day to symbolize his fall into the physical dimension. "Thou shalt not kill." is the sixth commandment.

The "Mark of the beast" is the number 666. The numerical symbol for the number six (6) resembles a pregnant mother. It represents the number one (1) that became pregnant. It symbolizes God giving birth or life to the physical dimension. To arrive in the physical dimension, one must "fall from God" or the spiritual dimension. In the elemental chart, the number six represents the element Carbon. Carbon is the basic element in the creation of the physical realm. When we die, our physical bodies stay in this dimension as our spirits return to the spiritual realm. This is represented by our funeral precessions of having six pall bearers, a six-sided coffin and being buried six feet underground.

SEVEN: Divine completion. This is where the term "Seventh Heaven" comes from. It is the number of spiritual perfection. God rested on the seventh day to symbolize the perfection in His work. Examples of seven in the physical dimension: There are seven colors in a spectrum; Jesus made seven statements on the cross; humans have seven layers of skin; there are seven chakras; there are seven key notes; there are seven seas, seven continents, seven parts of the brain and heart, seven deadly sins & virtues. The human body replaces all its cells every seven years. Seven is the Creator's personality expressed in the physical realm.

EIGHT: The number of eternity or infinity. The symbol for the number eight has no beginning & no ending. There were eight people on Noah's ark symbolizing God's promise to continue the human race. God made eight covenants with Abraham to show that He would be with His chosen people for eternity. The number eight turned on its side is the symbol for infinity in mathematics.

NINE: The symbol of judgment. The symbol for the number nine (9) represents the womb upside down or the number six (6) turned on its head. Numbers repeat themselves after you reach the number nine. One must pass the lessons of the number nine in order to move on to higher numbers or consciousness. Nine represents the five senses of man overcoming the four elements of the physical dimension to equal nine. Man takes 18 breaths per minute or 1+8= 9. Man has 72 pulses per minute or 7+2=9. Nine represents the struggle that one must endure and overcome to reach a higher place. Nine represents man's test to master his physical body to reach his higher spiritual consciousness.

TEN: The symbol of perfection. The number ten represents the number one (1) or man's higher consciousness, standing next to the zero (0), which represents 360 degrees of knowledge. The number represented by man mastering the Ten Commandments. The number ten represents the divine completion of the order of all things.

ELEVEN: (A Master number) This number represents a flawed addition to the perfect order represented by the number ten. It represents the number one (1) looking at its reflection (11). This number signifies the concept of duality. Eleven can represent too much of a good thing, which can be considered good or bad depending on the level of consciousness of the initiate and how he handles his successes or failures.

TWELVE: Symbol of perfect completion. There were twelve apostles and twelve tribes of Israel to symbolize God's completion of His task. There are twelve months in a year and twelve jurors in a court of law. The first mention of Jesus in the Bible was at the age of twelve, which represented the perfection and completion of the mastery of his physical body. Twelve represents the completion of a cycle or threshold that one must reach in order to achieve higher consciousness.

THIRTEEN: The number of resurrection or rebirth. The thirteenth month in the calendar is considered to be a new year. There were thirteen colonies in the "New World." There were thirteen stars & stripes on the original flag. White supremacy has demonized the number thirteen for fear of the Black man's resurrection from his mental slavery. This is supported by superstitions, such as Friday the 13th and not having any13th floors in high-rise buildings. Thirteen represents transformation. The New Testament has thirteen books.

FORTY: Number of trials or tests. Jesus was tested in the desert for 40 days and 40 nights. The children of Israel wandered in the desert for 40 years. The flood lasted for 40 days & 40 nights. Moses went to the mountaintop of 40 days. At the age of 40, one is considered "over the hill."

Look at numbers according to this key and you will see life more clearly. Use numbers as a blueprint or key to the map of life. One will find, once they are conscious of the numbers around them, that they will see the pattern of the reality that they choose to accept. Numbers don't lie. This science with numbers also produces very interesting results.

Use this key to assign numbers to letters:

A-1	J-10	S-19
B-2	K-11	T-20
C-3	L-12	U-21
D-4	M-13	V-22
E-5	N-14	W-23
F-6	O-15	X-24
G-7	P-16	Y-25
H-8	Q-17	Z-26
I-9	R-18	

Decode words, through the numbers, to unlock their invisible frequency to determine what level of vibration they give out. Use this science in your relationships. Numbers can tell you when to participate in, or withhold, Inner G. Use and interpret the numbers around you as road signs on the path that you are traveling on. If used properly, one can predict the future and even avoid hazards before they come into view.

Chapter 4:
Melanin: The Khemystery of Sex

"Partake of the forbidden fruit that you were taught to despise, for its
sweet nectar is the elixir to your salvation." — Nekhebet

You may ask yourself: why write a book about the secret science of BLACK male and female sex? Why not just write a book on the secret science of sex? I mean, aren't we all human? Don't we all have the same equipment and experience life with the same senses? I mean, there is no difference in the races. We all bleed, breathe and die the same. Absolutely not! There is a chemical in the body that separates people into two categories: Those who classify themselves as white, albino or European, and the rest of the human population that whites label as non-white or "people of color." People of color can be further categorized as Asian, Arab, Indian, Pacific Islander, Latino, Native American, Indigenous, Aborigines and Afrikan descent. As a rule, the darker the pigmentation of the skin, the more Melanin they have in their system. This would suggest that the Afrikan and people of Afrikan descent have the highest concentration of Melanin within their system.

Melanin is the root word for the word "chemistry". In Kemet, our ancestors called the color Black, which represents Melanin, Khem. When you break up the word "chemistry", one gets Chem- Mystery. This concept can be interpreted or defined as the mystery of Melanin. So the field or study of chemistry entails discovering the secret properties of Melanin and their characteristics when exposed to different environments.

What is Melanin? Put into simple or generic terms, Melanin is the chemical in the body that is produced by the Pineal gland that carries all the dominant traits in one's gene pool. When Melanin comes into contact with a recessive, non-Melanated gene or trait, Melanin is more apt to come out victorious. For example, if a Black man and a white woman have a child, the child will carry more of the Black man's dominant, Melanated genes, as opposed to the white woman's non-Melanated recessive genes. Dark or brown eyes are more dominant than recessive light or blue eyes. Kinky or curly dark hair is more dominant than straight, blonde or light hair. Full lips are more dominant than recessive thin lips. A wide nose is dominant over a recessive, narrow pointy nose. Afrikan, athletic and lean, muscular body type is dominant over the European, bulky, stout and recessive body type. A dark complexion of the skin is dominant over a recessive light or pink complexion of the skin.

So the child from these interracial parents, for example, may inherit 80% of its father's dominant Melanated genes and only 20% of the mother's recessive, non-Melanated genes.

Recessive genes can come from dominant genes, but dominant genes cannot come from recessive genes. This means that Black people can produce black, brown red, yellow and even white. White or Caucasian people can only produce white offspring. If there is no Melanin being introduced into the equation, then there is no color in the product being produced.

Lab rats are specifically and exclusively albino because they are the best genetic match to the Caucasian. All experiments on food, medicine and biological diseases are based on this albino prototype. Based on this ideology, disease and medicine, which are geared towards Caucasians, may have adverse effects on people of color, specifically Black people.

As Francis Cress Welsing points out in her book, *The Isis Papers*, this factor is the basis for white supremacy. Europeans, or people who classify themselves as white, make up roughly only 10% of the world's population. The other 90% of the world's population can be classified as people of color. Europeans or whites have a zero birth rate. That means for every white person who dies, only one other white person is born. So their population growth has become stagnant. The general white population is not growing or multiplying. Their population growth has flat lined. On the other hand, for Melanated people or people of color, for every one person who dies, two to three people are born! Melanated people's population is exploding! With this knowledge, subconsciously in the white man's psychology of self-preservation, he becomes defensive and bases his culture on this hostile mindset. The white man feels that he is constantly under attack. Throughout history, wherever the white man explored throughout the new world, he came in contact with Melanated people or people of color. His main objective, when in contact with these people, was genocide, oppression, manipulation and domination over them. The white man understood that if he intermingled with these people throughout the world, his recessive, non-Melanated genes that he so preciously loves and defines his superiority by, would be swallowed up by the sea of humanity that dominants the world. This is why he labeled the darker people of the world savages or heathens. In other words, if nature had its way without outside interference, the white race would be non-existent, let alone able to dominant the globe. So out of this mindset, white supremacy is born and continues to flourish.

"To open the blind eyes, to bring out the prisoners from the prison, and them that sit in darkness out of the prison house." — Isaiah 42:7 (King James Version)

Dominant traits of Melanin can be defined in these terms, "The Blacker the berry, the sweeter the juice." The properties of Melanin can be seen in moles and beauty marks on the skin. These spots on the skin contain high concentrations of Melanin. Usually in these spots, hair grows faster, thicker and stronger than in any other area of the skin. Melanin seems to act like a "super charger" to whatever it attaches itself to. In people of Afrikan descent, their skin sometimes develops keloids. This is a hard cluster of skin that usually manifests when the skin was initially damaged by a burn, cut or abrasion. These keloids also contain a high concentration of Melanin. It is as if the skin, super-charged by the Melanin in an attempt to protect itself from further damage, "over heals" by developing layer upon layer of tough skin on the damaged area. This creates the raised hard layer of skin clumped together called a keloid. So the keloid is an over-active chemical reaction of Melanin trying to protect the damaged area of the skin.

Also, you will notice that our reproductive organs, our areolas and nipples, are darker than the rest of our skin. These are the life-giving and life-sustaining, vital parts of our body. These parts also contain high concentrations of Melanin. You will notice that these parts of the body are also super-sensitive. This suggests to me that Melanin is very important to reproduction and to sustaining a healthy life.

Melanin can also be charged by any type of energy. All energy travels in waves or spirals. You will notice a person of Afrikan descent's hair is kinky or wavy. Its structure is a natural antenna to receive energy. You will also notice that manmade antennas copy this same design, whether you see them externally or internally. From cell phones, radios and TVs, all these electronic devices used to send and receive energy were initially black in color and have these spiral antennas.

The biggest Inner G source we have is the Sun. This is why Melanin is dominant in the skin. Melanin converts sunlight into energy for the mind, body and spirit to be used at its discretion. Have you ever noticed that when you are walking barefooted on the black top, how it is hotter than a lighter or white surface? This is because black or Melanin absorbs and holds energy, while white reflects energy. White surfaces do not absorb energy, they reflect it. The color black receives and holds Inner G the most efficiently. The skin in turn, becomes a darker pigment for protection against the Sun as well as to prepare the body to receive more energy. The Melanin then converts sunlight into vitamin D for the body to use. Vitamin D is a major supplement that keeps the body functioning, balanced and healthy. Melanin also converts music, colors, water, light, sound, and other energy sources that it is exposed to, into Inner G for the mind, body and spirit to use at its discretion. This is why people of Afrikan descent are so in tune with music when it is played in their presence. They can hear the beat between the beats, so they are receiving stimulation from the highest degrees. White people tend to miss the beats between the beats because they are lacking the Melanin to decipher the whole spectrum of sound and rhythm. Coincidently, Melanin cannot decipher higher Inner G or vibrations from lower energy or vibrations. So when drugs are introduced to the body, the Melanin will bind with them. Melanin is not prejudiced; it binds with "all" Inner G. This will make the "high" much higher, but the "lows" will be that much lower. It will also be harder for that person, who is exposed to the drug or lower level energy of vibration, to detoxify from it, as the Melanin has made it a permanent chemical addition to its structure. This can also be seen in lower level music, vocabulary, nutrition, thoughts and the media (television, radio, newspapers, etc.....) The Melanin will make all these Inner G sources its own reality, whether they are harmful or beneficial. The "powers that be" understand these properties of Melanin and use them to work against people of color.

Melanin is also the key chemical that attaches humans to each other, as well as the spiritual realm. Our ancestors would stimulate the Pineal gland which produces Melanin, through the use of meditation, mind-altering herbs and plants. This would induce a trance where they could communicate in the spiritual realm for guidance, understanding and inspiration. Melanin was the bridge to attach the physical realm with the spiritual dimension, so that our ancestors could cross at their discretion. This would allow our ancestors to see the connection of all life and relate it to the one divine source that incorporates the "All" in the seen and unseen worlds. So cultures of Melanated people would live in harmony with nature, not manipulate it or try to control or conquer it. There was no division of what was sacred and what was secular. God was nature and nature was God. With this concept, they believed, "I am because we are and because we are, therefore I am."-Ashanti Proverb. When introduced to Europeans, people of color assumed that they thought the same way and invited him into their way of life. The European or white man, because of his lack of Melanin, did not see the world with this mindset. Remember, the white man was always on the defensive because he viewed his reality as being under attack in his environment, whether it was biologically through his recessive genes, or in nature, because the Sun tried to destroy him. The natives were quickly subjected to the European or non-Melanated world view of control, conquer, cunningness and domination. Their worlds and cultures would never be the same after their introduction to the white man. People of color are still trying to recover today. Look at the state of so-called "third world countries." This is as true today as it was 2,000 years ago.

Once people of color realize that there are two very distinctive world views between them and white people, or Europeans, they will be able to work towards the restoration of their cultures, land and people. Also, the sooner we embrace our Melanin, Afrikan features and spirituality, the sooner we will be able to have strong, healthy and dynamic relationships with our own people.

Lab rats are specifically albino because they are the best genetic match to Caucasians. That is why all experiments are done on albino rats in regards to discovering cures and side effects of products that are being tested for human consumption. All science is based on a non-Melanated host to represent the people and their response to the exposure of the product being tested. Caucasians, or people who classify themselves as white, only make up 10% of the population, yet their genotype is the standard for the world in terms of health, beauty, intelligence, philosophy, religion, law, economics and all other facets of modern society. It is no secret that Melanated or Black babies, when compared to white babies, are more mature, stronger, and more aware and develop at a faster pace compared to their white counterparts. A Black premature baby has a higher survival rate than a white premature baby. This is because of the Melanin content within the Black baby and the lack of Melanin in the white baby.

We will now turn our attention to Kemet for the Afrocentric ideology of Melanin and its gifts, which was born here in Afrika. Our ancestors knew about this chemical we call Melanin and used it to its highest potential. Remember, Melanin connected man from the physical or seen world to the spiritual or unseen realm. I will now introduce one of the gods of our Kemetic ancestors, named Anpu. Anpu was known as the "Opener of the ways." "Opener" refers to the Pineal gland from which Melanin is produced. "The ways" refers to the bridge into the unseen or spiritual realm that a conscious man has access to. Anpu was portrayed as a black, jackal or dog-headed deity, with the body of a man. The majority of the deities in Kemet maintain the head of animals, while they kept their human bodies.

"But ask now the beasts, and they shall teach thee; and the fowls of the air, and they shall tell thee:"— Job 12:7 (King James Version)

The reason this image is promoted is the concept that man had to master and rule his lower self (the body) before he can access his higher consciousness (the brain). In other words, man must overcome his lower actions, desires, thoughts and urges, before he can become an enlightened being. Man must rule his body and not have his body rule him. Once this is achieved, man has the ability to access his higher consciousness, which is located above the neck. So once higher consciousness is achieved, our ancestors borrowed certain characteristics and idiosyncrasies from the animal kingdom, which represented traits or abilities that the enlightened being would have the ability to master as he saw fit. Anpu's ears are always pointing straight up, as if to be in tune with the unseen Inner G that we cannot decipher with our human ears. As you know, dogs can detect sounds, vibrations, decipher smells and have an overall awareness that we humans do not possess. These characteristics are properties of Melanin. Melanin is our sixth sense that we do not use anymore because we were brainwashed into thinking our intuition, spirituality and gut feelings were not valid in the white man's system. The white man didn't have access to these characteristics and traits, so he made you believe that they were not real.

Anpu represents the masculine principle of Melanin. The masculine principle can be defined as the "giving out" of Inner G. It is the positive end of the battery. It is more proactive and on the offense, as opposed to the feminine principle that receives Inner G and is more defensive than the negative end of a battery. So the characteristics of a dog are more masculine. Dogs are proactive explorers. They are always snooping and digging up something, putting something in their mouths, turning over rocks and sticking their noses in places you wouldn't think of going. They chase things and are aggressive when threatened or defending their territory. Dogs are used to guide the blind as well as to find missing people. Anpu, in Kemetic mythology, guides the individual in the afterlife so that one can enter heaven and achieve eternal life. Anpu takes you by the left hand, which activates the right brain, and guides you safely in your journey in the afterlife. We, as living beings, must also let our Melanin (intuition and spirituality) guide us in this physical dimension of logic, cognitive thinking and dominant, left-brain view of reality. The Pineal gland was called the first eye by our ancestors. That is because, in order for someone to truly see, they must blind themselves to the physical realm, the illusion, in order to fully internalize the unseen or spiritual world that is dominant around them. Roughly 10% of all Inner G is seen through our senses. The other 90% of Inner G cannot be deciphered by our five senses; thus, it is labeled as unseen Inner G. The opening up of the first eye, or the activation of the Pineal gland, allows one to see the world for what it really is. Melanin is your guide to consciousness in the seen and unseen realms. We have been tricked into believing that the 10% of seen Inner G, or the material world, is the only reality in our existence. The 90% of unseen Inner G is never accounted for, so one thinks that it does not exist. Once we acknowledge the spiritual or unseen realm, we are able to decipher what is real and what is not. What is more real: 10% of something or 90% of something? The choice to define one's reality is really only up to the individual.

Another one of Anpu's jobs is to prepare the body for burial. Anpu is responsible for preparing the individual to be able to cross over into the spiritual dimension, in order to find his way to eternal life. How does he prepare the deceased? Anpu mummifies the body by wrapping it up in strips of cloth to preserve the body. Similar to the caterpillar forming a chrysalis, or cocoon, around his body in preparation for his metamorphosis into a butterfly, so it is with the deceased body. Remember, the caterpillar is the lower self of the butterfly. It crawls amongst the mud, dirt, leaves and filth on the ground, only to recognize that it has the ability to transcend into a higher being with wings to raise his consciousness out of the gutter and fly high, thus changing his perception of reality. Anpu, who represents Melanin, has the capacity to do just that for the individual who puts in the time to master his lower self, activate his first eye and allow himself to shed his animalistic ways to transcend into higher consciousness, where his true reality can be deciphered.

"By deep intuition & insight one can change chaos into order, change danger into safety, change destruction into survival, change calamity into fortune. By strong action on the Way, one can bring the body into longevity, bring the mind to the sphere of mystery, bring the world to great peace, and bring tasks to great fulfillment." — The Book of Balance & Harmony (The Art of War)

As protector of the necropolis, Anpu was known as 'He Who is Upon the Mountain'. Dog is God spelled backwards.

The necropolis or cemetery was a symbol man's lower consciousness. A man who operated according to his lower, animalistic consciousness was already considered spiritually dead. In order to resurrect oneself, one needs to put to death their lower conscience in order to be reborn into their higher selves. The "mountain" that Anpu sits upon is none other than the Pineal Gland that produces the chemical Melanin, which is needed to achieve higher consciousness.

Another example of this symbolism can be found in the Bible.

The mountain or hill where the character of Jesus was crucified was called Golgotha. This word means, "The place of the skull." In other words, it represents your higher consciousness in the brain activated by the Pineal gland. As one can see, Melanin is the key. So what does this say about non-Melanated people, or people who classify themselves as white or European? I will quote a white man named David Wilcox. He says, "The Mark of the Beast is a calcified Pineal Gland." Let us break down this statement. The beast, antichrist or devil is not a character who lives underground in eternal fire. He is not in your closet or under your bed. The beast is the individual who defines himself by his lower self. It is our animalistic thoughts and deeds, such as greed, envy, jealously, selfishness, fear, hate, and so on. It is the butterfly in its lower state, represented by the worm or caterpillar. People who classify themselves as white or European have a calcified Pineal gland.

This is one of the traits of carrying the non-Melanated recessive gene pool. Remember, Melanin is produced by the Pineal gland. So if this is correct, then the lack of Melanin means a calcified Pineal gland, or a Pineal gland that doesn't produce Melanin!

So I interpret this state of the white man as not having the ability to transcend into the spiritual or unseen realm. He is lacking the "bridge" that connects the physical realm to the spiritual dimension. If this is true, the white man has no "Anpu" to guide him in the afterlife; thus, he cannot spiritually transcend into a higher dimension. In other words, Caucasians are stuck in the physical dimension. Is this why his system places so much value on material things in a material world? Is this why he came up with the slogan, "He who dies with the most toys wins"? There was a saying in ancient Kemet that said, "He who does not have a boat, cannot cross the river." I think that statement was referring to the outside invaders from Europe who tried to conquer Kemet from the moment they knew it was there. Caucasians cannot change their ways, because they know no other way. They may seem to change, but it will either be short-lived or a farce altogether. People of color need to quit thinking that white people will one day wake up and see the errors in their dealings with people of color throughout the world. It is not their fault. They are doing the best they can with what they have to work with. In fact, he has exceeded any expectations that anyone could have ever imagined this race of people could ever achieve. He has conquered the world by his might, cunning, ruthlessness and cold-heartedness. He has reached his epitome. Melanated people have just scratched the surface of what they can achieve. Don't limit yourself by adopting the white man's mindset, ways and culture. You have the ability to be so much more.

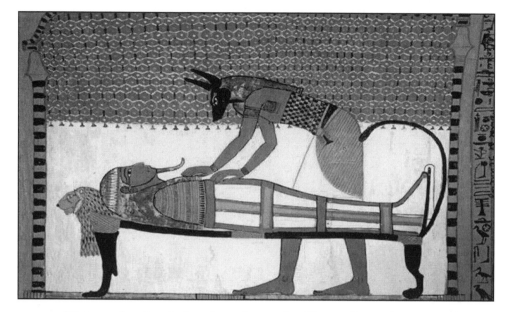

***Picture of wall painting from the tomb of Sennedjem. Anpu attending
the mummy of the deceased.***

Notice the position of the hands and feet of Anpu. Left hand on the
deceased heart represents the activation of the right brain and heart or love
frequency needed to be resurrected. When one operates from the heart, he
feels and thinks with the absence of the ego. He shows humility and places
other people's well being ahead of his own personal agenda. The right hand,
being placed on the solar plexus, represents the passion and desire of the
individual. They think and function in the physical plane with high moral
standards. This represents man's desire and passion to be righteous in the
physical dimension. He is dedicated to becoming a moral and righteous man
to lead others. Also, his tail touches the "soles or (soul) of the feet." This
image connects one's soul to their root chakra, which is located at the base of
the spine. The root chakra is your lowest self. So by connecting your lower
self to the soul, one is able to bypass or avoid lower level thoughts that lead
to lower level behavior. Lying on top of Sekhmet, or the lion goddess,

represents God's swift justice or wrath according to the life that one has led. There are also 16 black stripes on each pole, which are located on each side of the body. The poles represent the gateway, or the space between the spaces. The left pole symbolizes your past. The right pole symbolizes one's future. The body in the middle of each pole symbolizes the present or living in the now. The now is the only thing that really exists. It is the only thing we have. The deceased is being judged in the now. He cannot go back to the past to undo what he has done wrong and his future has not happened yet. All he can focus or worry about is the now. The contrast of white and black stripes on the poles represents the seen world and unseen worlds, or the physical dimension that one can decipher with their sixth senses and the spiritual dimension that we cannot see. The way to understand the spiritual dimension is through our intuition and activation of the right brain. The 16 rows of circles linked together above the figures represent the unseen realm that Anpu rules and dwells in. The number 16 represents the principle of the number seven. Seven stands for divine completion. So we are at the end or the completion of the life of God, represented in the physical body. This is who man represents. The 8 sections of the lower body represent man's eternal reward or the debt that he must pay according to the way he lived his life.

Anpu monitored the Scales of Truth from which the goddess Maat weighed your heart against her feather. So Anpu, representing your Melanin, which is your intuition and key to deciphering the unseen world, would be your conscience, which acts as a guardian protecting you from lower level or deviant behavior. Anpu or your Melanin protects from deception and eternal death. Anpu would "awaken" your consciousness in preparation for your final judgment, life after death. This was the method to achieve higher consciousness, which decided if one's soul was worthy to enter the underworld, or what Christians call heaven.

Anpu was also known as the God of orphans, travelers, and the lost. As a patron of magic, it was believed that he could foresee a person's destiny.

He was also considered a great messenger, one who carried messages from the Underworld to the Gods and Goddesses of the Heavens, as well as from these deities to mankind itself. All pay homage to Melanin's properties to guide the Black man into higher consciousness, if he is willing to embrace it and dedicate his life to higher consciousness.

BOOK OF THE DEAD

The Egyptian Book of the Dead is a collection of magic spells and formulas that was illustrated and written, usually on papyrus. It began to appear in Egyptian tombs around 1600 BC. The text was intended to be spoken by the deceased during their journey into the Underworld. It enabled the deceased to overcome obstacles in the afterlife. It did this by teaching passwords that allowed the deceased to turn into mythical creatures to navigate around hazards, while granting the help and protection of the gods, and proclaiming the deceased's identity with the gods.

The Egyptians believed that the human soul used the first night after death to travel into the afterlife. However, the body, which the Egyptians believed was an essential element to the afterlife had to be mummified. And this process took 72 days to perform properly. This also gave them time to put finishing touches on the tomb and to pack all the deceased's worldly possessions, which they would surely need in the afterlife. (http://members.aol.com/egyptart/ani.html)

Your guide in this life, as well as the afterlife, who the deceased would call upon, was the god Anpu. So if Anpu represents Melanin, then it is logical to say that the only way to transcend in the spiritual realm is if one is guided by Melanin. Caucasians, because of their lack of Melanin or the god Anpu, will be lost in the physical realm as well as the spiritual world. They cannot find their way to transcend to a higher realm, which Christians call heaven. So, all Melanated people quit letting Caucasians set the standards for your reality, for they are lost. You are following a doomed people who don't know how to attain higher consciousness or reach a higher spiritual realm. They are the blind leading you, the blind, who has a guide but refuses to acknowledge him.

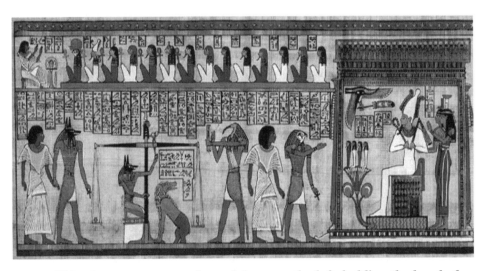

This picture represents the god Anpu on the left, holding the hand of
the deceased in his effort to guide him in the spiritual dimension.

Chapter Five:
The Pineal Gland: Was Blind but Now I See

"True vision materializes when one can see in the dark and is blinded by the light." — *Nekhebet*

He replied, "Because you have so little faith, I tell you the truth, if you have faith as small as a mustard seed, you can say to this mountain, move from here to there and it will move. Nothing will be impossible for you."
— *Matthew 17:20 (King James Version)*

The mustard seed that the Bible is talking about in the above scripture is referring to the Pineal gland that is located in one's brain. This is the gland that produces the miracle chemical called Melanin that Black people produce in abundance. If this gland is recognized and embraced for all its wonderful properties, people of color can create and manifest feats that are known as miracles. A miracle can be defined as the manifestation of one's thoughts and ideas into the physical dimension. This is the very gland that white supremacy must shut down in Black people in order to manipulate and control them. If Caucasians are able to continue to shut down the Pineal gland, they will be able to keep the darker peoples of the Earth in a state of dependency, oppression and operating at a lower level of consciousness.

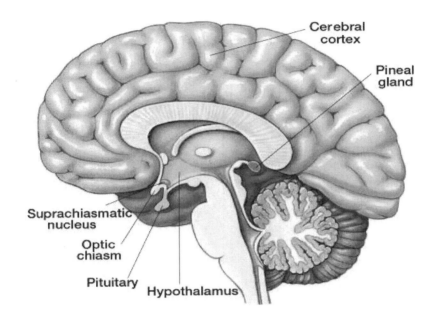

The Pineal Gland: Named after the shape of a Pine Cone, which it resembles. It was known as the "first eye" in ancient Kemet, because its activation was mandatory in order for a person to reach higher consciousness.

The Healing of a Blind Man at Bethsaida

They came to Bethsaida, and some people brought a blind man and begged Jesus to touch him. He took the blind man by the hand and led him outside the village. When he had spit on the man's eyes and put his hands on him, Jesus asked, "Do you see anything?" He looked up and said, "I see people; they look like trees walking around." Once more Jesus put his hands on the man's eyes. Then his eyes were opened, his sight was restored, and he saw everything clearly." — Mark 8:22-25

French philosopher, mathematician and physicist, Rene Descartes referred to the Pineal Gland as, *"The seat of the soul."* This European thinker knew that the Pineal gland in humans had a direct link to the spiritual realm and the higher consciousness that one could achieve or have access to if they raised their consciousness. If one were to locate the Pineal gland through the front of their skull, it would line up directly between their eyes on their forehead. This is the same location of the red dot that we see on Indian women of the Hindu religion. Our ancient Kemetic ancestors referred to this gland as the "first eye." It was later changed by the European to the "third eye" to take away the significance of its properties. The god Buddha is often also portrayed with a mark on his forehead that represents the Pineal gland. Catholics, on Ash Wednesday, will mark their foreheads with the ashes from palm leaves to represent the activation of this gland. The black ashes represent the Melanin produced by the Pineal gland.

So if the activation of the Pineal gland represents man's ability to transcend in the spiritual world through higher consciousness, what are the characteristics of an inactive or calcified Pineal gland? Without the concept of spirituality and higher consciousness, man is relegated to a beast, displaying lower consciousness or animalistic behavior. I refer to this state of mind as A.I. or Artificial Intelligence. Logic and intelligence, without any spirituality to guide it, is a deadly combination. This is the level of the white man's system as we know it today. Everything in this society is perceived as "just business"; nothing is supposed to be taken personally. Our Afrikan ancestors believed in the exact opposite. Everything was considered personal or a reflection of your consciousness. There was never any separation from the heart and the mind, which is responsible for the individual's behavior. Not one concept or ideology of higher consciousness or spirituality has ever come out of Europe, or for that matter, the United States. Not one thing. And if you think there has been, I promise you that there was a person of color behind the scenes that never got credit for it. World history has shown us that the more Melanin a person possesses, then the more humane and spiritual they have the capacity to be. If one looks around the world, they will witness this to be true. It is only after the European conquered the darker, indigenous people throughout the world did they display and adopt this lower level behavior that you see today. I am not saying that the darker people are incapable of lower level behavior or consciousness, as we all have freewill to decide for ourselves. What I do want to point out is that darker people have the "capacity", because of their higher concentration of Melanin, to be one with nature, and thus, closer to God consciousness.

The Indian god Krishna, the Kemetic god Anpu, the Christian god Jesus, the Asian gods Naga and Buddha, all represent Black or blackness. All these representations of God pertain to the chemical Melanin produced by the Pineal Gland.

The white man has always caused trouble, havoc and destruction wherever he showed up around the world, even among his own people. Why do you think there are so many countries in Europe? Why are there so many different states in the United States? Caucasians just can't seem to get along, not even among themselves, let alone with the darker people of the world. One may point out the fact that there are 54 countries on the continent of Afrika, so you just can't say this is a European trait of separation or division. Understand, people, until the European invaded Afrika and split up the land mass for itself, Afrika didn't need borders as we know today. The European divided Afrika amongst the Germans, Belgians, Italians, Spanish, Portuguese, Great Britain, the French and others for their own personal exploitation. I came across an interesting concept in my research. It was from a Caucasian man named David Wilcock. He is a professional lecturer, filmmaker and researcher of ancient civilizations, consciousness science, and new paradigms of matter and energy. He states that the concept of the *"Mark of the Beast" that the Bible refers to as the Anti-Christ in the book of Revelation is really the properties of having a calcified Pineal gland.* So he accentuates that those who do not have an active Pineal gland that produces Melanin will define themselves and their environment through their lower consciousness. They will behave like an animal with no humanity.

What he doesn't mention is the fact that the European or people, who classify themselves as white, share this condition of having a calcified Pineal gland.

Image of the pineal gland found in the center of one's brain. Its name comes from the gland resembling a Pine cone.

http://divinecosmos.com/index.php/videos/access-your-higher-self

"And he causeth all, both small and great, rich and poor, free and bond, to receive a mark in their right hand, or in their foreheads: And that no man might buy or sell, save he that had the mark, OR the name of the beast, or the number of his name. Here is wisdom. Let him that hath understanding count the number of the beast: for it is the number of a man; and his number is six hundred threescore and six" — Revelation 13:15-18 (King James Holy Bible)

So if the "Mark of the Beast" is the calcified Pineal gland located on the forehead, what is the mark on the right hand that this scripture is also alluding to? The right hand symbolizes man's lower self. It is man that defines himself through his animalistic desires and behaviors, whereas the left hand or left side of man's body represents his higher consciousness and spiritual side. Remember, the right hand is controlled by the left hemisphere of the brain, which our Kemetic ancestors believed represented man's lower self and consciousness. So the number of man, 666, is the number of the beast or the animalistic consciousness and behavior in man. Six, as you will recall in our Biblical numerology chapter, represents the spirit at its lowest level of existence, the physical dimension. The spirit incarnated in the physical body is the lowest level of existence that the spirit can descend to. According to our spirits, we are already in hell and don't even realize it because we define ourselves by our physical bodies. We are operating at the lowest level physically (6), mentally (6) and spiritually (6). These are the three properties that make up the physical dimension. It is in this physical world where the white man rules. This is his domain. This is where the white man wants to keep people of color, who have the ability to transcend into higher consciousness because of their activated Pineal glands.

Remember, the white man's level of higher consciousness and spirituality is limited by his calcified Pineal gland. He cannot transcend to the potential levels that we have access to in the spiritual world. The physical world is the European's foundation. That is why he holds on to it so tightly by way of promoting materialism, greed, selfishness, ego, oppression, and gluttony. This is where he came up with the concept of, "He who dies with the most toys wins." This is the premise that his system is designed for and at the expense of keeping people of color at their lower state of consciousness. The Caucasian needs Black people to participate in this lower consciousness system so that he can have his heaven here on Earth. "The White man's heaven is the Black man's hell." Since Melanin can be used to manifest thoughts and ideas in the physical dimension, the Caucasian needs to hijack people of color's Melanin in order to create the physical world that he wants to live in. Because of his lack of Melanin, he feels that he has no other choice than to force people of color to build the civilization he desires but cannot manifest on his own. And the only way he knows how to do this is to embrace his lower, animalistic consciousness. One thing that the Caucasian missed when he was exposed to people of color, which would have worked in his favor, is this: All he had to do was ask for help and we would have volunteered to help him build, educate and uplift his people. But since he embraces his lower self, he felt compelled to enslave, deceive, poison, rape, kill and maim people of color in order to forcefully achieve his goals.

The Biblical "Mark of the Beast" represented by the calcified Pineal gland on the forehead and the activation of the left hemisphere of the brain by marking the right hand.

"To open the blind eyes, to bring out the prisoners from the prison, and them that sit in darkness out of the prison house." — Isaiah 42:7 (King James Bible)

The white power structure understands this science and uses it against us on a daily basis. Caucasians innately know they are not going anywhere after their physical death but right back to being reincarnated in the lower physical dimension. However, people of color have the capacity to access many dimensions in the spiritual realm, depending on the life lessons they have learned here in the physical realm. The physical dimension is the proving ground or litmus test for people of color. We cannot achieve higher spiritual realms until we master our physical bodies and the physical dimension. This dimension is as far as the spirit can fall. Why do you think the white man holds on to this material world so drastically? His motto is, "He who dies with the most toys wins." This is as good as it gets for him, so he invests his time and Inner G in the material world to have some semblance of a life experience in the lowest level of consciousness there is. His system is designed to keep Black people and people of color here as well. Who else is going to create the heaven here on Earth for him to partake and indulge in? Understand, Black people, he never intended for you to be equal or included in his physical world, which he claims mastery over. So people of color might as well work on transcending from the physical dimension and see what higher, spiritual dimensions have in store for them. Our goal should always be to achieve and be dedicated to reaching higher, spiritual consciousness. We should never take the low road or we will be doomed to travel it throughout eternity.

In the Bible scripture 1 Samuel 17 is the story of David and Goliath. David representing the Caucasian slew the giant, who represented the Black man, by hitting him in the forehead with a stone. The forehead symbolizes the activation of the Black man's Pineal gland. This is how the white man oppresses and controls the Black man. The Caucasian purposely suppresses and destroys the Black man's ability to reach his higher consciousness by attacking the properties of his Pineal gland. This act keeps the Black man from achieving his status of a "giant", otherwise known as a person of higher consciousness in the physical dimension. The system is designed to keep the Black man preoccupied with his lower consciousness so that he will never recognize his higher self, which is portrayed by Goliath being represented as a "giant."

The Biblical parable of David and Goliath is really about the
suppression of the Pineal gland of the Black race by the Caucasian.

The Pineal gland has also been represented by the pine cone. The pine cone is roughly the same shape as the Pineal gland. In ancient Sumerian texts, it shows the Annukai raising the pine cone with one hand as if to squeeze it like an orange to retrieve its Melanin. There is a giant statue of a pine cone in Vatican City, the head of the Catholic Church. On the Pope's staff, it has the crucifixion of Jesus on the cross, standing on a pine cone. This is why we decorate the Christmas tree with lights. Light always symbolizes higher consciousness in the ancient world. Pine trees are used as Christmas trees so that people would subconsciously worship the pine cone, which represents the Pineal gland. They put presents under the tree so that the person would have to bow down to the pine cone if they wanted to retrieve their gift. The gift under the pine tree represents the "gift" of higher spiritual consciousness. The character of Buddha is always displayed with a hairstyle resembling a pine cone.

The pine tree used to celebrate Christmas is really the worshipping of the Pineal Gland. One bends over, or "bows" down to it, in order to retrieve the gifts underneath.

The pope also glorifies the Pineal Gland. On his staff, he has the Christ figure standing on top of a pine cone to represent KRST consciousness. The Pineal gland is the foundation for achieving higher consciousness.

The Buddha figure has a hairstyle in the shape of a pine cone, which represents the Pineal Gland. Notice the dot in the middle of the forehead, which symbolizes what our ancestors called the "First Eye" or the activation of the Pineal Gland. The picture on the left is a giant pine cone statue found in the courtyard of the Vatican.

Stanford University's mascot is the pine tree, symbolizing the activation of the Pineal Gland on the left. Stanford is one of the most prestigious universities in the country. The Sumerian god Marduk, on the right, is seen holding a pine cone, representing higher consciousness and life held in the activation of one's Pineal Gland.

The pine cone on the staff of Dionysus on the left and the staff of the Kemetic god, Ausar on the right.

The pine cone on the left of the photo on top of the staff of the Greek of the god Dionysus. According to Greek mythology, Dionysus traveled to Egypt, otherwise known as Kemet, the land of the Black people. He was the god of wine, which represented his Melanated blood and festivities.

So how does one obtain access to this wonderful gift that the Creator has bestowed upon people of color? It seems everyone who doesn't have it knows about its properties and uses them against the very people who are fortunate to have access to it. How can the people of color, who actually manufacture it, make it work for our benefit and not against our own best interests? The answer to this question can be found in this scripture in the Bible:

"That night Jacob got up and took his two wives, his two maidservants and his eleven sons and crossed the ford of the Jabbok.[23] After he had sent them across the stream, he sent over all his possessions. [24] So Jacob was left alone, and a man wrestled with him till daybreak. [25] When the man saw that he could not overpower him, he touched the socket of Jacob's hip so

*that his hip was wrenched as he wrestled with the man. *[26]* Then the man said, "Let me go, for it is daybreak."*

But Jacob replied, "I will not let you go unless you bless me."

[27] The man asked him, "What is your name?"

"Jacob," he answered.

[28] Then the man said, "Your name will no longer be Jacob, but Israel, [a] because you have struggled with God and with men and have overcome."

[29] Jacob said, "Please tell me your name."

But he replied, "Why do you ask my name?" Then he blessed him there.

[30] So Jacob called the place Peniel, [b] saying, "It is because I saw God face to face, and yet my life was spared."

[31] The sun rose above him as he passed Peniel, [c] and he was limping because of his hip. — Genesis 32:22-31

The name Jacob means to supplant another man and take his place to usurp his power and status. Jacob symbolizes man's perpetual struggle to define himself through his higher self or his lower self. All men are born of freewill, from which to define themselves. Jacob represents man's struggle within himself. We all are familiar with the cartoon below that shows an angel on one shoulder and a devil on the other. It symbolizes man's the freewill to decide which side of himself he will embrace. His higher consciousness on his left, represented by the angel or the lower consciousness on his right represented by the devil.

That night, Jacob sent his 2 wives, 2 maid servants and 11 sons across the river. In Biblical numerology, these numbers add up to 15, which equal 6. Remember, six represents man's lower self. So by isolating himself from his physical vices or characteristics, he is now able to concentrate on his higher, spiritual self. ***He then proceeds to send his possessions away as well.*** Jacob now relieves himself of all superficial materialism that feeds his ego. Jacob is now humbling himself to go into deep meditation to achieve higher consciousness. In order to find one's true self, one must get rid of material things, which one uses to define him or herself on the outside, and look within for the true knowledge of self. ***So now, Jacob wrestles with his lower self throughout the night until daybreak.*** Remember, consciousness or enlightenment is represented by the sun or sunlight, in this case, daybreak. Jacob is now an enlightened being as soon as the Sun rises.

When Jacob's ego realizes that he has been defeated, Jacob is touched on his right leg and acquires a limp. The injury to the right leg symbolizes Jacob defining himself through his higher self and not his lower self. Jacob has killed his ego or lower self represented by the right leg. The left leg represents one's higher self.

Jacob forces his ego to bless him. Just then, the ego names his true self Israel, Isis, RA & EL. These are Kemetic terms with higher consciousness at their core.

Jacob asks the man, which is his ego, "What is your name?" The ego, being a figment of his imagination, does not answer because it does not exist.

So this place in which Jacob achieved higher consciousness, he called Peniel, another spelling of the same word for Pineal gland. He calls it by this name because this is where he saw God face to face. This is the KRST consciousness, also known as Christ consciousness.

The Sun rose above him as it passed Peniel. This refers to the Pineal gland being activated by the Sun's energy in order for higher consciousness to take place. Melanin uses the Sun's energy to activate the Pineal gland.

And he was limping because of his hip. Our ancient, Kemetic ancestors had a saying, "Left foot forward to trample down evil so that the heart can move forward" (taken from Ashwra Kwesi lecture). The left foot moving forward activates the right brain, which represents one's higher or spiritual consciousness. As we know, the left side of the body is controlled by the right hemisphere of the brain. So the limping signifies the favoring of the left leg over the right, or the choice to activate one's higher self over their lower self.

"Brain fluid and seminal fluid are made up of the same substance. Man can only serve one master at a time, his higher head or his lower head." —Nekhebet

Anointing Oil

I relate the anointing oil in the Bible to the activation of the Pineal gland, which produces the chemical called Melanin. Melanin is the anointing oil. The Greek term for anointing oil is called Chrism. This leads us back to the KRST or Christ consciousness that we discussed in earlier chapters of the book. Let us further delve into the theory of KRST consciousness and how it relates to the Pineal gland and the manufacturing of Melanin.

"Kerast is a 'Chaldean' (Iraqi) Word for 'oil'...as in 'anoint or caress with oil.' It is also the base of the Chaldean word 'Chris', which means 'sun'. The connection between 'oil' (as in fuel) and the burning 'sun' as its symbol is unmistakable."

So according to these definitions, one can receive KRST consciousness by activating one's Pineal gland to produce Melanin, by exposing it to the Sun. Keras in Hebrew comes from a primary Kar (the hair of the head), a horn like from an animal. **Strong's #2768:** Keras points back to the head and also represents a horn of an animal. So here we have another source of the word Keras that represents the region of the head. When we combine this definition with the other meanings of Keras, we can conclude that the production of oil is connected or activated by the Sun and takes place in the region of the head. Another legend states as follows:

"Ancient legends advise the Island was inhabited by a tribe called the 'Kares' since about 3,000 BC. Ironically, the word 'Kares' in Hebrew means a 'divinely inspired premature death (kharmic justice?) decreed by the Jewish Torah for certain transgressions.' One of the 'punishments equivalent to death' in the Torah is 'exile' or 'Banishment' onto a foreign land... literally doomed to wander a 'stranger in a strange land.'"

So if Kares in Hebrew means a divinely inspired premature death or banishment, it seems that living life with a calcified Pineal gland is equivalent to death, banishment, and being lost and doomed. It is the life of the European species, who are unable to raise their consciousness to a level that transcends the physical dimension. So not being able to transcend into higher consciousness is the motivation behind the white man's lower level behavior and his brutal mindset to rule the world by the oppression and devastation of Black people and people of color. Since the white man has been "exiled" or "banished" from higher, spiritual consciousness because of his calcified Pineal gland, he must embrace the physical dimension as "his" world to master, dominate, manipulate and control.

<u>Luke 11:34</u> Your eye (the Pineal gland) is the lamp of your body. When your eyes are good, your whole body also is full of light. But when they are bad, your body also is full of darkness.

<u>Matthew 6: 22</u> The light of the body is the eye: if therefore thine eye be single, thy whole body shall be full of light

Chapter Six: Man vs. Mankind
(kind of a man)

"The difference between man and mankind is Black and white."
— Nekhebet

I will break down the difference between Afrocentricity (Eastern Philosophy) versus Eurocentricity (Western Philosophy). Mind you, Western or European thought is the basis or foundation that dominates how the world sees itself and operates, and it controls all facets in this global society. It is the system of white supremacy and thought that rules the world as we know it. Needless to say, this system of European thought is grossly flawed, given the horrendous conditions of the world today. This philosophy has been put in place so that Caucasians would have the advantage or upper hand when dealing with the darker peoples of the world. Melanated people of color, as we covered earlier, naturally operate and decipher their reality dominated by the right hemisphere of the brain or their higher spiritual selves. Because the European is deficient in Melanin and cannot reach the level of spirituality that Melanated people can, he must establish a playing field in his favor which is based on the left hemisphere of the brain. This understanding and interpretation of the world and reality gives the European the upper hand in politics, sociology, economics, biology, chemistry, nutrition, medicine, philosophy, war, religion, history, education and the sciences.

Dr. Wade Nobles, my professor at San Francisco State University, lectured me on the comparison and contrast of Afrikan (Black) thought vs. Eurocentric (white) thought. These are his findings and interpretations:

AFROCENTRIC IDEOLOGY VS. EUROCENTRIC IDEOLOGY

Manifestation of the Creator	Product of the Creator
Sees himself as an extension of nature	Opposes & tries to conquer nature.
I am because we are and because we are, therefore I am	Survival of the fittest. Individuality.
Everything in the Universe is connected	Isolate & dissect the Universe.
Elders & children are closer to God	Elders & children are weaker stages in life.
Cosmological view & Ideology.	Separation & Domination mentality.
We are spirits having a human experience.	We are humans having spiritual moments.
Misconduct leads to separation from God.	Man's destiny determined by hostility.
Ideas of Ascension.	Ideas of Domination.
Capacity to Change & Transcend.	Ability to define difference & separation.
Capacity to renew & grow beyond self.	Ability to Manipulate.

As you can see, it really is a white man's world because he has put the world in its "unnatural" state as it exists today. He has influenced or strong-armed all the darker people in the world to act according to his ideology. He has convinced them that it is his natural inheritance, or his ordained right, to rule the world as he sees fit without any questions to his authority.

> Eurocentric ideology has to create a common enemy for Caucasians to bond together and co-exist with one another. That is the only way white people can be united. They need to have an "Us against a common enemy" mentality, for if they do not have a common enemy, they will war with one another. This will initiate their own

demise and the self-destruction of the white race. If they do not unite against a "perceived" common enemy, then they will try to destroy each other. That is why Europe, being a relatively small land mass, has several countries or "tribes" of Europeans with different languages and cultures. The white man's history shows that he is a people of war and destruction, even against his own people. But he must tolerate his own people if he wants to continue to oppress the darker people of the world. For him, it is an evil necessity for him to remain in power.

The Caucasian has held the darker people of the world hostage to his belief system. Believe it or not, there was a time in the history of the world when white people did not exist. This planet was an exclusively Black or Melanated world. Can you imagine a time when reality was defined through the Afrocentric ideology and not Eurocentric? It was no wonder that these ancient civilizations were the most advanced in the history of man. It is only after the Europeans crawled out of the caves of Europe that the world was slowly and methodically hijacked and transformed into the Eurocentric school of thought ruled by lower consciousness. This is the basis of white supremacy. This is why the white man has to keep his foot on the necks of all the darker people on the planet. If the system switched back to an Afrocentric ideology, the white man would eventually be banished to the place from which he came. Either that or he would be swallowed up by the genetic gene pool of the darker people of the planet. The white man thinks too highly of himself to ever let that happen. He has vowed that he will put up a fight for his life. Although his blending into the darker gene pool is inevitable, he has made a pact to take as many people as he can with him. As the conscious rap group of my generation, Public Enemy, once stated, the white man has a fear of a Black planet and genetic annihilation. The white man's thought process is: if he cannot rule the world, there will be no world for others to rule. He has vowed that his destruction will mean the destruction of the world, as well.

We need to understand that the present mindset that Black people possess is not our original thought pattern, or the way God intended for us to perceive ourselves and our reality. Our "right" minds have been hijacked and switched with the inferior, slave mind. On the road to recovery, the first thing one must do is to acknowledge that he is not well. In order to get well, one must address the symptoms of their mind first. We, as people of Afrikan descent, need to admit that we are not in our right minds and seek the help that we need.

Foundation of White Supremacy

- People who label themselves "White" make up less than 10% of the world's total population, but control 90% of the world's resources.
- Caucasians have a zero percent birth rate. For every Caucasian that dies, only one Caucasian is born. For every one person of color that dies, 2 to 3 persons of color are born.
- Caucasians define their supremacy by the characteristics of their recessive genes, which are the direct result of their lack of Melanin.
- In order for the Caucasian race to survive, they must protect their gene pool while destroying the gene pools of all people of color.
- The source of the white man's fear of the Black man is the genetic potency of the Black man's DNA that has the potential to annihilate him as a race through sexual integration.
- If nature had its way, the white race would be eliminated. The Caucasian is constantly being attacked and destroyed by the Sun (nature) and from the DNA of people of color.
- The white man vows that he will not go down without a fight.
- The white man is driven by his ego or lower self. He always knows what's best for everyone at the expense of everyone but himself.
- The white man cannot admit that he is wrong. He will never fully give credit to or listen to a person of color.
- The white man never apologizes for his thoughts or actions. He will justify what he does or blame the victim.

- The white man never forgives but always wants forgiveness from the very people whom he oppresses, people of color.
- In order for the white man to feel good about himself, he must subject others under his perceived "superior" power.

Man vs. Mankind

Throughout time, history records only the winner's story; the loser's version is never told. Since the white man has assumed his position as the ruler of the world, our history has been falsified, denied, forgotten and manipulated. In order to stay in power, the white man must subject his rule over the people he has conquered. In this chapter, I want to concentrate on the white man's history and not the Afrikans'. Let's take a look at how and when the white man came on the scene and why he is the exact opposite of Melanated people or people of Afrikan descent. When we look into the white man's history, which has never been objectively addressed in his school system, we will come up with a better understanding of how and why he thinks and processes his reality the way he does. Remember, legitimate control and manipulation starts when one not only has the power to enforce what is talked about, but more importantly, what is not addressed.

"History is a set of lies agreed upon." — Napoleon Bonaparte

Remember a few years back a scientist discovered an Afrikan female, human remains in the country of Ethiopia? "The fossilized remains were discovered in 1974 in the remote, desert-like Afar region in northeastern Ethiopia. Lucy is classified as an Australopithecus Afarensis, which lived in Africa between about 4 million and 3 million years ago, and is the earliest known hominid." So the history of the Afrikan can be traced back to at least 3 million to four million years ago. What is the farthest back in time that we can trace Caucasians' history? I have heard estimates of time as far back as 80,000 years ago. What I want to point out is that, whether they want to believe it or not, Caucasians come from Afrikans. It is impossible for

Caucasians to produce darker or Melanated offspring. Whether they want to acknowledge this fact or not, Afrikans are their parents. That means their way of life for the last 2,000 years is very infantile and immature when one looks at how old Afrikan civilizations have been around. What they view as progress, our ancient ancestors saw as a dysfunctional baby that has not yet begun to mature, let alone fend for itself.

Let us break down the word "human". The root words are "Hue" and "Man".

Hue- a shade of color or pigment; complexion

Man- of the human species. The compound idea of infinite Spirit. The spiritual image and likeness of God; the full representation of Mind.

According to the definitions of these two words, in order for one to be considered human, they must have pigment or color. Pigmentation is caused by the chemical Melanin produced by the Pineal gland. The definition of white is the absence of pigmentation or color. This is the condition of having no Melanin because of the calcified Pineal gland. One is either born with Melanin or not. An individual cannot acquire Melanin after they are born. Man was defined by our Afrikan ancestors as the full representation of the mind. If this is true, then man must be able to access the right brain and left brain with equal balance in their view of reality in the physical dimension. The right brain is man's spiritual interpretation of reality and the left brain is man's physical interpretation of reality. The Caucasian, as we discussed before, is left-brain dominant. The Caucasian does not have the capacity to interpret the physical or lower plane according to a higher, spiritual nature. According to our definition of human, the Caucasian does not qualify. So if the Caucasian cannot be considered human, what are they?

"History will be kind to me for I intend to write it" — Winston Churchill

According to the Moorish Master Teacher, Taj Tarik Bey, the Caucasian race is a species described as "kind of a man", otherwise known as "Mankind." Very distinctive and not to be confused with the state of being human.

Definitions of Mankind, according to the Strong Concordance Bible:

Masculine, Bold; Cruel

- *Pertaining to all of man.*
- *Kind — Nature, family, lineage, manner; essence.*
- *A doubtful or barely admissible member of a category.*
- *"Kind of a Man"*

So let's also refer to the King James Version of the Bible in order to break down the metaphysical definition that separates man from mankind or (kind of a man.) Who was Adam? Some Biblical scholars say that the time Adam was created was between 6,000 to 12,000 years ago. Mind you, this is a short amount of time compared to Afrikan Lucy's remains of 3 to 4 million years ago. The story of Adam begins in the Book of Genesis, otherwise known as the "Genes of Isis." Genesis, the first book of the Bible, is an abbreviation for "Genes of Isis." Isis is the Greek name for the Kemetic goddess, Auset. Auset was the Afrikan goddess that the Bible refers to as Mary, the mother of Jesus. So basically, man and mankind originated and came into existence through the genes of the Black woman. Remember, a Black woman can create Black, brown, red, yellow and white pigmentation offspring. The white woman can only produce white offspring. She cannot produce color. *The Strong Concordance Bible defines Adam as such: red in the face. Earthy. Ruddy or pinkish in color, flushed. Generic name for man. As a symbol of original sin. Frailty. Formed from the ground. Meaning "mankind." One who becomes easily angered.*

There is no one man on Earth who fits this description more than the Caucasian. According to our Afrikan ancestors, Black people come from the spiritual dimension or from the heavens. According to the stories in the Bible, the white man was created in the physical dimension. Adam was made from the Earth's soil. The spiritual realm represents man's higher self and the physical realm represents man's lower self. One can conclude that the Afrikan contains man's higher consciousness and the European represents man's lower consciousness at their essence.

In the Bible, Genesis chapter 1:26 says, "Let **US** make Man." I pose this question to the reader: Who is the "**US**" the Bible is referring to? This Bible verse suggests that there was more than one God or person involved in the creation of man. The numbers of the chapter and verses of this information comes out to be the number nine when we decipher the numbers according to the science of Biblical numerology. The number nine, according to the science, equals judgment. Was the white man created to test the humanity of the Black race in their effort to achieve higher consciousness by surviving the brutality of white supremacy? Are we being judged by the way we handle our oppression and enslavement, in our pursuit to return to higher consciousness in the spiritual dimension? Do we need to be subjected to the fire of oppression in an effort to purify us in our evolution to a higher consciousness? Did we purposely make a lower conscious being in order for them to test our humanity in our efforts to return to the spiritual realm?

The Bible also says that on the 6th day, God created Man. Remember, the number six in Biblical numerology represents the spirit in its lowest state of existence, reincarnated in the physical body in the physical dimension.

The Bible also says that Adam was formed from the Earth. This suggests that Adam is a worldly being, not in the image of God. Afrikan or Kemetic mythology always views the Black man and woman coming down from the heavens to have a physical experience. Not physical beings having spiritual moments. We are not of this world but from the higher spiritual dimension. We are just having a human experience and will soon return back to the heavens when we "transcend" the moment that our physical bodies die.

The Bible also relegates Adam, who represents the white man or mankind, as being made lower than the angels. Remember, the Bible and the Quran also state that the angels are supposed to serve man. Adam, or the white race, must be different from man, because the angels cannot serve someone who is lower than themselves.

All these definitions unequivocally describe the characteristics of the white man. These definitions would suggest that the Black race has been here for as long as anyone can remember. The white race coming from the Black race such a short time ago, suggests that something very drastic had to take place in history for the white race to have lost all their Melanin and their ability to produce it. Also, what took place in history that made Caucasians so infuriated that they despise the Black man so much to inflict the greatest tragedy in the history of the world and do not want to be accountable for their actions? What would turn a child against their parents?

The Lineage of Man & Mankind

The common ancestor of man and mankind is called Homoheidelbergensis. He, of course, lived in Afrika some 500,000 years ago.

400,000 years ago, there was a divergence in time that separated the Afrikan or modern human form this new species, the Neanderthal Man (see illustration). Modern humans come from the Afrikan species that appeared at least 190,000 years ago. Subsequently, the Neanderthal man shows up in the Neander Valley in the European country of Germany. Then it seems, for no reason, the Neanderthal becomes extinct, never to be heard from again. Or did he?

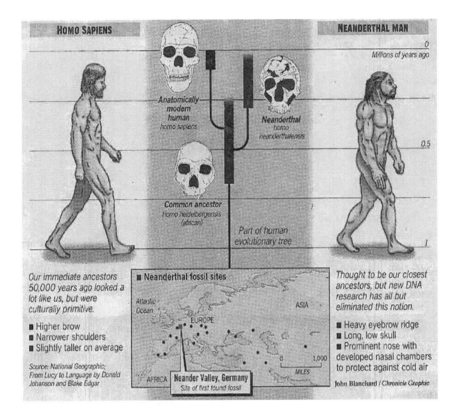

HOMO SAPIENS

NEANDERTHAL MAN

0

Millions of years ago

Anatomically
modern
human
homo sapiens

Neanderthal
homo
neanderthalensis

0.5

Common ancestor
homo heidelbergensis
(african)

Part of human
evolutionary tree

Our immediate ancestors
50,000 years ago looked a
lot like us, but were
culturally primitive.

■ Higher brow
■ Narrower shoulders
■ Slightly taller on average

Source: National Geographic;
From Lucy to Language by Donald
Johanson and Blake Edgar

■ Neanderthal fossil sites

Atlantic
Ocean

EUROPE

ASIA

AFRICA | Neander Valley, Germany
Site of first found fossil

Thought to be our closest
ancestors, but new DNA
research has all but
eliminated this notion.

■ Heavy eyebrow ridge
■ Long, low skull
■ Prominent nose with
developed nasal chambers
to protect against cold air

John Blanchard / Chronicle Graphic

While man, the Afrikan, was building the most advanced civilization ever in Afrika over 50,000 years ago, mankind was still living in the caves of Europe. How is it that one group of man was living in advanced technology and sciences, while the other group, mankind, was walking on all fours, not knowing how to bathe, cook its food, or use language? This is an interesting note about the Neanderthal. Throughout the entire animal kingdom, no species has ever started out at an advanced level, and over time, gradually sank into barbarism. This species is what we now know as the Caucasian race.

The Neanderthal, from day one of their existence, has slowly regressed to a lower animalistic state. In nature, species always evolve over time, not devolve as the Neanderthal did. This tells me that they were once a product or offspring of a higher evolved Afrikan species. When they left or were banished to fend for themselves in Europe, they slowly lost their humanity or human spirit and continued to practice barbarism.

"Mankind must put an end to war before war puts an end to mankind." –JFK

The European Dark Ages were in 7th to 14th Century AD. The Moors were a people of Afrikan descent.

- In 711 AD, the Afrikan Moors conquered Spain.
- Europe, with the Catholic Church in power, was in complete barbarism.
- 90% of Europe was illiterate, did not bathe and were uncivilized.
- The Moors reintroduced hygiene, mathematics, medicine, architecture, religion, education, government, agriculture and the physical sciences.
- The Moors built Universities, public baths, paved streets, sewage systems, aqueducts, developed industries for textiles, metals, food production and hydraulic engineering.
- Moors got rid of the Roman Numeral System and introduced the number zero and the decimal point. This implementation was necessary in order to decipher advanced mathematics and engineering.
- Even in Europe, Afrikan people had to civilize, teach and show Caucasians how to be human. Coincidently, there was never a Dark Age in Afrika! Afrikans had to civilize the Caucasian race, not the other way around, as they would have you believe.

"One Small Step for Man, One Giant Leap for Mankind." –Neil Armstrong

The above quote gives insight into the separation of man and mankind being different concepts. The term "man", representing the Afrikan, has achieved the highest level of civilization and science that the world as ever known, as signified by the pyramids and other great Afrikan civilizations. His knowledge is vast and ancient, so going to the moon was not a great accomplishment compared to the other achievements he has made. It was just a "small step" for him. Coincidently, mankind, representing the Caucasian race that came out of the caves of Europe on all fours, going to the moon was a "giant leap" in his history.

Elijah Muhammad's Blue-Eyed Devil Theory

There was born a genius whose name was Yakub. At a young age, Yakub wanted to be a scientist. Yakub's plan was to graft the weakest germ out of the Black man to create a "lesser" man to rule over the Earth. Yakub discovered that the Black man was composed of two germs, one black and one brown. The brown germ was a weaker version of the Black germ. From the brown germ, he grafted the red germ. From the red germ, he grafted the yellow and from the yellow germ, the white germ. He then gave the white germ all the science and knowledge of the Black man. The new, white race now uses this knowledge to rule over the Black man. This new white race only has 6,000 years to rule before they will die out. The white race was only made as a temporary species and was not to live beyond a certain time. Yakub did this so that the Black race would be forced to rise up and surpass its highest expectations.

Yacub, an evil Black scientist, created the white man through a series of gene splicing and manipulation of the germ. Evolution is the stages of the experiments to make the beast into the "kind of a man" creature that we call the "white man." According to Elijah Muhammed of the Nation of Islam, the white race is the product of Afrikan blood that, over time, a scientist deliberately and gradually eliminated all the Melanin from the blood. The result is the white race you see today. Because the Melanin was eliminated from the human, the final product is the Caucasian, or the "blue-eyed devil." The "devil" is the term used to describe someone who defines themselves and operates according to their lowest levels mentally, spiritually and physically. Elijah Muhammad's theory adds another piece to the puzzle of the origination of the white man and why he is so different from the rest of the Melanated people who are the majority on Earth. His theory supports the splitting of the Afrikan species of man and the European species of "kind of a man".

> *"then the priest shall consider; and indeed if leprosy has covered all his body, he shall pronounce him clean who has the sore. It has turned 'white.' He is clean." — Levitcus 13:13*

Dr. Frances Cress Welsing, the author of *The Isis Papers*, also has an interesting theory to add to the equation. **Dr. Welsing states that the white race began with the genetically recessive Afrikan albino.** She suggests that there had to be a catastrophe at some point in history, within the Afrikan race, that produced an abundance of albino offspring. She suggests that the albinos were gathered from Afrika and transported up north to Europe where they could survive because the cold, fog and caves would protect them from the sun that was trying to kill them in their native land. Coincidently, this is where you get the term of leprosy in the Bible. Leprosy is a state of albinism. Without parental love and guidance, these Afrikan albino mutants plunged into a world of chaos and animalistic behavior when they were isolated from Afrikan society and civilization. They would later gain strength and live to avenge their parents, who had forsaken them. Dr. Welsing suggests the psychology behind the European's brutal and deviant behavior towards the Afrikan stems from deep-rooted feelings of abandonment, neglect and being disowned from the parents who gathered them up and left them for dead in the hills and caves of Europe. This theory would not only explain the mindset and behavior of the European towards darker people of the world, but would also explain their loss of Melanin.

Let's Combine the Theories

1. Darwin's Theory states that mankind evolved from apes. Notice the term "mankind" or "kind of a man." Black people have always believed, throughout their existence, that they came from the heavens and not a beast or from the earth.

2. Evolution is the stages of the genetic blending. –Elijah Muhammad. Could it be that the "stages" that Darwin and Elijah Muhammad are referring to are the conditions of the white man's transformation over time?

3. The white man originated in the Caucasus Mountains in Southern Europe. The name "Caucasian" refers to the Caucasus Mountains. It is in this region that the Bible mentions as the birthplace of the people we label as white today.

4. The Afrikan albinos were ostracized and expelled to Europe.-Dr. Welsing. Could it be that the place the Afrikan albinos were expelled to was directly north across the desert, into the Caucasus Mountains?

5. Moses "escaped" out of Egypt, and crossed the burning sands to find the "Promised Land" for the "chosen people." Interpretation: Afrikan albinos "escaped" the effects of the Sun in Kemet by crossing the North Afrikan desert to get to the Caucasus Mountains, in order to find shelter in the caves from the Sun and the other natural elements that were harmful to their recessive genetic makeup.

6. Adam means reddish & one who becomes easily angered. He was made 6,000 to 12,000 years ago.-Strong Concordance Bible. The Black man and woman were here hundreds of thousands of years before the making of the white man. Adam refers to the birth or inception of the white race, not the Black man or people of color. They are two separate species.

7. Adam was kicked out of Paradise (Afrika) & discovered he was "naked." This Biblical story of Adam and Eve getting "kicked out" of the Garden of Eden refers to the exodus of leaving Afrika by being kicked out, or escaping, the effects of the Sun. The phrase "discovering that they were

naked," refers to finding out that his albinism did not contain Melanin to protect him.

8. The ostracized, albino Afrikan because of their self-hate, experimented with apes to genetically get rid of their recessive genes.- Tarik El Bey. Because the albino Afrikan wanted his color or Melanin back, he experimented in bestiality. He believed that if he intermingled with the monkey and/or the dog, he would somehow capture the color or Melanin that he was born without. Most of the Melanin in animals is contained in their fur and not their skin. Under their skin, they are very pale. Because of this attribute, the albino Afrikan only became more hairy but their skin remained pale.

9. Neanderthals are the only species to begin being humane and civilized, and over time, they became more brutal, barbaric & beastlike. The Neanderthal was the offspring of the albino Afrikan. Once they were ostracized and isolated from Afrikan civilization, the albino Afrikan began to practice barbarism, incest and bestiality. This caused the Neanderthal to fall deeper into his barbaric and animalistic nature as time went on. This is the origin of the white race.

10. The Neanderthal supposedly disappeared off the face of the Earth without any warning or trace. The Neanderthal did not disappear. He simply blended in with the human or Black race. This is where his DNA hides and infiltrates the human race today. But his true, barbaric nature will never fully disappear from his behavior. The white man will always be ruled by his lower, animalistic consciousness. This is where he is most suitable in nature.

11. The white man subconsciously has a hate for his parents, the Afrikan. They feel hurt and betrayed because the Afrikan shunned and turned their backs on him when they needed them the most. Thus, he is in a vengeful state & in an eternal retaliation mode. – Dr. Welsing. It is this psychology that fuels the white man's barbaric nature towards all people of color. Check out your history books. Whenever he has come into

contact with the darker people of the world, he has destroyed them and their way of life.

Genesis 10:1-2

This is the account of Shem, Ham and Japheth, Noah's sons, who themselves had sons after the flood.

The sons of Japheth:

Gomer, Magog, Madai, Javan, Tubal, Meshech and Tiras. These are supposedly the origins of the people we call Caucasians today according to the interpretation of the Bible. Notice the word Caucasian, comes from the place they inhabited called the "Caucasus Mountains," which is in the country known as Turkey today.

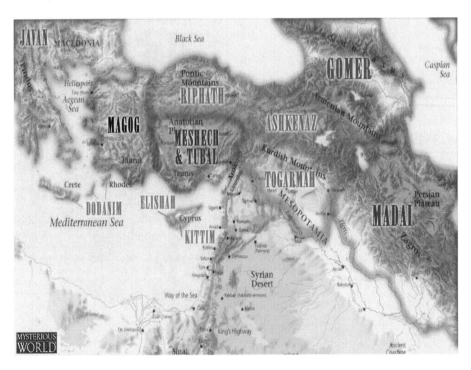

The character of Jacob in the Bible is another important clue to discovering the lineage and creation of the white race. Let us break down this character metaphysically:

Genesis 25:23 — The Lord said to her, "Two nations are in your womb, and two peoples within you will be separated; one people will be stronger than the other, and the older will serve the younger." This lays further evidence to our theory of the white race being genetically separated from the Black race. Two different species of man come from the same Afrikan womb or lineage. One race is stronger than the other, and the older race, the Afrikan, will serve the younger race, the European. This is the state of the world as we know it. The older, darker people of the world are being oppressed by the younger, white race.

Definition of the Biblical name *Jacob- to take the place of another, as through force, scheming or strategy, or the like.* This clearly alludes to the European using the Afrikan's sciences and technologies, which he stole from him to subdue, manipulate and oppress the Afrikan. The Afrikan was the ruler, god, or king of the world before the Caucasian came into existence. The white man has now made himself the ruler, god and king of all darker people of the world, at the expense of the Afrikan, through conniving force, strategy, brainwashing and manipulation. The European has now usurped the power of the once mighty Afrikan people and now uses this power against him.

Let us look further into the Biblical scriptures that describe the character of Jacob and how it relates to the Afrikan and Caucasian races being two separate entities:

Genesis24:25 [24] *When the time came for her to give birth, there were twin boys in her womb.* [25] *The first to come out was red, and his whole body was like a hairy garment; so they named him Esau.*[d]

I believe Esau represents the white race. The definition of **Esau is already made** — **he was already made a man, from the point of his birth; there would be no changing, no building or reshaping him. Esau was who he was going to be from day one.** This definition supports my claim that the Caucasian, because of their lack of Melanin, cannot transcend into higher consciousness. He is the man that he is going to be at birth, with no chance of evolving into higher consciousness because he has a calcified Pineal gland. He is described as red in pigment, has hair all over his body, a hunter and a carnivore. He would go on hunts, killing wild beasts, and had a reputation of being a cunning and courageous hunter. These are all attributes of someone who embraces his lower or animalistic consciousness. These are characteristics of the Caucasian. Even though this scripture says that he was born first, I believe this is just propaganda to justify the white man's self-imposed birth right of dominating the Earth and all that dwell in it. Esau's brother, Jacob, is described as having skin that was smooth and tender. Afrikans have little hair on their bodies. Their skin is smooth and hairless. Jacob was described as quiet and reserved. He kept to himself and looked out for his father's flock of sheep. He was a very peaceful man. Once again, these are attributes of indigenous people. They do not look to oppress or colonize Europeans. They are content in their culture and do not need anything outside of what the Earth provides for them in nature.

Furthermore, Isaac, the boy's father, favored Esau over his son Jacob. He believed Esau was more like himself, whereas Jacob possessed the characteristics of his mother. Isaac, the father, represents the masculine principle of Inner G, and Rebekah, the mother, represents the feminine principle of Inner G. This is very important because masculine Inner G represents lower consciousness of man, whereas feminine Inner G represents the higher consciousness of man. This means that Esau embraces his lower, animalistic consciousness and Jacob embraces his higher, spiritual consciousness. These two points further support my claim of the separation of the two races: one Caucasian, which embraces man's lower, animalistic consciousness and one Afrikan, which embraces man's higher, spiritual consciousness.

Genesis 24:26 — **[264]*After this, his brother came out, with his hand grasping Esau's heel; so he was named Jacob.***

Esau was born with his twin brother holding his older brother's heel. This signifies that Jacob, the white man, was trying to oppress his brother by limiting his potential to discover the powers of his right brain function. As you recall in a previous chapter, the left foot activates the right brain. By holding the heel or the left foot of his brother, he cannot access the power of his right brain functions.

The main excuse that the European made for the enslavement of the Black race was that the Black man was a savage and a heathen. They, like Jacob in the Bible, switched places with his brother. Afrikans became the heathen and the savage and the white man proclaimed themselves the civilized or more advanced race.

"I refuse to accept the view that mankind is so tragically bound to the starless midnight of racism; that the bright day break of peace and brotherhood can never become a reality....I believe that unarmed truth and unconditional love will have the final word." — Martin Luther King Jr.

In conclusion, my agenda is not to prove that the Afrikan race is superior over the European race. This is not my objective. My point is to get Black people to realize that we don't naturally possess the same view of the world or ourselves that our Caucasian counterparts maintain. We have tried to fit into their system, which we were forced to participate in, and we have plummeted to the lowest state that Black people have maintained in the history of the world. My focus is on Black people embracing their Melanin and higher consciousness for the blueprint that deciphers what they define as their reality. Quit trying to be white. By that I mean measuring yourself and defining your reality through what the white man has set as being normal or appropriate. Black people have become better white men than the white man himself! Their strategy is to keep us preoccupied by trying to reach their standards. If we do this, we will be oblivious to the fact that we were the original standard that they could never attain! They were outcasts in our civilization because they could not reach the level of humanity needed to function in our illustrious and advanced society. Now, the savage has come back to avenge the very people who rejected him and his sub-culture, the original Afrikan. Let us set our own agenda. If we define our own worldview and definitions of reality, they could not compete, let alone enslave and oppress the darker people of the world. Embrace, love, cherish and protect your Afrikan right mind and it will embrace, love, cherish and protect you.

"The European and his behavior as a living organism act like a cancer to the one earth body. He is a natural-born killer wherever he has gone." —Nekhebet

The white man's mentality: A definition of a Psychopath.

The psychopath is one of the most fascinating and distressing problems of human experience. For the most part, a psychopath never remains attached to anyone or anything. They live a "predatory" lifestyle. They feel little or no regret, and little or no remorse — except when they are caught. They need relationships, but see people as obstacles to overcome and be eliminated. If not, they see people in terms of how they can be used. They use people for stimulation, to build their self-esteem and they invariably value people in terms of their material value (money, property, etc...)

A psychopath can have high verbal intelligence, but they typically lack "emotional intelligence". They can be expert in manipulating others by playing to their emotions. There is a shallow quality to the emotional aspect of their stories (i.e., how they felt, why they felt that way, or how others may have felt and why). The lack of emotional intelligence is the first good sign you may be dealing with a psychopath. A history of criminal behavior in which they do not seem to learn from their experience, but merely think about ways to not get caught is the second best sign.

Caucasian Mythology Reveals His Mentality

The Caucasian's mythology tells a lot about how he views himself and the world around him. It gives you a blueprint on how he thinks and his worldview. It is my conclusion that there would be no concept of a "monster" in the world if the white man didn't create him. All mythologies of people of color recognize a lower level consciousness and contrast it to a character of higher consciousness. The lower level mythology of these "bad" characters are used to balance the reality of freewill that one has in their decision to practice righteousness. People of color use these "bad" characters in their mythology to contrast the karma and repercussions when such behavior is embraced, as opposed to practicing higher consciousness of their "good" characters.

Caucasians glorify their monsters or characters of lower level consciousness. They worship them by making movies about them, action figures and memorabilia. They promote and embrace their lower level behavior and show a favorable outcome from this devious behavior. Characters such as: Jason from Friday the 13th, Freddie Kruger, Chuckie, Pin Head from Hell Raiser, Michael Myers from Halloween, Hannibal Lector, Leather Face, Candy Man, Jig Saw from Saw, Damien, The Knoxes from Natural Born Killers, Norman Bates from *Psycho,* and many more!

The white man's legendry monsters reveal more about his mentality and psychological makeup. The character of Dracula is an example of his behavior. Dracula is a vampire from the European country of Transylvania. The white man also comes from Europe. In order for Dracula to survive, he must suck the blood, or life force, out of his victims. The European also sucks the life force out of people of color — by means of slavery, oppression and colonialism — in his efforts to survive and conquer the world. Dracula cannot come out in the daytime for fear that the Sun will kill him. People of European descent must also avoid the Sun for fear of dying from skin cancer. Dracula is relegated to having immortality in the lower, physical dimension and cannot transcend into higher, spiritual consciousness. Because of the Caucasian's lack of melanin, he also cannot transcend into higher, spiritual consciousness.

Other monster characters that reveal the white man's personality and psychological makeup are: the wolf man that shows his tendency to embrace his lower self. This is displayed by the wolf man's transformation when there is a full moon and his thirst for blood is insatiable. Other characters include: Frankenstein, the Mummy, Zombies and Dr. Jekyll and Mr. Hyde. Look further into the leading characters of monster movies and it will reveal the psychological makeup of the Caucasian and the inner workings of how he perceives himself and the world around him.

Chapter Seven:
Seen & Unseen Sexual Inner "G"

"The faster Inner G vibrates, the more information it contains. Raise your vibration and you expand your capacity to decipher unlimited access to knowledge." — Nekhebet

By now, you are probably wondering why I spell the concept of energy as Inner G. I borrowed the term from my good friend of mine, Kelli Dillon. She has a way of combining sounds, symbols and meanings of words to enhance their meanings from a more profound, yet simple, definition. She is a wordsmith. Inner G was one of those words that resonated in me when she introduced it to me. Let us break it down. Energy can neither be created nor destroyed. This sounds to me like the definition of the concept of the one God or Creator. God is described in terms of being the Alpha and the Omega. So that must mean that God and the concept of energy are one in the same. With this foundation, I turned to the letter "G" in the symbol of Freemasonry. Freemasons state that the letter "G" in their symbol possesses many definitions, according to the degree the initiate has obtained, just like the concept of God has many names and different connotations, depending on the knowledge and faith of the believer. They say the "G" stands for God: of course, this definition is self-explanatory. It is the simplest meaning on the most mundane level. They also say the "G" stands for the sacred Geometry that the Great Architect of the Universe used to create the physical dimension. This is a higher degree of knowledge as the initiate is exposed to higher knowledge. He is exposed to Universal laws that expose reality on the level of geometrical equations or theorems.

Symbol of Freemasonry with the letter "G" having many meanings according to the degree of the initiate.

The universe cannot be read until we have learned the language and become familiar with the characters in which it is written. It is written in mathematical language, and the letters are triangles, circles, and other geometrical figures, without which means it is humanly impossible to comprehend a single word. — Galileo Galilei (1564-1642)

Geometry-

The mathematics of the properties, measurement, and relationships of points, lines, angles, surfaces, and solids.

This definition can also be applied to energy. The characteristics of energy can be changed, manipulated and controlled by the same properties that describe the mathematics of geometry. Energy can be expressed with unique characteristics by exposing it or manipulating it by using different measurements, points, waves, angles, surfaces and matter.

Freemasons also say the "G" stands for Gnostic.

The definition *of **Gnostic: Relating to knowledge, from the Greek gnosis (knowledge or investigation), which is also the root for 'cognitive' and 'cognition'. Gnosticism, in general, is a form of religious belief, assuming privileged knowledge of the spiritual world — knowledge considered superior to the science of the day.***

Based on these definitions, one can conclude that to know God or Inner G, one has to obtain privileged knowledge of the spiritual (unseen) world. This is the world in which Inner G is most abundant. A human can only decipher less than 10% of Inner G through our five senses. There exists in our reality over 90% of Inner G that we cannot see, touch, hear, taste or smell. Possessors of knowledge of unseen energy would be considered superior to the science that we are allowed to pursue today. So Gnostic, otherwise known as a Mystic, possesses secret knowledge of Inner G, hidden from the people. Your oppressor uses this science to manipulate and control the masses, and in particular, people of Afrikan descent. The Gnostic or mystic understands that each individual has the capacity to tap into this hidden energy from within in order to transcend into higher, spiritual knowledge. If this is true, then one simply has to understand and master their Inner G in order to free themselves from their hidden slave masters. Gnosticism, therefore, is the secret knowledge of Inner G, which we all call God.

So if Inner G is God and God is Inner G, then we all have the potential to access this universal power that permeates through us and all things in the universe. To know God is to know the different personalities of Inner G. Plain and simple, one cannot know God if one does not understand how the elements, the molecules and the atoms, your body, the plant life, the planets, the solar system, the Sun and the universe work. It is impossible to understand the one creative life force that can be found in the microcosm and macrocosm of the universe. Uni-Verse — this word can be broken down to "Uni", which means one, and "Verse", which can be defined as one line of poetry. Poetry can be defined as using sound, rhythm, cadence and vibration through words to project the ideas and emotions of the writer. When we add these three definitions together, Universe can be defined as the one version of sound, cadence, rhythm and vibration used to create and project the ideas and emotions of the one Creator.

They say our bodies are God's temple. This implies that God lives in, through and around all of us. If God lives in all of us, then we should be able to access the God or Inner G that resides in ourselves. This is the concept of Inner "G". We all have the power to utilize and manifest the God or Inner "G" in ourselves. To know and comprehend all the mysteries of the universe, all one has to do is know and comprehend the Inner "G" in oneself. The Great Architect of the Universe used simple building blocks from which to create this vast universe. From the smallest sub-atomic particle to the largest Sun, all objects must adhere to the one universal law. The universe is made up of the same material as you are. Learn the basic laws and principles of Inner G and one has the ability to know God from within. Know God from within and one discovers their destiny and purpose in life!

The Concept of Planting the See'd.

I had the pleasure of meeting a beautiful and wonderful sister named Karen Johnson. She is the owner of Marcus Books in San Francisco, Ca. I would always wind up having profound conversations with her when I visited her store to get my knowledge. The thing I liked about the Inner G we shared was that it was spontaneous and chaotic at the same time. Subjects, ideas and concepts were always sparked by the time and the moment and without contemplation. One day, in our conversation, she broke down to me a concept she had about the word "seed." I will paraphrase because this conversation took place several years ago but it always stayed with me, for some reason. She said the word "seed" is really spelled "see'd" as in the past tense of "to see", but not the word "saw". The word "saw" is used to describe a tool used to cut or separate things from themselves. It represents the separation from the seed. Her word, "see'd", is the same seed that one plants in a garden or the seed a man impregnates a woman with to create life. Within this small see'd contains all the DNA and genetic information of over 100,000 years that's needed in order to fully manifest its full potential once it grows. She spelled it see'd because the information that is contained in it has already "saw" the full potential this object can ever be once it is fully mature. Remember that a see'd contains information from every experience and thought that said object has ever experienced throughout its entire physical existence. So I related this concept to support my Inner "G" theory. One does not have to look outside of oneself for answers to the mysteries of the universe. All one has to do is access the information that is already imbedded in their DNA. We all started out as a see'd. All we have to do is reconnect with the information and unlock the answers to the mysteries it contains.

[7]Now to each one the manifestation of the Spirit is given for the common good. [8]To one there is given through the Spirit the message of wisdom, to another the message of knowledge by means of the same Spirit, [9]to another faith by the same Spirit, to another gifts of healing by that one Spirit, [10]to another miraculous powers, to another prophecy, to another distinguishing between spirits, to another speaking in different kinds of tongues,[a] and to still another the interpretation of tongues.[b] [11]All these are the work of one and the same Spirit, and he gives them to each one, just as he determines. — 1 Corinthians 12:7-11 (New International Version)

All things in the Universe travel in spirals or waves. Inner G does not express itself in nature linearly. Nothing in the universe moves from point A to point B in a straight line. Inner G expresses itself in such forms as microwaves, infrared, X Rays, Gamma rays, light, radio waves, VHF & UHF, colors of the spectrum, etc..... All Inner G must adhere to the same laws. Electrons revolve around protons. Atoms revolve around other atoms to create molecules. Molecules revolve around other molecules to create elements. Elements revolve to make gases, vapors and mass. The moon revolves around the Earth. The Earth revolves around the Sun. The Sun revolves, and so on and so on. Nothing in the Universe is standing still; everything is in constant elliptical motion. In the previous chapter about Melanin, we discovered that the spiral or curly structure of Black people's hair is the optimal instrument for picking up and receiving Inner G in nature. In other words, Afrikan or Black hair in its natural state is the best antenna for receiving information from God. Its spiral or kinky structure has the same structure and formation as all Inner G expressed in its natural state. Thus, Black people have the ability and potential to access many more frequencies in nature than non-Melanated people. So life experiences for Black people are richer, more fulfilling and contain infinite possibilities, which are not accessible to non-Melanated people.

In nature, the lower the frequency, the lower the vibration. Low frequencies can be identified by their big looping wave structure. (See illustration #1 & #2.) The physical dimension houses the slowest frequencies and the spiritual realm contains the highest frequencies. Velocity has to be slowed down in order for Inner G to exist in the physical plane. So the lower the frequency, the bigger the wave or loop pattern and the further apart the spirit or God is expressed between loops. This low-level Inner G represents our lower, animalistic desires and thoughts. Higher frequencies, on the other hand, can be identified by their rapid or quick, smaller loop patterns. (See illustration #5 & #6.) The higher the frequency, the higher the vibration. The higher the frequency, the smaller and more frequent the loop pattern becomes. This higher level Inner G represents our higher, spiritual selves. One is able to recognize the omnipotence of God at a more frequent rate. So by this knowledge, one can determine that, in order for a person to transcend beyond the physical plane after death, one has to acquire enough velocity, in their lifetime, to escape the physical dimension. A person "acquires" enough "velocity" through participation in higher level Inner G and thoughts. This leads the person down the righteous path, the path to open higher dimensions in the spiritual realm once one leaves the physical body, otherwise known as death.

The Earth is trapped inside a vacuum in space. In order to escape, we must acquire enough velocity to break the gravitational barrier that keeps us in this physical dimension. Raise your vibration and one raises their velocity. The root word for "gravity" is the word "grave". So in actuality, we are experiencing the death of the spirit, otherwise known as the physical dimension. The physical dimension is the "grave-yard" of the spirit. Our spirits contained in our physical bodies are consumed by the effects and the laws of the "grave" or gravity. In order for one to be "resurrected" from the grave, called the physical dimension, one needs to raise their vibration in order to escape the "grave-itational" pull that was designed to trap them here. Love is the highest vibration and fear is the lowest. The chemical Melanin, in people of color, is the key to reaching and acquiring higher vibrations or frequencies, which are necessary for resurrecting one's spirit from the grave or the law of gravity.

Wavelength is the distance of one full cycle of the oscillation. Longer wavelength waves, such as radio waves, carry lower Inner G; this is why we can listen to the radio without any harmful consequences. Shorter wavelength waves, such as x-rays, carry higher Inner G, which can be hazardous to our physical bodies because our bodies vibrate at such a low frequency.

These shorter wavelengths are hazardous to our physical bodies. We are only able to decipher and communicate with shorter wavelengths within in the spiritual realm. Our physical bodies cannot hold the information contained in these shorter wavelengths so the body goes into overload and starts to turn on itself. To enter the realm of higher frequencies or Inner G, we must let go of our physical bodies and the physical realm. In other words, we must stop defining ourselves and our reality through the laws of the physical world and start to focus and invest our time and Inner G in our spiritual selves. The same is also true of sound. The higher the frequency, the higher the note sounds. We cannot hear higher notes because our physical ears cannot decipher higher vibrations. Imagine the sounds we will be able to hear after we leave our physical bodies in the spiritual dimension. This is what is described in the Bible as the trumpets sounding in the opening of the gates of Heaven

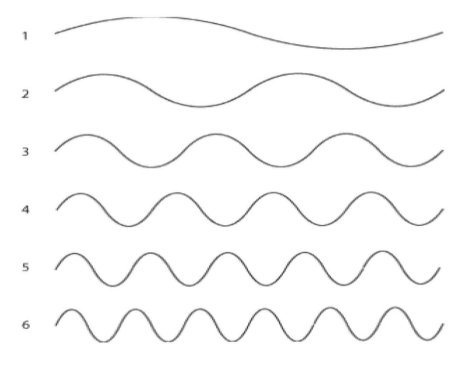

If love can be seen as Inner G, it would look like the higher vibration of smaller, more frequent waves banned closer apart. (See illustration line #6.) Love would look like the last wavelength at the bottom of the illustration. The opposite of love, which is fear and not hate, would look like a lower vibration frequency of bigger loops that are farther apart. Fear would be the first wavelength or the first line in the illustration. Picture yourself as a horizontal line that dissects both wavelengths right down the middle. The person exposed to the higher frequency of the love vibration would dissect each wave numerous times. This person would be wide open in receiving all the Inner G that is around him. This is why people who are experiencing love are always smiling, walking on air, smelling the flowers blooming, hearing the birds singing and are very jovial and full of life. The love Inner G vibration is bombarding their senses at such a rapid rate that they experience being "high" on life. They are able to experience and recognize "God" more frequently in their everyday lives.

On the other hand, if a person is exposed to a fear vibration, which most people interpret as hate, then they automatically or instinctively close up their senses as a means to protect themselves. If you dissect that same horizontal line through the middle of the lower frequency fear vibration, then it would dissect each wave only a few times. An example of this is somebody watching a scary movie. When scared or threatened, that person will immediately cover their eyes, so as to not let the Inner G inside them. When a person has a nervous breakdown or is being physically attacked and cannot defend themselves, they will instinctively ball up in a fetal position to protect themselves from the low-level Inner G that wants to cause them harm. This person will totally close and block all their receptors as a means of survival from the Inner G it deems as a threat. This is nature's way of protecting ourselves. It is the "fight or flight" response. Our heart rate will start racing; we may begin to sweat; our hair stands up on end and our adrenaline starts pumping. These are also the symptoms of stress. Stress is nature's way of protecting the body. Stress is a survival mechanism that is only supposed to last as long as the person is in danger. In nature, dangerous or life-threatening situations rarely last over five minutes. Once the danger is eliminated, the body goes back to its natural state. In the Black community, we are in a state of stress 24 hours a day and 7 days a week, all year long. This is by design so that we will never reach our higher consciousness or see

"God" within ourselves or our community. We now relate the symptoms of this stressful state as having a "ghetto mentality." This mental state of being can be described as a person in a perpetual state of self-survival. One cannot be in a defensive mode and raise their vibration at the same time. If one is motivated by fear, they cannot reach higher consciousness. Fear closes oneself or shuts down one's ability to communicate with "God" or achieve higher consciousness withheld in higher vibrations of Inner G.

FREQUENCIES OF HUMAN EMOTIONS

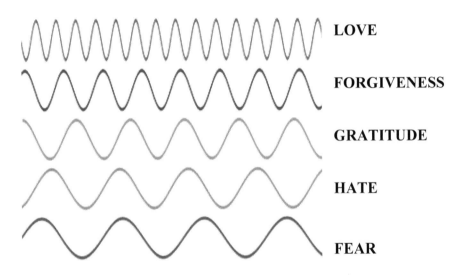

LOVE

FORGIVENESS

GRATITUDE

HATE

FEAR

In ancient mythology, specifically from Kemet, the snake represented the unseen, or enlightenment of the spiritual or unseen world. The snake moves just like invisible Inner G, in waves or spirals. When you see a snake slither in the sand, you can distinctively see the wave patterns he leaves behind. In the pictures above of King Tutankhamen and the Hindu goddess Shiva, it shows the cobra on their foreheads, symbolizing the activation of their Pineal glands. Shiva's hair is even styled in the shape of a pine cone. In the Bible, the snake was the one to tempt Eve into partaking of the Tree of Knowledge or Life. I never understood why acquiring knowledge was such a bad thing. Because of Eve's feminine Inner G or intuition, she was able to recognize and decipher unseen Inner G, portrayed by the snake. Christianity portrays the snake as the devil in an effort to keep Black people from the knowledge of themselves and of the universe they live in. All the snake really represents in mythology is knowledge and understanding of unseen Inner G, which makes up over 90% of our reality.

The picture above is a snake track found in the desert. The spiral pattern is similar to how all Inner G moves throughout the cosmos.

So one who is aware of this science can manipulate this unseen Inner G and dictate the behavior of their target group without them being aware of it. The Black community is bombarded with this lower level, unseen Inner G, and does not even know it. In fact, Black people in the community embrace it and define themselves by this lower level frequency. This lower level Inner G permeates the Black community through the food (processed fast food, red meat, sugar and the history of a slave diet); in the music (hip hop or gangster rap); miseducation (public school system); law enforcement (fear of police brutality and murder); inundated with guns & drugs (physical & psychological trauma); the images of disrespect against Black women (psychological warfare); vaccines (biological warfare); influx of liquor stores, smoke shops and churches; as well as the introduction of gossip and slander as normal forms of communication. All these institutions in the Black community are accepted consequences of their reality. They not only internalize these vibrations as part of their culture but they also define themselves through the consequences of these Inner G's. The term "ghetto" was once a concept one had to overcome to succeed. The Black community pride themselves on overcoming the pitfalls and adversity that the ghetto had to offer; now it is a term that one seeks to become. The ghetto was an environment that made you strong through one's commitment and perseverance to overcome the adversity to get out of it. People now aspire to become it. It is now the goal that one aspires to internalize and dictate one's behavior. "Ghetto mentality" can be defined as a person operating at the lower level frequency from which to define their existence. This level of consciousness is motivated by self-survival, greed, selfishness and cold-heartedness. It is the lowest vibration or frequency at which one can live their life and define their reality.

Frequencies of the Human Body in MHz

Normal brain frequency (head) 6:00am to 6:00pm is 70-78 MHz
Brain frequency at 80-82 MHz, indicates a genius
Healthy body (neck down) 6:00 am to 6:00 pm is 62-68 MHz

Heart is 67-70 MHz
Lungs are 58-65 MHz
Liver is 55-60 MHz

Stomach is 58-65 MHz

Disease begins; colds invade at 59-60 MHz

Flu-like symptoms at 58 MHz
Viral Infection at 55 MHz

Cancer at 42 MHz

Death begins at 20 MHz

Human cells start to mutate when their frequency drops below 62 MHz. Low frequency also indicates a pH imbalance:

Abundance 78 MHz

Acceptance 102 MHz

Clarity 101 MHz

Forgiveness 192 MHz

Grounding 140 MHz

Harmony 101 MHz

Hope 98 MHz

Humility 88 MHz

Inspiration 141 MHz

Joy 188 MHz

Peace & Calming 105 MHz

The concept of angels and demons in religion and ancient mythologies is nothing more than names or characters given to specific frequencies or vibrations that represent the characteristics of that given unseen Inner G. Angels and demons are nothing more than higher and lower invisible wavelengths and their proscribed personalities or characteristics represent the attributes of that particular wavelength. Angels, being described as coming from the heavens, represent higher frequencies, whereas demons, coming from Hell or the underworld, represent lower frequencies. All frequencies or vibrations have unique effects on humans, affecting our minds, bodies and spirits. Our oppressor has access to this hidden science and uses this knowledge to keep the Black man and woman in a lower frequency or dead state of consciousness in our communities. The Black community is being preyed upon to keep our spirits trapped in the physical dimension, where the white man rules, in order to serve his agenda of having his "heaven" here on earth.

Black people must be aware of their space, surroundings and environment. Protect it and make it sacred. Understand that you have the power to control and manipulate your own unseen Inner G and have it work in your favor. When one comes together with their mate, make sure you are in a good space. Remember, you have been bombarded with all this lower level Inner G all day. One needs to "detox" their aura before they engage in any type of activity with their mate, let alone sex. To detox, one should collect their thoughts. Take time out to clear your head of everything that took place throughout the day. Remember, your thoughts dictate your reality. Fill your thoughts and intentions with higher frequency vibrations. The best way to do this is to show humility. Be humble about your dealings that you had throughout the day. Always look within for the reason you had lower level Inner G exchanges with people. Remember, we attract a part of ourselves, disguised as other people whom we meet on a daily basis. Never be the victim and never give yourself an excuse to engage in lower level activities with anyone, no matter what the situation dictates, for what you are experiencing is but a reflection of a part of what frequency you are operating on. Always be the "better or bigger" person. Never justify lower level behavior because there is no justification. These moments are your opportunity to suppress the lower vibration that lives in you. Also, put the well-being of your mate ahead of your own personal issues and concerns. Your mate will also follow the same procedure as yourself. By both raising your vibrations for the betterment of each other, you can now come together in harmony. This balance will raise both of your consciousnesses and fill the space between the spaces with higher frequency thoughts and intentions, so miracles can manifest in the physical realm. It will be like depositing your intentions in a bank of the unseen or invisible realm, only to have them compound interest for future withdrawals later in your life in the seen or physical world.

It is very difficult for one to switch from a lower frequency to a higher vibration. One literally has to change their perception of what is real by destroying their personal definition of reality and ignoring their pacified level of accepted comfort. One must embrace their uncertainty and fears of the unknown, voluntarily give up their level of understanding, and admit to themselves that their present state of mind is an illusion. Examples of people operating at lower vibrations can be witnessed in those who fight obesity, drug abuse and alcoholism, criminal activity, compulsive and impulsive behavior such as gambling, lying, stealing, cheating, pornography, Jesus freaks and workaholics, to name a few. These people define themselves by their compulsive lower level behavior, otherwise known as addiction, and not their higher selves. For example, a man addicted to drugs defines himself through the "high" he gets from the drug and not the feeling when he is sober. A compulsive over-eater defines themselves by the pleasure that food gives them while they are eating and tries to suppress their state of mind between meals. A man who cheats on his wife defines himself by the excitement and pleasure he gets from sleeping with other women and getting away with it, and not the time he spends with his wife. Religious zealots define themselves by the time they spend at their church, temple, mosque or synagogue, and not their time away from it. A criminal defines himself by the crimes he commits and gets away with, and not the time he has between committing those crimes. As one can see, it is hard for these people who are engaged in lower frequency behavior to change, because they define themselves by the very act they participate in and neglect their higher selves.

In order to change frequencies, one must follow the blueprint in the Bible that explains the crucifixion of Jesus Christ. We discussed this procedure in an earlier chapter in the book. One must be willing to let go of all they think they know and expose all their insecurities and weaknesses in order to be "resurrected" into a higher vibration. This is called "killing the ego", which contains one's lower self or lower consciousness. One cannot hold on to a lower frequency and reach a higher one at the same time. One must fully let go of one to reach the other. Frequencies are independent unto themselves. It is impossible to be on two different frequencies at the same time. Each frequency has a unique vibration unto itself. There is only one form of communication per frequency. Different frequencies cannot recognize or communicate with other frequencies. They can only communicate with similar or the same frequency as itself. This is how we attract and repel certain people and situations in our everyday lives. We are in a constant stage of attracting and repelling people and things all around us that reflect our level of consciousness, in order to communicate with them. It is in this communication that we form our version or definition of ourselves and the world we live in. This is the basis for the formation of our reality. One must completely relinquish their lower frequency in order to "put it to death." This is the threshold that one needs to experience and embrace in order to be "resurrected" into a higher vibration. There is no other way to achieve higher consciousness. This is what is meant when we talk about a drug abuser "bottoming out." If he does not completely reject his present state of mind or dependency on drugs, he will never let go of his addiction. The same is true for all lower level behavior. The process is similar to chemotherapy treatment on a cancer patient. The patient's infected area is bombarded with toxins in an effort to kill off the cancer. Unfortunately, in the process, the chemotherapy also kills off the person's "healthy" cells. So it is with us when we want to change frequencies. We must "kill" our lower selves in an effort to transcend into a higher vibration. This is the process or steps in rehabilitation. This is why a person who is addicted to drugs, alcohol or any other lower level frequency feels like they are dying when they are so-called sobering up or detoxing. A part of them is literally dying so that their higher selves can maintain and operate at a higher frequency.

Unseen Inner G, as we have discussed, starts with the basic building block of the physical dimension, which is known as the atom. The atom, or Atum in ancient Kemet, means the life force or Inner G that permeates all things in the universe. It is the one common denominator that is the sole source in all expressions of life. It is the way or the intent of the Creator manifested in the physical dimension. With this hidden Inner G, behind the scenes, let us refer back to the concept of the electron revolving around the proton. As the planets revolve around the Sun, so the electrons rotate around the proton or nucleus of the atom. What is not discussed is the space between the electrons in relation to the nucleus of the atom. Mercury is the closest planet to the Sun. Pluto is the furthest planet from the Sun, whereas Earth is the third planet closest to the Sun. Each of these planet's distances affects the relationship they have with the Sun. Mercury is the hottest planet and Pluto is the coldest because of their positions in relation to the Sun. The Earth is coincidently in the exact position in relation to the Sun in order to manifest life as we know it. Any subtle change in the Earth's position to the Sun would affect life drastically. We are living in a delicate balance that permeates all things in the universe.

With that said, I want to focus on the vast amounts of space between the electrons in regards to their positions to the protons. Each electron is positioned as the planets are to the Sun. Some may be like Mercury, very close to the Sun, and others like Pluto, far away from the Sun. Remember the basic building block of life is the atom. The atom's function is the synergy of male and female energy, sex, and the product or personality that energy produces. In our junior high science class, we are taught that all things are a solid, liquid or gas. The solid is denser and gas is the least dense. Density is the ratio of the mass of an object to its volume. My interpretation of density is the weight of an object in regards to how many atoms it holds in its given space. The more atoms compacted in an object, the denser or heavy that object becomes. For example, lead is denser than cotton candy. Cotton candy is sugar that has been liquefied and injected with air to make it light and fluffy. Lead contains less space between its molecules. What we weren't taught in school was that the densest object still maintains vast distances between its electrons and protons in the unseen world. If one could enlarge an atom, one would see that the closet electron that revolves around the proton/neutron nucleus may be miles away from its center. This electron could be the closest out of all the other electrons revolving around the nucleus! So, the question I must ask is: what is the purpose of the vast amount of space between the electron, represented as feminine Inner G, and the proton, represented by masculine Inner G?

The universe or space is represented by 95% of what scientists call Dark Matter. When we look up at the sky at night, we see the stars twinkling but we don't see the space between the stars. This is the Dark Matter of the universe. This is Melanin! If this is the case, then people of color have the ability to fill the void of the space between the spaces in the unseen world. People of color can access this dimension of reality. So how does one access this reality? Remember that in our Melanin chapter, we discussed how the Sun's energy supplies the fuel for the intent of the person who is being exposed to the Sun. The Sun is consciousness and Melanin is the receiver of said consciousness. Black people, through our thoughts and intentions, can be fueled by the Sun to create our reality relative to those said thoughts and intentions. Higher level thoughts and intentions manifest a higher level reality in the physical dimension. Lower level thoughts and intentions manifest lower level reality in the physical dimension. So one would conclude, in order to oppress and enslave a people, the most proficient and efficient way is to control said people's thoughts and intentions. *The author Carter G. Woodson alluded to this in his book, "The Miseducation of the Negro":* If one takes a slave's chains off and tells him he is free, but one still enslaves and oppresses his mind, then he is still a slave and he will exhibit the behavior of a slave who still wears his chains.

Remember that Melanin is a gift from the Creator. Let us embrace it and have it work miracles in the physical dimension. We have to reclaim that which was lost, stolen or hidden from us. Let us access the space in-between the spaces. Remember, only 5% of reality is seen Inner G. We have 95% of unseen Inner G that has been neglected or ignored. We are like a gallon container, but we only think we can hold a cup of water. Be mindful of your thoughts and intentions. Ward off lower level Inner G and egotistical environments. Keep your space between the spaces sacred. When relating to your significant other, come together with the intention of uplifting each other. Be conscious of the Inner G that you share, which will be used to fill this space. We have so much potential within us already that we don't need to look outside of ourselves for solutions to our problems. Get kissed by the Sun as often as you can. Meditate, sit still and be quiet in the Sun's presence. Let it be your guide as it recharges your thoughts and intentions. Give the Sun the opportunity to fuel the miracles you desire in the physical realm. Let the Sun be the rushing river and let yourself be the leaf riding on that river. Let go completely. Let it take you over the rocks into still waters, over mountains and through valleys.

Don't try to hold on to the sides of the riverbank for fear of turbulent waters ahead, for if you hold on too tightly, you will surely drown.

We are made up of 85% water. When we are exposed to the Sun, it gives consciousness to the water that makes up our bodies. The water is the perfect receiver for the Sun to relay its message of higher consciousness to us. When water is exposed to sunlight in nature, it automatically wants to raise its vibration and become closer to the Sun. It does this in the form of evaporation. The water transforms into a less dense substance called vapor. The vapor, being light or without burden, automatically rises to meet the Sun at a higher frequency in the atmosphere. Thus, it is true with the water withheld in our bodies. The Sun's message is relayed to our bodies; it is always uplifting us, through our bodies' water, to attain a higher level of consciousness. People without Melanin cannot access this dimension. Non-Melanated people, who are exposed to the Sun, cannot retrieve the consciousness that the Sun holds. So the Sun damages and destroys their bodies through skin cancer, if they are overexposed to it. The Sun's consciousness is actually toxic to non-Melanated people. Think about that for a minute. Non-Melanated people are limited in their ability to raise themselves into higher consciousness through exposure to the Sun.

After the Sun has given our body its intent through its consciousness, sunlight, it has done its job. Now it is up to the moon to play its role. If it was the Sun's job to give you the consciousness with which to fill the void in the space between the spaces, then it is the moon's job to put that consciousness into motion. Remember, the moon is responsible for moving the water on the Earth. The moon is the catalyst that affects the ocean's tides. So it is with our bodies. It controls the ebb and flow of our consciousness held in the water of our bodies. The moon communicates with us through our dreams, for the right time and place to manifest our desires. It is up to us to decipher the images and symbols in our dreams to better understand and grasp the road map or blueprint that the moon has laid out for us to navigate the space in-between the spaces. One must pay very close intention to one's dreams. Do not take them lightly or just brush them off as superficial. They are the keys to our life's destiny. They represent the unseen world's communication with you to guide you in the physical dimension. Remember, the Sun infused in your Melanin the intent to manifest your reality in the physical plane. The moon sets that intent in motion if you are open to receiving its instruction. Melanin is activated at night for this sole purpose.

Put this theory into effect when it comes to having sex with your partner. Remember, the sole purpose of engaging in sex is to pay homage to our higher selves and uplift our partners. In doing so, you pay homage and uplift your higher or true self, which raises one's vibration or frequency. Be very aware and concerned with keeping the space between the spaces that you share with your mate, sacred and pure. Understand that once you are conscious of this space, you will be held accountable for what you put into it. It takes two people with the same level of consciousness to manifest their reality in the physical dimension. A chain is only as strong as its weakest link. Be mindful of who you give access to this space and what you put into the space yourself. Such is one of life's miracles. Black people are very fortunate to be given this gift to access this space. There are infinite possibilities in regards to creating our own reality.

As we raise our vibration or consciousness, our DNA changes within that given frequency. The opposite can also be true. If we lower our vibration or consciousness, our DNA also changes with that given frequency. We will use the example of talking to your plants. Studies have shown that when one exhibits a high vibration when talking to their plants, they respond to that vibration and are healthier for it. The plant, representing a living entity, responds immediately to the vibrations they are exposed to. The same can be said about us humans. Our DNA, which we have inherited, contains 100's of thousands of years of information from our mothers and fathers. We are the byproduct of our ancestors' legacy, through our parents, whether it is perceived as good or bad. We can access this information by resonating at the same level or frequency of that acquired knowledge. If I live my life at a low level, I do not have access to the vast knowledge of information contained in my DNA. Thus, I limit my potential for higher consciousness, which in turn limits my quality of life. If I raise my vibration to a higher level, more information or knowledge will be available for me to tap into, which enhances my quality of life.

97% of our DNA is not active. It is called "Junk DNA." It is in this so-called Junk DNA that Caucasians have labeled Black people to have access to, because of the Melanin content in their skin. In their very bodies contain a dimension or universe that Black people have access to from which to define themselves and their reality.

"Less than 3% of DNA's function involves protein manufacture and more than 90% functions in the realm of bioacoustics and bioelectric signaling."- Dr Leonard Horowitz

The symbol of the Flax Twist in Kemet, pictured below on the left, was used to describe the feminine words "her", "who" and also "placenta". I believe it represented the genes or DNA passed on to the child through the mother carrying and nurturing the child in the womb. It looks just like the double helix of the DNA strand.

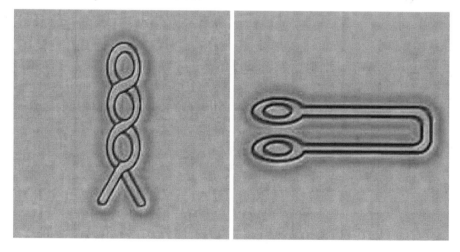

The Tethered Rope symbol in Kemet, on the right, stood for the word "child", usually displayed as twisted ropes. I believe it represented the child's potential in the physical realm according to his DNA. One end of the rope represents the mother and father's DNA that anchors the child to the physical realm. The other end of the rope is attached to the child. So the rope or DNA limits what a child can accomplish and the potential they have in the physical dimension, depending on what traits or genes are passed on to him from his parents.

Now we will examine how "male" and "female" Inner G works in its natural state. We were never taught that there were specific properties on how each gender expresses itself. How do we expect to have healthy relationships if we don't even know how each sex works in its natural state? It is like trying to work on your car without a mechanic or any knowledge of combustible engines. When one lifts up the hood, everything seems foreign to them. You might as well be blind. Thus, when we try to "lift up the hood" in our relationships and try to fix our problems, we have no clue as to the inner workings of the engine or the dynamics of male and female energies. One must understand how each gender behaves naturally, in order to appreciate and build a healthy relationship.

So let us break down the specific characteristics and properties of each of these Inner G's. We will start with the atom because this is the basic building block of the material world. Remember, everything in the universe must adhere to the same principles and laws. From the biggest Sun to the smallest subatomic particle, all things in nature must obey the same laws. So to understand the macrocosm of the universe and all that it entails, you must pay attention and dissect the microcosm as well. This is what our ancestors did thousands of years ago, when the Black man and Black woman ruled the world as king and queen. This is where we aspire to return to.

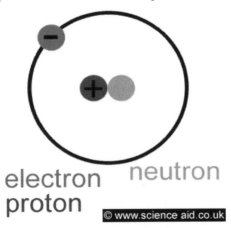

electron   neutron
proton
© www.science aid.co.uk

The male (masculine Inner G) is electric, symbolized by the (+) plus sign. The plus sign represents the male phallus in its rested, as well as, its excited state. The penis is represented by the vertical line; it is in its rested state, below the horizontal line, and in its aroused state, above the horizontal line. The horizontal line that crosses the vertical line represents the testes. So, together, they represent the male phallus ready to give out Inner G. Male Inner G is labeled as positive. Positive implies to "give out" Inner G. ***The definition of positive means, to post or to sit still.*** It is represented by the proton in the atom. The proton sits still or posts up in its natural state. This is characterized by the male erection. The erection must be able to sit still and be upright, in order to give out Inner G. It does this so that the electron, or female Inner G, can revolve around it and create the unique synergy between the two. This is the concept of sex. The outcome of this relationship is the creation of a unique Inner G that expresses itself and exhibits qualities and traits relative to the male and female Inner G emerging as one. Thus, this is the expression of life.

Male Inner G is in its natural state, or closer to God, when it gives out and produces Inner G. This is why the male genitals are on the outside of his body. This is why males are external beings. Males are made for the sole purpose of "giving out" Inner G to produce or manifest specific life forces. Males are visual, outgoing, analytical and external beings. Males must be able to produce in order to feel satisfied or feel at one with nature or God. If you take away their ability to produce, they go against nature and thus fall from God. If the male remains in this state, it is impossible for him to manifest anything that is balanced and healthy. This includes relationships. This is what has been done to the Black man in America and the world. From slavery to the present, the Black man has been relegated to a child to be taken advantage of. He is not allowed to produce anything of benefit for his own community. He is only allowed to produce for his oppressor. This is why the Black man is not allowed to have ownership of any institutions that benefit his community.   For example, the Black man dominates the entertainment, music, sports and fashion industries, but is not allowed to have substantial ownership in any of these venues. Black people do not even own Black Entertainment Television!

This is all done by design to keep the Black man away from his natural state in order to divide and conquer his people.

If a man is not allowed to produce for his woman and children, his nation is already conquered. When I mean produce, I don't mean a job. A job implies that your time and energy are invested in the owner's vision and ideologies. A job does nothing for a Black man's ability to be free or be closer to God in his natural state. He is only giving his most precious resource, his time and Inner G, into the manifestation of another man's goals and dreams.   He may feel fulfilled because a man must work at accomplishing something.   But in the end, he still hasn't produced for himself. A man must see that his time, Inner G and work, has produced something of value.   If he does not see his reflection, he is simply "masturbating" on an atomic level. He is just going through the motions of life expression, but hasn't produced anything of substance for himself or his people.   His feelings of satisfaction and contentment will always be temporary until he gets the opportunity to pacify himself again.

People may say that this is a cop out. That we live in the land of milk and honey. This is a lie, which states that the American Dream is attainable for anyone who works hard and has the audacity to make their dreams come true. We see people from other countries come here and are seemingly in a better position than we are. Looks can be deceiving. Every Black man that promoted Black Nationalism was ostracized, institutionalized, castrated and/or killed. From the Honorable Marcus Garvey, to Black Wall Street and the Black Panther Party, all organizations were sabotaged, shut down, disbanded and destroyed. The European fears the potential of the Black man, so he works night and day to suppress his ability to transcend to higher consciousness. This is done by design. The Black man to the Caucasian is Public Enemy #1!

The Female (feminine Inner G) is magnetic, symbolized by the (-) negative sign. This symbol represents the vagina of the woman. The vagina is the ultimate gateway and gives life on the highest level. It is the bridge that brings the spiritual world into the physical dimension. In order for a male to manifest anything in this physical realm, he must use feminine Inner G to usher it into existence. The word "magnetic" implies "to receive" Inner G. Female Inner G, in its natural state, is closer to God or nature when it receives Inner G and shows the reflection of that Inner G. Females must be able to receive and reflect Inner G in order to be content. If she is not receiving and reflecting Inner G, she goes against nature and distances herself from God. Thus, she will remain unhappy and unfulfilled.

Because of the sexist and chauvinist views of the European male, negative or feminine Inner G is defined as something that is bad or lower level. Afrikan culture is a matriarchal society. It was the woman who chose the next king. It was the woman's family that maintained the wealth. So the man had to prove himself worthy to be selected by the woman to be king. The European culture is a patriarchal society. It is a society where the European man subjects and oppresses the woman under his rule. Please note that this is same man who gave his slave the right to vote before he gave his own woman.

Negative actually means, ***"To have no gates or boundaries."*** It has infinite possibilities and no limitations. This is displayed by the electron in the atom. The electron (female Inner G) will find a proton (male Inner G) that it is attracted to and will revolve around that proton to create a specific Inner G that is beneficial for the two. The electron needs to have no limitations or gates to move freely around the proton. Thus, the electron has the potential for infinite possibilities. This Inner G is needed in order for the proton to manifest its will. This negative Inner G is labeled as magnetic. This is why women are called "attractive." This property can be seen whenever an "attractive" woman walks by a male or electric Inner G on the street. As soon as she walks by, the male Inner G has an uncontrollable urge to look back and change his original direction that he was going, in order to follow the woman. The term "I can't take my eyes off of you" is another term which supports this property. Just as the magnet pulls metals towards its direction, so does the female or magnetic Inner G attract the male. This is the unseen power that women have. The power of attraction. Many women know it and use it to benefit themselves. They may not know the inner workings of the power, but they recognize it and use it nonetheless. The woman, being magnetic, holds these characteristics: she is internal; she needs to express her innermost thoughts; she feels; she is sensitive; she is emotional; she craves affection; she wants to be wanted; she wants attachment and she needs to give life to ideas and dreams yet to come.

In the Strong Concordance Bible, it lists the definition of the name Eve, as the solution. Eve, of course, is the representative of the first woman or feminine energy in this dimension. Eve means the answer to the problem. I believe this specifically relates to the feminine or magnetic Inner G being the key to manifesting the male or electric Inner G. Because feminine Inner G has no gates or boundaries, it has infinite possibilities for male Inner G to tap into.

Let's look at it from this perspective. The woman is the vehicle. She has the capacity to take the male, the driver, anywhere he wants to go. But there is one thing that needs to be addressed. The woman is the vehicle without a battery or fuel. This being the case, the woman needs masculine or electric Inner G to charge and fill her, in order for her to move. Contrary to popular belief, the woman cannot jumpstart or refuel herself. She needs the right key to fit her ignition in order for her to manifest. The male, being the spark, also cannot go anywhere on his own. The male, holding the fuel and the electricity, cannot do anything with it if he does not have the vehicle to take him there. Whatever he dreams cannot fully manifest, unless he has the vehicle, feminine Inner G, to take him there.

We are brainwashed through the media, especially in music, that we don't need each other in order to accomplish our dreams or be happy. Songs that promote and celebrate the ideal of the Independent Woman — *I Don't Need a Man, Men Can Do Nothing for Me* and *I Got My Own* — all are detrimental. Also, songs that lower women as sexual objects to be used promote the same ideology. This system will promote the division of the Black male and female and we will unknowingly celebrate these ideals as if it's something to be proud of. WE NEED EACH OTHER! Anything that goes against this statement is detrimental to our community and relationships. It is an equal balance in the universe of male (electric) and female (magnetic) Inner G that makes the world function at its highest level.

We will also use the example of a battery. The end of the battery that protrudes is the male or positive end of the battery. The other end of the battery that has an indentation is the female or negative end of the battery. When you put batteries in any electronics, you need to lay the batteries side by side, in opposite directions, for the energy or electrical current to properly flow through. This is where we get the old adage of opposites attracting.

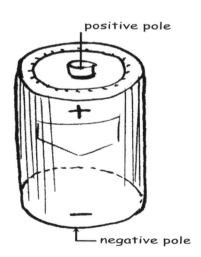

positive pole

negative pole

The battery representing positive or male Inner G (+) and negative or feminine Inner G (-).

If this is the case, then homosexuality goes against Universal law or nature. Electrons, or feminine Inner G, repel each other in nature. Protons, or masculine Inner G, repel each other in nature. Electrons and protons attract each other in nature. It is that simple. If you lay the same batteries side by side, in the same position, they will not hold a current. Their Inner G's will repel each other. Current is the continuous flow of Inner G. The current or Inner G will start to work against itself. It will literally turn against itself. Like the opposite sides of a magnet, they will naturally repel each other. In nature, opposites attract and likes repel. This is the law that holds the Universe together. This is the blueprint or key to all mysteries of this physical dimension. I do not wish to preach the morals or values of individuals who engage in this behavior. That is not my purpose. My purpose is to state the law that our ancestors abided by when we were at our highest level in the history of the world. My main concern is to resurrect the Black man and the Black woman in our relationships with each other. Relationships build marriages, marriages build families, families build communities and communities build a nation! That is my only goal and objective. Let us return to our past in order to move forward!

Male and female couples have a unique relationship with one another. Have you ever admired how two beautiful couples seem to get along so well as one group? Let's break down the science. When you have two protons (males) of the same amount of energy, they can literally share two electrons (females) at the same time. Let's clarify this. Whenever a male and female relate to each other on any level, they are metaphysically having sex. Let's break this down. Sex can be defined as male Inner G that fully engages with female Inner G in order to create a synergy that is a byproduct of their union. In nature, the proton or male, sits still. The electron or the female, minding its own business, will float on by the proton. The proton will display its power and Inner G to the electron. The electron will decide to revolve around the proton because it gets positive Inner G from the proton. The electron will then internalize that Inner G and reflect it back, so the proton can see itself. If the electron does not care for or need the Inner G that the proton is giving out, then it will keep moving until it finds a proton that satisfies it. If this is the case, a simple conversation with someone of the opposite sex can produce an orgasmic-type Inner G without even touching.

Women are more aware of this than men. Remember, women were built to receive Inner G. So our two couples are basically sharing feminine Inner G. The two female Inner G's are revolving around the two males simultaneously. Picture a figure eight lying on its side. The two spaces or holes in the figure eight are the men. The pattern around the figure eight is the continuous path of the female's Inner G circling the men. Both females are well aware of each other and keep their distance as they complete their figure eight patterns. Each female will subconsciously keep the furthest possible distance from one another in regards to reflecting both men's Inner G. I believe this to be a beautiful thing. Every person involved in this exchange of energy benefits from it. One thing must remain constant for this action to stay balanced and healthy: both males must be equal in their Inner G's. If not, the weaker or smaller Inner G will be excluded or ignored in favor of the stronger or more brilliant Inner G.

Why are women competitive when it comes to finding and keeping a man? When a woman finds a man that she is attracted to, she will revolve around him, meaning she becomes the reflection of his Inner G. A woman can only revolve around one man at a time. If he is sufficient for her, there is no need to look elsewhere for her Inner G or her reflection. When another female is naturally attracted to "her" male, she will naturally try to repel the other woman. Remember, likes repel. The "other" woman will naturally be pulled into the male's space because of her magnetism to the male's Inner G. The first woman knows that once the other female is in the "space" of the male, she is now forced to share his Inner G and his reflection. Sharing male Inner G doesn't necessarily mean sex in a physical sense. As we alluded to before, a simple conversation is "sharing" male Inner G with another woman. This is the same as having "sex" on an atomic level. Sex can be defined as the giving out and receiving of Inner G between masculine and feminine principles. This is why the woman will always blame the other woman first, if she finds out her man has been cheating on her. The other woman will initially receive the majority of her Inner G and focus if she is present. She will hold the other woman more accountable than the man. This is the science behind the scenario. It is only natural.

Once we know the principles of how male and female Inner G relate to each other, then we can start addressing the issues in our relationships. Let's review the basic principles before we move on, as they are the foundation of our relationships:

1) Male is electric, meaning he was made to give out Inner G.
2) Female is magnetic, meaning she was made to receive Inner G.
3) Males need to see their reflection in their women. If he does not see his full reflection in her, he will find whatever she is lacking outside the relationship.
4) Females need to be sustained by the male Inner G that she reflects. If his Inner G does not satisfy her, she will look for it elsewhere.
5) Males, being electric, are positive, external beings.
6) Females, being magnetic, are negative, internal beings.
7) Male & females need each other to manifest their dreams and desires. One cannot be complete or exist without the other.
8) Males & females are opposites of the same Inner G. We complete the equation of life.
9) Men start fast and end quicker.
10) Women start slow and end slower.

BONDING BASICS

In order to have a healthy relationship of any kind on any level, one must first understand the laws and functions of how matter and Inner G relates to each other in terms of the concept of basic bonding. All matter is made up of molecules. These molecules are in a perpetual motion of constantly attracting and repelling each other, depending on the molecular structure of the matter. Have you ever met someone for the first time and had an immediate attraction to that person, as if you have known them all your life? On the flip side, have you ever met someone for the first time and were immediately repelled or offended just by their very presence, without them saying a word? These are both examples of molecules in yourself and the other person either attracting or repelling each other based on your molecular structure. Understand that the same molecules repel and opposite molecules attract. That is why, in nature, females, representing negative Inner G, attract males, representing positive Inner G. But let's look deeper into the science of this concept in terms of two people's Inner G's bonding with each other.

We will first look into bonding in terms of solutions versus mixtures. Solutions are groups of molecules that are mixed up in a completely even distribution. Solutions have an even concentration throughout the system. So solutions, in regards to the relationship between two people, are evenly distributed Inner G from the two individuals that create a balance of the two when they are combined as one. *So·lu·tion- the act of solving a problem, question, etc.* It is no wonder that the generic definition for the word "solution" refers to solving or completing a problem or question. When two people come together in a balanced relationship and their Inner G's are evenly displayed and supported in the union, their problems are naturally solved! Their relationship seems effortless. They have each found their solutions in their relationship and in each other! When elements join and become compounds, they lose their individual traits. In solutions, one sees the benefit of giving up their individual Inner G because they see the best in themselves when they are united or combined with their partner's Inner G. We are all looking for solutions or relationships that address all our problems as individuals. This is the goal of individuals who participate in relationships. Everyone is searching for their solution.

The other relationship that two individuals can participate in is called a mixture. Mixtures can have less or higher concentrations of one individual's Inner G when compared to the other person in the relationship. Mixtures are unbalanced. One person's Inner G dominates the relationship, while the other person's Inner G is inhibited or suppressed. The key point here is that these two individuals do not blend naturally, thus their union must be forced and manipulated for them to remain together. For example: Sugar in water vs. sand in water. Sugar dissolves and is spread evenly throughout the glass of water. The sugar naturally wants to give up its individual Inner G because the water accepts and embraces its properties. The water naturally finds cohesion and balance in the sugar, so it allows itself to be molded and defined by the introduction of the sugar's Inner G. As a result, the compound of the sugar/water is balanced throughout the solution. If one were to take a sample of the water from the top of the glass, the middle and the bottom, then one would find an even distribution of both sugar and water throughout the glass. In terms of relationships, this can be translated to mean that in the good times of the relationship (i.e. the top of the glass), or when the relationship is stagnant (i.e. the middle), or when the relationship is going through hard times (i.e. the bottom), then the couple will continue to naturally be balanced and united throughout the trials and tribulations of their relationship. The sugar-water could be considered a "solution" to their problems.

Now, let's take the sand and water mixture. When one puts sand and water into a glass and shakes it up, it will look like an evenly distributed solution of the two. But over time, as these two Inner G's become comfortable, they naturally separate. The sand will naturally fall to the bottom of the glass and the water will naturally rise to the top of the sand. The only way these two Inner G's can stay together is through constant agitation. If there was no unnatural or outside interference to keep the two together, they would naturally separate. These couples are in constant conflict with each other. Each person is forcing the other to accept their Inner G that does not come naturally to them. It is a constant struggle to stay together. This has nothing to do with the person's sincerity to want a balanced relationship. This is just a natural progression of these two Inner G's trying to combine together, when in their natural state they repel each other's Inner G. One should not take it personally or look badly at the other person if they cannot understand, communicate or accept that person in their natural state. These couples may experience awesome "make-up" sex after a fight, but they can never maintain the Inner G balance long enough before they will naturally separate from each other. The couple will need constant and unnatural agitation or outside interference to stay together. This may come in the form of gifts, food, vacations, drugs, lies, sex toys, awesome make-up sex and/or rewards for unnatural behavior. Inevitably, the couple or mixture will be doomed to have an unbalanced relationship. Another example of this mixture is called emulsion. Let's examine a bottle of salad dressing. Before you mix it, there are two separate layers of liquids; one is oil-based and the other is water-based. When you shake the bottle, you create an emulsion. As time passes, the oil and water will separate into their original states. It is inevitable. It may take longer than the sand and water to separate, but nonetheless, it is still a mixture. Don't be fooled in your relationship. Time will reveal if your relationship is a mixture or a solution. Do not settle for mixtures. A healthy and balanced relationship is impossible, no matter how hard you want it to work. Find your solution and never settle for a mixture.

Let's take the concept of sex one step further now that we are familiar with the science. As one can see, sex is the way of the cosmos. In the seen, as well as the unseen realm, sex is the expression of life. The cosmos is one giant orgy! Every living entity is either giving out Inner G or receiving Inner G. This is the basic concept of sex. From the smallest sub-atomic particle, to the largest galaxies in the largest universe, sex is equivalent to life experience as we know it. If one is not practicing sex, they cannot live. Sex is the definition of life. One can find sex in everyday, normal activities. This is the basic definition of sex. Sex is the female principle of receiving Inner G and the male principle of giving out Inner G, working in a synergistic and cooperative relationship that keeps the balance of life. Sex is not dirty. Sex is not a sin. Sex is the act of knowing you are A-LIVE! But the European has brainwashed us into thinking sex is a bad thing. Remember LIVE backwards, in his language, spells EVIL. So his definition of evil goes against life in its natural state, abiding by universal law. Again, more proof that the European goes against nature in his mindset and definition of reality. Remember, according to our ancestors, nature and God meant the same thing. So the European's mindset and system goes against God.

Let us look further into the ancient Kemetic philosophy of how Inner G expresses itself. I will refer to a book called, ***"The Kybalion." The Kybalion: Hermetic Philosophy is a 1908 book claiming to be the essence of the teachings.***

This book represents the ancient Kemetic Tehuti text, who the Greeks called the god Hermes. Tehuti, in Kemet, represented the divine knowledge and wisdom of God or Inner G. Listed here are the seven principles of Inner G and how they relate to Black male and female relationships:

KEMETIC MYSTERY SYSTEM OF INNER G

DETERMINISM:

"He who knows these understandingly, possesses the Magic Key, before whose touch all the doors to the temple fly open."-The Kybalion

1) **The Principle of MENTALISM** – *The Universe is mental. All is the mind.*

- All that is experienced through our physical senses is spirit.
- The spirit is the infinite, universal, living mind.
- Whatever we visualize becomes reality.
- Whatever I project outwardly, I will attract internally.

Understand and internalize this principle. The physical world is made up of seen Inner G and unseen Inner G. Seen Inner G is only 10% of this reality. This is the Inner G that we can decipher with our five senses: Sight, Touch, Taste, Smell & Hearing. We are taught that these energies make up 100% of our reality. This is a bold and blatant lie. 90% of unseen Inner G is unaccounted for. Examples of this Inner G are radio waves, microwaves, X-rays, infrared light, UHF & VHF, etc.... These Inner G's affect us on a day-to-day basis, but we are oblivious to their properties and characteristics. Ways that we can decipher this Inner G include: right brain thinking, intuition, visualization, meditation, imagination, free will, inclinations, fearlessness and improvisation.

If one can access this Inner G or spirit world, then we will understand the power it has in manifesting our heart's desires in this physical realm. If you do not acknowledge this Inner G, you are basically operating in a retarded state. Understand that the universe conspires to help you succeed and accomplish your heart's desires. It yearns for you to access, believe and acknowledge it. Beginner's luck is the universe coaxing and encouraging you to step outside the box, in order for you to reach and attain your goals. Athletes who access this Inner G define it as, "being in the zone." They describe it as everything seeming to be in slow motion, i.e. similar to Keanu Reeve's character, Neo, in the movie, "The Matrix." They describe a euphoria and effortlessness. They describe superhuman strength and perceptions that seem to be like a dream state. They have no concept of being tired or any other physical ailments. It is described as an out-of-body experience while inside of your body. This is the Inner G we want to tap into when we engage in sex with our significant other. Can you imagine the experience of literally holding your partner's heart in your hand? For one to be able to look at their partner's soul face to face, for the first time? To get lost and be consumed by them so that you lose yourself in the bond you are engaged in? To lose consciousness of where you begin and where they end? This is what engaging in sex is supposed to be about.

2) The Principle of CORRESPONDENCE - *As above, so below. All objects in the universe must adhere to the same laws.*
This is the hidden secret of nature. Everything is everything.

- Nothing is above the law.

Once we understand this law, we can work within it to further our agenda. We will understand that there are no "short cuts" or "easy way outs" in life. What one puts into life or their relationships, that's what they will receive. They will also be shown signs and clues if the relationship does not have their best interests at heart. It will then be up to the individual to act accordingly. You can never blame your partner for hurting you, because the signs were there for you to see, but you chose to ignore them. We will be able to access information from within and not look outside of ourselves for solutions. In our relationships, we will see our significant other as an extension of ourselves. We will realize that, if I hurt or harm my partner, I am hurting myself. The same can be said if we take care, honor and love our partners, then we, in turn, take care, honor and love ourselves.

3)   **The Principle of VIBRATION** – *Nothing rests, everything in the universe is in motion.* Reason for the season.

- Matter, energy, mind & spirit are only different rates of vibrations.
- "He who understands the principle of vibration has grasped the scepter of power."

If one can attain this level of consciousness, then nothing shall be impossible unto them. If one can decipher vibration, then one can access their partners' feelings, thoughts and actions before they can express them. Have you ever experienced somebody giving you something you desired or needed before you could verbally express it to them? Have you experienced a person picking up the phone before the phone had a chance to ring and knew it was you on the other line? These are examples of the principle of vibration. Have you ever experienced having sex with someone and they knew all the right places to touch at all the right times and with the perfect amount of pressure? They had grasped the principle of vibration, and in so doing, they held your soul in their hands. This is what sex is supposed to be like. It means to be fully engrossed in your partner's vibration. To have the power to play them like a musical instrument that soothes their soul by plucking each string in rhythm, as you send them traveling into the edges of space and time. To finely tune a musical instrument, you must first decipher and have the ability to reach and embrace its vibrational frequency.

4)   **The Principle of POLARITY** – *Opposites must attract. Everything has its pair in the universe & must adhere to that relationship.*

- -There are two sides to everything.
- -Objects are identical in nature, but different in degree.
- -Opposites are really extreme differences of the same thing.

This principle relates to knowing and understanding that your partner is really an extension of yourself. What you love in your partner is really a reflection of what you love in yourself. Consequently, what you do not like in your partner is the same characteristics that you don't like in yourself. You are the mirror image of your partner. It is critical in having a healthy relationship to pick your mirror wisely. You do not want to have a partial reflection of yourself in your partner, because you will look elsewhere to find the missing parts of your reflection in others. This is not the fault of your partner. It is our own fault for trying to fit our partner's reflection into our own mirrors. We pick partners for the wrong reason. Our decisions are based on physical appearances, insecurities and our egos. One shouldn't have to work at seeing their reflection in their significant other if they are being honest with themselves. It should be a natural occurrence from which to build upon. Everything after that should be both partners polishing and refining each other's reflection.

5)   The Principle of RHYTHM – *Everything in the universe has its ebb & flow.*

- -There is rhythm in every pair of opposites.
- -For every action there is a reaction.
- -Everything flows out and in; all things rise and fall, ebb and flow, to and fro.

This is very important when it comes to relationships. We must understand, in nature, everything is done in its proper place and time. We need to recognize when to reap and when to sow. We need to understand our partner's rhythm. We need to know when to give them space and when to smother them. We need to understand when to motivate them and also when to discourage them. We need to recognize the space or time they are in and act accordingly. Once we understand our partner's rhythm, we can tap into their source. Knowing our partner is half the battle. If we do not recognize these characteristics, then it will lead to miscommunication, strife and eventually the parting of ways. Although this seems like it should come naturally to us, it does not. We are so off-base that we have to really concentrate and work at being in tune with our partner's rhythm. As a side note, just because you know all of your partner's "spots" and erogenous zones in the bedroom, doesn't necessarily mean you know your partner's rhythm in the spiritual realm. It takes dedication, understanding and commitment. You need to ask yourself: is it worth it?

6) **The Principle of CAUSE & EFFECT** *– Chance is but a name for a law not recognized. There are no coincidences, just the illusion of coincidence.*

- -Chance is but a name for a law not recognized.
- -There is a cause for every effect, and for every effect, there is a cause.

One must always be conscious of the signs and omens that are around them in their everyday lives. Consciousness means what we invest our time and Inner G into focusing on a particular thing. We are conscious of our jobs, cars and homes. But are we conscious of the stars, our children, the birds or trees? Once we are more aware of our surroundings and learn how to decipher the signs around us, then the more we will understand that there is a road map to our reality that we can access. We will be in a better position to manifest the things we want in life. We will be able to choose better partners in our relationships. We will not have to repeat lessons in life that seems to always follow us. Remember that there are no coincidences. If you meet someone at a particular place and time, then understand that person is there to teach you a lesson. Now, what that lesson entails may not be the one you want to learn. Understand that the Universe will either move things out of our way, or bring things in our path, according to the lesson we need to learn on our life's journey. It is our job to let go and walk out on faith, knowing that we are going to be better off for it, whichever way it turns. There are no bad lessons. All lessons have value. There are only bad judgments. Just make sure you don't repeat that lesson over and over. There are no bad lessons, just lower level reactions to the lesson.

7) **The Principle of GENDER** – *Masculine & Feminine principles manifest on all planes of existence. They are building blocks of the universe.- Kybalion*

- -There is a masculine & feminine principle in everything.
- -The masculine principle wants to express or give out.
- -The female principle is always in the direction of receiving impressions.
- -Both working in conjunction with one another creates balance and harmony.

We covered this topic earlier in the book. I will express this principle in a different light than before. Forgive me if I offend anyone with my lack of sensitivity to this topic, but this idea seems to resonate inside of me.

As we covered before, the female gender wants to receive Inner G just as the male wants to give out Inner G. What happens in today's society is that the system has switched the roles of the Black male and Black female. This has been implemented on purpose to create confusion and division among the two. Switching roles and expecting each to act according to those roles is an act of extreme violence to the very nature of a person's being. When you force the woman to act as a man, you are raping her spirit, which yearns to be feminine. This is accepted in today's society. Because of this, the Black woman's womb suffers, because she expresses masculine attributes. Her womb goes into a state of shock by the imbalance of feminine Inner G. Side effects of this are fibroid tumors, painful menstruation and cancer. It is like the physical rape of a woman. The perpetrator is "forcing" her to receive his Inner G when she does not want to. Similarly, the male is also being spiritually "raped" when a woman forces him to engage in communication, verbal arguments, getting up in his face and testing his manhood. The man just wanted to be left alone and this should be honored. But the woman will keep pushing because of the imbalance of her energies and not recognizing herself and her man as well. Each scenario is an act of rape and carries the same weight in the cosmos or unseen realm. Gender is the natural personality of things in creation and should be respected and honored as such. The Black man and woman must reeducate themselves and learn the roles that nature intended for them to embrace.

Everything to Me

"Boy if you ever left my
My Side
It be like taking the
Sun from the sky
I'd probably die without
You in my life cause I need you to shine, shine your light".--Monica

Did you know that the word for "son", a male child, comes from the word "Sun"? It makes sense when you know the science behind male and female Inner G. The Sun is the biggest giver of Inner G in our solar system. Every planet and moon receives the Sun's life-giving Inner G in order to be sustained. Giving out Inner G is the natural characteristic of all men.

"The true power of the Sun is expressed at its core. It is internal. That's where it burns the hottest. The Sun's Inner G is seen on the outside but its power is in its center. Its true Inner G is camouflaged by its outside appearance. So is the male." —Nekhebet

It defines the masculine trait. If this is the case, the daughter, or female child, is represented by the planets and the moons. Remember, feminine Inner G is a natural receiver of all Inner G. The Sun shines on the planets. The planets, in turn, give life from that Inner G, which the Sun gave them. The planet or moon then reflects that Inner G back to the Sun, so that the Sun can understand and appreciate its own brilliance and power. The glow or light of the planets and the moon are nothing but reflections of the Sun's Inner G. If a woman has a glow about her, there is usually a man in her life that is giving her good Inner G. If the woman is depressed, tired or looks lifeless, then there is probably a lack of male Inner G or the male Inner G that she revolves around is toxic to her well being. We all know that particular woman who stays with a no-good man and suffers because of it. She wears it on her person. There is no denying it, no matter how hard she tries to hide it.

"The true power of the Moon is expressed on its surface. Its power and Inner G is displayed on its surface. Its Inner G is fully displayed for all to see. Nothing is hidden. There is no need to look further in its core. What you see is what you get. The same holds true for the female."
— Nekhebet

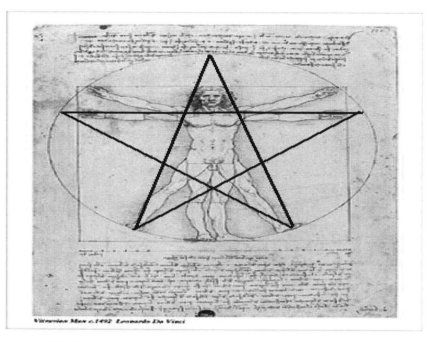

In this illustration of man by Leonardo Da Vinci, we see man as a 5-pointed star or the Sun. Arm, Leg, Leg, Arm, Head are the 5 points, spelling ALLAH frontwards and backwards, the Arabic word for God.

Because of European brainwashing, we now view polygamy as something to look down upon. Let us be reminded that, at the time of the highest civilization known to man, we were practicing polygamy. But let us understand the concept which produced this behavior. First of all, man had to be brilliant, powerful, strong and disciplined enough to exude enough energy to support his wives. So fellas, don't get too excited. Not every man or Sun has the capacity to give life to more than one planet. It is an ongoing process to uplift and recognize the knowledge of self. If the man was not capable of "supporting" each female — mentally, physically and spiritually — then he would not be allowed to practice polygamy. Remember, the purpose of marriage for our ancestors was to create gods here on Earth. That is why there were arranged marriages. Not just to keep the wealth in the bloodline, but to also further the God consciousness in their bloodlines or DNA. This is where the real wealth was located. So the elders would take into consideration the positioning of the stars at the birth of the couple. They would look at each family's lineage. The purpose was to match the genetic codes of the male and female to infuse the potential of their union, to produce a human being of the highest level of God consciousness. Certain family bloodlines or lineages were specifically designed to raise consciousness after every generation. Generations after generations of this practice produced the highest quality of a human being that had the potential to reach God consciousness. God consciousness simply means to internalize, master and recognize all the attributes of nature and to eliminate the ego. So for generations, the sole purpose of the mother and father was to raise the consciousness of their child. When that child was old enough to have children, he was matched with a mate of the same potential. Their child would be nurtured to reach God consciousness, and thus, the cycle kept repeating itself. Can you imagine what type of union and offspring this couple would bring forth?

It is an incredible and amazing concept to grasp! Lost in this concept is our Western or European version of marrying for love or selfishness. We practice a foolish form of so-called love that produces an over 50% failure rate. Yet, we hold on to this concept and aspire to have this definition in our own lives. We never question this practice. We just blindly accept it as the best thing for us while we ignore the destruction it brings to our community. What would you rather have: a love driven by your ego or the ability to create gods and goddesses?

When analyzing polygamy, keep these attributes as your focal point. Don't get me wrong, I believe any Afrikan system that is implemented in the United States will be a dysfunctional failure. The overall environment of this country is at such a low level that anything sacred has to be compromised and undermined. Like my teacher once told me about politics, "The only way not to get dirty in a cesspool is to not jump in." You can't avoid being contaminated in this country. We are all tampered with because of the overall environment this system operates on. There is no escaping this lower vibration. All we can hope to do is survive it and focus on higher levels, as time will usher in a new age of consciousness. One thing I realize in life is that the closer we understand and embrace nature, God, then the closer we are to the solutions to our problems.

Orange Moon
Songwriters: Lacy, Braylon; Martin, Shawn; Wright, Erica;
I'm an orange moon
Reflecting the light of the sun.
Then he turned to me
He saw his reflection in me
And he smiled at me when he turned to me
Then he said to me
How good it is, how good it is
Shine so bright
He ruled the day, I ruled the night
Shine, shine, shine
How good it is, how good it is
I'm an orange moon
I'm brighter than before, brighter
Reflecting the light of the sun
Smile at me. – Erykah Badu

Christianity uses this symbolism to show this characteristic in its religious figures when it puts them in paintings, sculptures or pictures. You will see a halo over the head or sun rays emitting from the back of the head of Jesus Christ, the saints or other important characters in the Bible. They are enlightened or brilliant beings. The Sun or light always has underlining meanings referring to consciousness. We see the light bulb above people's heads in comic books when they have an epiphany or brilliant revelation, in the form of an idea. This is the power of the Sun. This is the masculine Inner G of man. It means to give life to higher consciousness, to be reflected by feminine Inner G. When a teacher wants to describe a student as intelligent, they will say that the student is bright. To be enlightened means to fully understand a concept or idea. It means that a light has been turned on when there used to be darkness. Now they are able to see the truth for what it really is. The light has been shined on the object being studied. So if this is true, then nature practices polygamy! There is one Sun that sustains and supports nine planets.

Remember, when our ancestors referred to nature, they were speaking about the concept of God. One Sun is positioned in the solar system as its center. The planets all revolve around the Sun. Just like the atom where the proton is the nucleus and the electrons revolve around it. The planets do not collide with each other or compete with each other, just like the electrons that orbit around the proton. They do not interfere with the other electrons that are also orbiting around it. There is a synergistic relation in the group. As long as each planet is receiving the Inner G it needs to sustain it, it will continue to revolve around its Sun. Let's look at other systems in nature that practice polygamy; there is one male lion and several female lions in a pride. A woman releases one egg approximately every 28 days, whereas a man produces billions of sperm during that time.

We also know brothers who are defeated in their relationships because the woman tries to outshine them or inhibits their Inner G. We refer to this as the "woman wearing the pants" in the relationship. We will address this concept later on in the book.

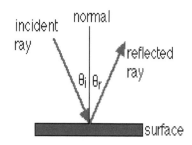

law of reflection : $\theta_r = \theta_i$

The Law of Reflection

Objects can be seen by the light they emit, or, more often, by the light they reflect. Reflected light obeys the law of reflection, that the angle of reflection equals the angle of incidence.

Let's look at this law according to the Black man and woman's relationship. Man needs the woman to reflect his light. If there is no woman present, a man cannot define himself or his purpose, for he cannot visualize himself. He will become lost, feel alone and have low self-esteem. The woman needs the man to give her his Inner G. In order for her to manifest anything in the physical dimension, she needs a man's Inner G to fuel and inspire her. If she doesn't have a man around her, then she becomes stagnant, confused and disorientated. The concept of the law of reflection applies in this relationship.

For objects such as mirrors with a smaller wavelength of light, the law of reflection applies on a large scale. All the light travelling in one direction and reflecting from the mirror is reflected in one direction; reflection from such objects is known as specular reflection.

If the man's Inner G is smaller than the woman, who is reflecting his Inner G, the woman has the capacity to reflect 100% of the man's Inner G. The woman has the capacity to absorb and reflect all of the man's Inner G that he gives to her. This is similar to looking at a mirror and seeing one's entire image reflected back. A man will not look outside of his relationship to see himself because his woman reflects all his Inner G. He is satisfied and content with the reflection that he sees of himself, which is displayed by her.

Most objects exhibit diffuse reflection, with light being reflected in all directions. All objects obey the law of reflection on a microscopic level, but if the irregularities on the surface of an object are larger than the wavelength of light, which is usually the case, the light reflects off in all directions.

Most men contain within themselves more Inner G than the woman has the capacity of reflecting back to him. The woman does not have the capacity to reflect 100% of the man's Inner G. The light or Inner G from the man will reflect off in all directions. This is the Inner G that the woman, who is reflecting him, did not have the capacity to absorb and reflect back to him. This is the Inner G that another person, place or thing can and will reflect back to him. It is the law. A man, by nature, needs to see 100% of his reflection in his life. If a woman does not have the capacity to reflect 100% of the man's Inner G, then he will seek to find his reflection somewhere else. This doesn't mean the man is dissatisfied with the woman, who contains the majority of his reflection. In actuality, it has nothing to do with her. This law is not personal, so don't take it as such. The woman is doing all that she has the capacity to do. The woman has two choices: Limit the Inner G your man can display, which will lead you and him to a controlling and manipulating relationship and contempt, or help him explore and manifest the things you do not have the capacity to reflect in him. Remember, seeing his reflection does not necessarily mean another woman. He can see it in places he likes to attend, as well as business ventures and hobbies that bring him satisfaction and contentment. Understand the law of reflection and use it to determine the quality of your relationship.

Let us now look into the science of attraction to learn why atoms, representing male and female relationships, bond together. We will use the concept called "Happy Atoms." Scientists use letters to name the orbitals or shells around the nucleus of the atom. They use the letters "k,l,m,n,o,p, and q". The "k" shell is the one closest to the nucleus and "q" is the farthest away. The nucleus contains the protons, or masculine Inner G, and the shells contain electrons, which represent feminine Inner G.

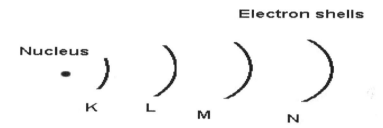

Atomic shells around atoms yearn to be full. Some atoms have too many electrons (one or two extra). These atoms like to give up their electrons. Some atoms are really close to having a full shell. Those atoms go around looking for other atoms that want to give up an electron. They can either give up electrons or receive electrons. Not all shells hold the same number of electrons. For the first eighteen elements, there are some easy rules. The k-shell only holds two electrons. The l-shell only holds eight electrons. The m-shell only holds eight electrons. The m-shell can actually hold up to 18 electrons as you move farther along the periodic table. The maximum number of electrons that you will find in any shell is 32. (See illustration on next page.)

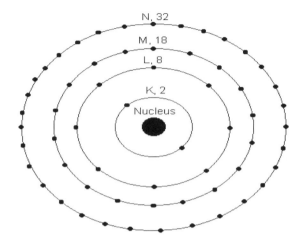

The main goal of an atom is to become a "Happy Atom" with completely filled electron orbitals or shells. Once the atom has completely filled its shells, it will become stable and content. Now the atom becomes electrically "attractive." Other electrically charged atoms (ions) are now looking at it and seeing a good partner to bond with.

So let us relate this science to Black male and female relationships. The nucleus of the atom contains protons, which represent the masculine Inner G of the Black male. The electrons in the shells revolving around the nucleus represent the feminine Inner G of the Black female. The nucleus or male Inner G of the atom is constantly looking for electrons or feminine Inner G to see its reflection and power. The electrons are also searching for protons or male Inner G to give it enough Inner G to sustain and support them. As we mentioned earlier, the shell closest to the nucleus or male Inner G, labeled "m", can only contain a maximum of two electrons or two entities of feminine Inner G. This means that the Black male can only supply enough masculine Inner G to support and sustain a maximum of two females in his immediate circle or area. However, in his outer shells, the male can support between 8 to 32 female entities, depending on how much Inner G he was born with in his nucleus or core. A man is born with a set amount of masculine Inner G in his being. He cannot acquire more along the way. This is why some men can sustain and support many more women while others have a hard time keeping one woman.

The outer shells of the atom that contain feminine Inner G, although they may be in the "background" of the male in regards to being acknowledged in the relationship, are still nonetheless revolving around that male Inner G and are being sustained and supported by it. It may not be to the degree of the female Inner G in the first shell, but she is receiving his Inner G on a different scale. All females share masculine Inner G in nature, whether they want to or not. It is only in the Caucasian's definition of a healthy relationship that state that one male must only share his Inner G with one female. Don't get me wrong; "sharing" a man's Inner G does not necessarily mean having sexual intercourse. Remember, sex is the engagement of masculine and feminine Inner G used to create a unique synergy of life between the two. It does not just mean sexual intercourse on a physical level. All females, whether married or single, share masculine Inner G with every man in their circle. Just like all men, whether married or not, support and sustain more than one female at a time according to the capacity of his innate, masculine Inner G.

The word *"Valence" is a measure of how much atoms want to bond with other atoms.* This describes the principles of the atoms we have been discussing. When one looks further into this definition, it sounds like the scientific definition of the concept that we call love. If this is the case, then the feeling that we call love can actually be broken down and deciphered on the atomic level. Love is real. It has a formula and laws that it must adhere to. It can be recognized, appreciated and deciphered.

Male & Female Principles of the One

Let us go back to the origin of masculine and feminine principles of Inner G. Ancient Afrikan mythology expresses its concept of God in terms of the feminine, never the masculine. Throughout the Diaspora, darker peoples of the world refer to God as a female. Not only are ancient definitions of God a woman, but they refer to Her as a Black woman! There are many creation stories that are based on Afrikan spirituality, otherwise known as metaphysics. All come with the same concepts; they just have different stories to illustrate the science. Here is one according to master teacher Dr. Phil Valentine. I paraphrase: "One day, God was sitting around, pondering over how perfect She was. Inevitably, God got bored in Her perfection. There was nothing for God to improve or work on, nothing for God to keep busy in the state of perfection. God had nothing to contemplate about. She was perfect. So, in a perfectly, boring bliss, God wanted to have an experience outside of Herself. She did this by creating the material universe or physical dimension as we know it. God then separated herself. She called one part feminine and the other part masculine. She did this so that she could acknowledge, embrace and appreciate both aspects of Herself. Thus, the male and female principles of Inner G were born."

First, the feminine principle of the one God fell from the unseen or spiritual world to have a human experience in the physical dimension. Remember, one needs this principle in order to create or bring forth new life or Inner G. The feminine principle, being magnetic, attracted or collected all the materials in the universe to make a physical body from the ethers, similar to a rain cloud collecting moisture in the atmosphere. When a rain cloud gathers enough moisture from the atmosphere it becomes too heavy and falls to the Earth in the form of rain. The heavier the elements or materials in the ethers, the denser the form becomes. This is how God's spirit came down to the physical dimension to have a human experience. When the Bible says that Lucifer, otherwise known as the Light Bearer, the Morning Star or the Fallen Angel, was kicked out of heaven and fell to the Earth, this is what it was alluding to. You are the Light Bearer. You are the Morning Star. You are the Fallen Angel. Bear with me, people, stay focused. I said that you will have to show humility and be courageous on this journey to the truth. And as we know, truth sets us free. All these titles refer to the science that we have been studying. Take religion out of the equation and look at the science. I promise you, you will be closer to God than any religion can ever take you. We will get further into this concept later on in the book. But understand this point before we move on. Your enemy knows that, innately, Black people are a spiritual people. So he uses this to his advantage. He will hide solutions for overcoming your oppression in subjects that you dare not try to understand. One of these subjects is what he calls devil worship. I can see you turning back already. Like Harriet Tubman in the Underground Railroad, put so eloquently by Erykah Badu in song, "I got that shotgun on yo' back." Harriet Tubman did not carry a shotgun to kill the slave masters. She carried it to force those cowardly, ungrateful Negroes, who wanted to turn back to massa, to keep going to reach the Promised Land! They thanked her later.

The Masculine Principle of the One God was resurrected from the Earth to become reunited with the Feminine Principle. This story is alluded to in the creation of Adam in the Bible. Remember Adam or Atom was made from the Earth; he didn't fall from the heavens as God's feminine side did. So if this is true, it gives credibility that the first concept of God was a woman. God needed the feminine principle or magnetism first to enter the physical dimension. It is after She arrived here that She created Her masculine principle from the Earth, unlike what the Bible preaches, that the woman came from man. This is far from the case. All men came from a woman, even the one Creator. Remember, the European wants to subject his rule and world dominion over all women, so he made her think that she was inferior to him. The Bible is sexist because the white man, who manipulates and interprets its contents, is sexist, not God. So now you have the one God, in human form, separated from Itself. He called one half "woman", and the other half she called "man."

Through the European's manipulation of history, the true history of the Afrikan woman has been suppressed and hidden. Eve did not come from Adam, Adam came from Eve. The Afrikan woman now accepts her oppressor's definitions of herself as if she came up with it on her own. This internalized slave mentality has led her to be unbalanced in her mind, body & spirit. In order to recapture her knowledge of self, she must embrace her feminine principle & Inner G. The woman is the Creator's original recipe and must be recognized and honored as such. Sistas, trust and embrace your intuition & it will guide you to your higher self. Know that you were a goddess first in the spiritual world before you decided to create this physical plane of existence. Listed below are a few facts that reveal your strength, power & divine characteristics. Remember, it is only through you that the Black man will rise to one day assume the throne that he has fallen from. Only you can put him back together, and in so doing, place yourself as his Queen, side by side.

- **There are more widows than widowers.**
- **There are more women over 100 years old than men.**
- **Women age slower than men.**
- **The hardening of the arteries, ulcers & heart attacks are less frequent in women.**
- **Women can hold their breath longer than men.**
- **Women's muscle capacity can carry more oxygen than men.**
- **Women have a stronger endurance & stamina than men.**
- **Women can have unlimited orgasms while her counterpart is spent after the first one.**

- All human life in its early stages start out as female
- The mother determines the sex of the child, not the father.
- Women have two X chromosomes, while men only have one, plus an exaggerated or mutated X chromosome called Y.
- Because females are made to receive Inner G, one needs to be stronger to receive than to give out Inner G.
- The original Creator's life form on this material existence was a woman.
- The first concept of God, in Afrika, was a woman.
- Women's brains, on average, are more dense and heavier than a man's brain.
- A female can create life without a male (scarab beetle, honey bee, and others).
- Today's so-called menstruation is really the female hemorrhaging. This is designed to keep the woman weak and subservient. In Ancient Afrika, the women did not menstruate.
- Women have more taste buds than men.
- Vessels such as boats, ships, airplanes and cars are named after women to promote the feminine principle of Inner G.
- The planet is inundated with positive or electrical Inner G. We need to be more magnetic to raise our vibration into higher consciousness. A male-dominated society equals lower vibration.
- The female heart beats ten times faster per minute than a male's heart.
- Seven in 100 men suffer from color blindness, while this only affects one in a 1,000 women.

Chapter Eight:

Biggest Sexual Organ is between Your Ears Not Your Legs

"If you masturbate, your pleasure will be quick and temporary, but if you play with your mind, your pleasure will be limitless and have infinite possibilities." — Nekhebet

The brain and its functions is one of the biggest mysteries of the human body. Little is known about the functions and multiple purposes of the brain. Our ancestors went to great lengths to honor, study and internalize the great mysteries of the brain. They understood that the brain was the epicenter of information, which the body was obligated to listen to and obey. So if one was able to comprehend and master the functions of the brain, then one's body, and the physical dimension it dwells in, must conform to what the brain commands. They figured out that the power of thought can create physical reality. The brain contains billions of neurons which fire electricity in the form of neurotransmitters. They communicate through electrical impulses that relate the reaction and behavior that the body must respond to and obey. ***There are over 100,000 chemical reactions in the brain every second. The brain is also a radio transmitter, which sends out measurable electrical wave signals.***

Every thought that an individual has creates an electrical pulse that penetrates not only every cell in the body, but also communicates with the immediate environment outside of the individual. Mind you, this happens millions of times a second! You are constantly controlling and manipulating your body and the environment around you, even if you are unaware of it. With the mastery of this concept by our ancestors, they were able to create their own reality on the physical, mental and spiritual plane. We see some semblance of this today when we look at the concept of likes attracting. The individual creates the environment in his body in the form of health, as well as the people, places and things that make up his environment. You notice that "birds of a feather do flock together." A person, who always complains by saying, "Why are things always happening to me?" will find, under close scrutiny, that they are attracting the same Inner G around them. They are the cause of their own unhappiness and misery. In the sports world, you will hear athletes talk about "being in the zone." This is the time and space where their activation of Melanin is aligned with their thoughts to produce a physical reality they want. This is the space and time where Michael Jordan seems to fly to the hoop or can't miss seemingly impossible shots that he takes anywhere on the court. This is when baseball player, Barry Bonds, knows he is going to hit a home run the moment he walks into the batter's box. This is the state of existence where jazz musicians intuitively create masterpieces on stage in an impromptu jazz session. Also, in hip hop, when the rapper free flows to a beat and creates a synergistic rhythm that connects his thoughts and the beat infuses into one fluid Inner G that has purpose and intent. We have the power to create our own quality of life, instead of our oppressor creating their own definition of our lives for us to believe in.

Also, the individual, armed with this knowledge, will be able to decipher when, where and how lower-level Inner G comes into his aura. Have you ever met a person for the first time and something didn't feel right about them? Or even vice-versa, where there is an immediate attraction upon meeting them for the first time. It's like you have known them all of your life. What you are feeling is the electrical pulses that a person's body is emitting into you and your immediate environment. You are also giving out your own Inner G frequency as well. Inner G can repel as well as be absorbed, according to the relationship of the two frequencies. The repelling of the Inner G frequency is the feeling of uneasiness that one gets when meeting a person. The natural absorption of Inner G is the result of the same Inner G's complementing each other. The Caucasians now bombard the Black community with low-level Inner G to create lower level thoughts that produce lower level behavior. Lower level Inner G can be described in terms of promoting, nurturing and manifesting drug abuse, pollution, bad nutrition, stress, unemployment, lower level music, jealousy, distrust, low self-esteem, guns, violence, fear, hate, materialism, ignorance, self-survival and others.

Imagine if the Black man and woman were bombarded with higher levels of Inner G. The Black man and woman would produce higher conscious thoughts, which would lead to higher consciousness displayed in their behavior. Our communities would be transformed overnight! Protect your Inner G as much as possible. Be very careful who you allow in your immediate circle. Be very demanding of the people who you choose to communicate with on a daily basis. Do not allow anybody to contaminate your sacred space. Protect it as if your life depended on it, because it really does. When you engage in a relationship with someone, always keep this as a motivating factor in your decision to share your Inner G with them. When you do come together, remember how sacred and life-changing the Inner G you share will impact your reality. Do not engage in sex with the primary motivation being to satisfy your selfish, animalistic or lower desires. Always think about the reality you want to create with your partner and your sexual satisfaction will explode exponentially. If you have sex to satisfy the body, then you might have an orgasm and then it will be over. The satisfaction will only be temporary. But if one has sex using the mind as the sexual organ to higher consciousness, then one's orgasm, whether male and female, will be nurturing, inspirational, healing and infinite. I encourage all Black people to be responsible and create their sacred realities with their partner when engaged in sex or otherwise. Let the biggest sexual organ you have be between your ears and not your legs!

Our brains are divided into two sections: The right hemisphere & the left hemisphere of the brain. One can only activate one side of the brain at any given time. The left side of your body is controlled by the right side of your brain & the right side of your body is controlled by the left side of your brain. Each side of your brain serves as different functions of your perceptions of reality.

LEFT BRAIN	**RIGHT BRAIN**
uses logic	uses feelings
details	abstract "big picture"
facts	imagination rules
words, language	symbols, images
present, past	present, future
math, science	philosophy
order, patterns	faith, beliefs
perception	appreciates possibilities
names	spatial, risks
safe	not detailed
reality, defined	fantasy
rationality	intuition
formal intelligence	spirituality
positive (Post or sit)	negative (no gates)

Left Brain is the defined sense of your personal self.
Right Brain is the oneness of infinite creative energy.

Society rewards left-brained people. Our school system is designed to produce left-brain thinking, as it suppresses right-brain functions. As a result, society rewards those who can get in line and do what they are told & taught to do. Our school system trains us to be good sheep. Always raise your hand & get permission to speak. Wait in line to get what you want. Dress, talk, behave & think like we want you to. Be able to regurgitate the information we uploaded to your brain. No thinking outside the box. Left-handed people are dominated by their right brain. This is why they used to demonize them in the past. Right-brain-dominated people do not make good sheep. They even burned them at the stake and called them demons or witches.

To this day, the European still practices rituals to suppress right brain thought. When we introduce ourselves to a person, we shake with our right hand. This activates the left hemisphere of the brain. This automatically distances and lowers the exchange of Inner G between the two individuals. Our first meeting is not based on love or higher consciousness for your fellow man, but based on self-survival and analytical thinking. When one recites the pledge of allegiance, they place their right hand over our hearts. By covering their hearts, this ritual promotes that the decisions one makes will be influenced by self-survival and not the higher consciousness of love. This ritual takes the heart or the humanity out of our decision making and promotes a blind allegiance for our country, no matter the circumstances we find ourselves in. Our allegiance is based on lower level consciousness and not the compassion that dwells within our hearts. Also, by raising our right hands when we give an oath, we operate from our lower self, located in the left brain. This again takes our compassion and love of fellow man out of our thinking process, in order to serve the agenda we had sworn to uphold.

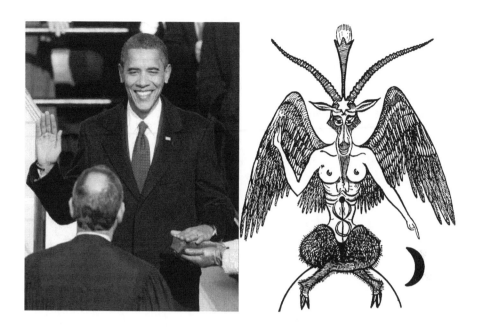

The picture of President Obama, on the left, taking the "oath" to become the President of the United States. Notice that the Freemason god Baphomet, in the picture on the right, is giving the same pose or stance. The right hand pointing up signifies the promotion of lower consciousness housed in the left hemisphere of the brain, and the left arm pointing down symbolizes the suppression of higher consciousness housed in the right hemisphere of the brain. This is the conspiracy that secret societies implement in order to control and manipulate the masses into embracing their lower consciousness, while at the same time, never letting them acknowledge their higher selves.

Even in our vocabulary, the word "Right" signifies: *one who is correct, good, opposite of wrong, opposite of left, just, good or proper; preferable, socially acceptable, being in good physical or mental health or order and in his right mind; qualities (as adherence to duty or obedience to lawful authority) that together constitute the ideal of moral propriety or merit, moral approval.*

Our ancestors knew of this knowledge and fought hard to correct this human condition. Master teacher Ashra Kwesi states that they had a procedure in Kemet to correct this human nature. It states, "Left foot forward to trample down evil, so that the heart can move forward." See illustration:

As you can see in the illustration, all the figures in the Metu Neter are walking in the same direction. Each figure is leading with their left foot forward. As we covered earlier, the left side of our body is controlled by the right hemisphere of our brain. The right side of our body is controlled by the left hemisphere of our brain. So to always activate our higher, spiritual self, we need to activate the right side of our brains. We do this by moving the left side of our bodies first and foremost. In theory, one can suppress their lower selves by favoring the left side of their bodies. Since Europeans lack the capacity to reach higher spiritual consciousness, they will always remain left-brain dominant by favoring the right side of their bodies. The goal of our ancestors was to live life and make decisions based on the compassion and love of the heart. There was no separation from the heart in all of life's predicaments, lessons or circumstances. The heart is the first level of higher consciousness. One did this by favoring the left side of their bodies.

In Dr. Jewel Pookrum's lecture, The Seven Circuits of the Brain, she covers and explains seven levels of consciousness that one has the ability to tap into if one is willing to raise their consciousness. We only use a very small percentage of our brains. Western medicine and science never seems to think that this fact is of any concern. Our ancestors were able to access all regions of their brains. Because of this, they were able to accomplish great feats in the past that are still a mystery to modern man. Black men and women are literally operating at a level of mental retardation when compared to our Kemetic ancestors. The educational system is meant to enslave and prepare you for slavery, otherwise known as the work force, not to enlighten or free you. Once you have access to different parts of your brain, your reality changes immediately. The system wants to keep you on lockdown so they control the parameters of what you define as your reality. If they have the ability to keep you mentally in a box, then they will control your actions in regards to the individual always reacting to their given environment and not acting on their own freewill. Simply stated, if you control one's thoughts, then you can control one's actions. The best way to enslave an individual is to have them believe that they are free. Dr. Pookrum addresses the parts or circuits of the brain that our ancestors had access to, which lay dormant in our collective Black minds in the present day.

Pituitary and Pineal Glands

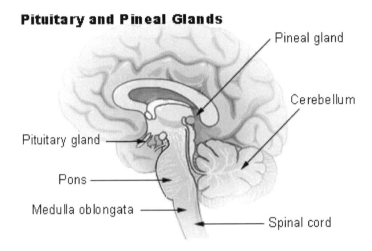

First Circuit: The first and most primitive level of the brain is located in the brain stem. The brain stem is also known as the "reptilian brain." When we are in our mother's womb, we all start out having a tail, like a reptilian. We look just like a tadpole. We even breathe liquid or water before we are able to breathe air. After we are born, some of us still simulate this reptilian behavior in the form of our thought process. Reptilians are preoccupied with their own safety, selfishness and well being. Reptilians are so selfish, they do not have families. If a reptilian offspring stays around too long, the mother will eat them. Reptilians only come together to mate. Otherwise, they are relegated to a life of solitude. Reptilian behavior is motivated by fear and self-preservation. They go through their whole lives driven by satisfying the basic necessities of life: food, shelter and safety.

If one was to try to have a relationship with this type of person, it would virtually be impossible, unless the other person was also operating at the first circuit of the brain. Each person in the relationship would have their own space within their perceived shared space. They would virtually live independent lives from each other, although they live with each other. They would only share their resources and energy for the basic necessities of life, such as procreation, food, shelter and transportation. We all know couples who operate in this type of circumstance. One person claims ownership to one part of the house and the other claims another part of the house. They will definitely have separate bank accounts. This type of person is incapable of sharing a healthy and nurturing relationship. In the end, they will always look out for themselves above their mates. This mindset cannot have a relationship based on higher consciousness. It would be impossible.

Second Circuit: The second circuit of the brain is activated in the Medulla Oblongata. This circuit houses the consciousness of the insect world. Insects define themselves through groups. Every member of the group has a particular role to play. That is their bond and their bond alone. There are no emotional ties or personal investments in other participants in their group. Their work and the role they play within the group is their sole purpose for living. In other words, these people define themselves through their job titles or the power that their positions have in the work environment. Outside of that preconceived job title, they are lost and unsatisfied. These are the individuals who die six months to three years after they retire from their occupations. Also, these are the church-going people. They spend more time and Inner G at their church than they do at home. Their home is usually in disarray and neglected because of it. Thus, they do not want to stay at home. Their spouses will usually try to attach themselves to places, people or things outside the house to find the satisfaction that they are not receiving at home. These people tend to gossip about other members of the group because there is no real emotional bond to their peers. If this person, for some reason, has to leave the group, they will suffer significantly and be miserable until they attach themselves to another group. These people will also ostracize other members of the group who have been dismembered. They will be cold and merciless in their dealings with disbanded members. They will act like they are strangers to excommunicated members, even if they have known them for a long period of time. A relationship with this type of person is either a feast or a famine. It all depends on whether you are part of the group or not. The main focus of the relationship is how to stay together, no matter if the relationship is fulfilling or not.

Third Circuit: The third circuit of the brain is located in the Cerebellum. This area of the brain is ruled by the fowl species. This is where we get the term "bird brain." This type of individual may display a significant amount of intelligence and logic. These are the people who become experts too soon. These people can be dangerous because they possess a significant amount of intelligence, but they are arrogant in their wisdom. They feel that they know it all, so no one can tell them anything. If one does present knowledge to these individuals, then they would want you to show them proof of your findings. These people are the "prove it to me" type. They want to know the resources of your knowledge and if you can't tell them your resource, then your information is not valid to them. In the animal kingdom, birds fly the highest in the sky. They have developed the habit of always looking down on others. Birds fear other birds that fly higher, faster and stronger than themselves. If you get into a relationship with this type of individual, be prepared to always apologize for your misunderstandings, even when you are in the right. This is where the super ego dwells. Be prepared to put them at ease by not outshining them in any of life's adventures. As long as they perceive you as being below them, they will be content. Never challenge them in all their wisdom, because it will be perceived as a threat or sign of disrespect. People in this relationship are not interested in uplifting their mates. They are only interested in feeding their own egos and subjecting their mates under their rule without questioning their authority.

Fourth Circuit: This part of the brain connects the thought process based on the emotions of the heart. This is the first circuit of higher consciousness. The final decisions in all thoughts that determine behavior are filtered through the heart. There is no separation between thought and the heart. This part of the brain is where an individual thinks with his heart and feels with his mind. This is the first level of the enlightened individual. This is where true and healthy relationships begin. They operate without the preconceived confines of the ego. There is no fear, worry or stress to poison the relationship before it has the chance to grow. Each person who is operating at this level will always put their partner's feelings, thoughts and actions ahead of their own. They will always sacrifice themselves for the good of their partner. When the two combine their Inner G's together, they will be able to manifest miracles and create god children as a result of their union.

Fifth Circuit: This part of the brain houses the capability to transcend into other, higher dimensions of reality. All of life's thoughts and actions are connected to the one life force that permeates all things. This is where the individual makes the connection and is able to tap into that one, divine Inner G. It is the level of pure knowingness. One can perceive the past, present and future dimensions all at the same time. This is the sixth sense operating at its highest level. It is more powerful in understanding and interpreting reality than the other five senses combined. This is where true and healthy relationships begin, because each partner will now sense each other's needs and wants instantaneously.

Sixth Circuit: This circuit of the brain is located in the Temporal Lobes of the brain. This is where higher consciousness is mastered. A person who is activated at this level of the brain can have access to multiple dimensions. They will be able to astro-project themselves to any dimension. They will have the ability to communicate using the totality of all their extra sensory perceptions. In this relationship, the individuals will be able to see each other outside of their physical bodies. They will be able to see each other's souls. Once you acknowledge and recognize the soul of your mate, one will be able to travel and experience other dimensions while they are engaged in sex. Infinite possibilities will be the outcome of this relationship.

Seventh Circuit: This circuit of the brain is housed in the Frontal Lobes of the brain. A person who is activated at this level of consciousness would have "access and the ability to utilize the entire electromagnetic structure as we know it." This person would have the ability to fly. They would be able to grow any organs or limbs on their bodies that need repair. They would be able to exhibit super-human strength and do super-human feats at will. One cannot comment on a relationship with this type of person, but understand that our ancestors in Kemet had to be operating at a high level of consciousness in order to produce the civilization that they built and that we still cannot figure out how they did it.

Christ Consciousness:

As we covered in an earlier chapter about KRST consciousness or what the Christian figure of Jesus Christ represents, here is a dissected view of the brain that shows you where this concept was taken from. In Dr. Phil Valentine's lecture on the movie *The Passion of the Christ*, he breaks down the metaphysical theory of the crucifixion of Jesus Christ. The place where Jesus was crucified was called Golgotha.

> *John 19:17* ***And he bearing his cross went forth into a place called [the place] of a skull, which is called in the Hebrew*** Golgotha***:***

So as we alluded to in an earlier chapter, the crucifixion of Christ is really the method or journey that an individual must undertake to reach higher or Christ consciousness. Where does this journey always begin within the individual? It always starts in the mind — always in the brain, or as it is referred to in the Bible, Golgotha, which means "The Place of the Skull." This is the place where the character of Jesus in the Bible was able to put to death lower level behavior and was resurrected into higher consciousness. In the illustration below of the anatomy of the brain, you will see a dissected view of the human brain. Notice that in the middle of the brain, between the two hemispheres, you will see what appears to be a man hanging on a cross. He is made up of the Fornix and the Sub thalamic Nucleus. Notice what appears to be behind the head of the figure: an illuminated Pineal gland. Remember the Pineal gland produces Melanin, which is needed in order to accelerate your vibration in order to achieve higher consciousness. Remember, if one has a calcified Pineal gland, like the Caucasian race, it cannot produce the quality of Melanin necessary to accelerate one's vibration to a higher frequency, in order to transcend into higher consciousness. This is one of the reasons why, whenever you see images of Jesus or other enlightened beings, they always seem to have the back of their heads illuminated with light, similar to the Sun, or a halo over their heads.

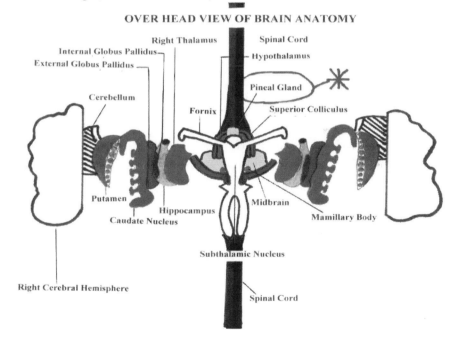

OVER HEAD VIEW OF BRAIN ANATOMY

So the metaphysical concept of the crucifixion story of Jesus Christ is the ability of the individual to put to death their lower level consciousness and deeds in order to embrace their higher, spiritual consciousness. One must master their animalistic behaviors, such as selfishness, greed, fear, hate, addiction and the ego.   Once this is mastered, the gateway to higher consciousness will be attainable. This is the place where man can master his physical self and environment to produce miracles. On both sides of the Christ figure were two thieves. The one on the left wanted Christ to prove that he was the son of God by taking himself off the cross and saving himself. The thief on the left, representing our left brain, wanted physical proof of Christ's power. The thief on the left believed that if there was no physical proof, then it did not exist nor could it be true. The thief on the right, representing the right brain, didn't need physical proof to believe that he was the son of God. All the thief had to do was believe and have faith in that belief, and it would be so.

Christ told him that because he believed and had faith, he would save a place in heaven for him.

Our right brain houses our higher or spiritual selves. It does not limit its reality and capabilities according to the rules of the physical dimension. On the other hand, our left brain only recognizes what is real based on our five senses. Its reality is limited to the physical dimension. So the object of man is to cross over from predominately using the left brain to defining his reality through his right brain. This is why Christ had to die. His death symbolized the transformation from being left-brain dominant to being right-brain dominant; from his lower physical consciousness, to his higher, spiritual consciousness. The illustration shows the crucifixion of Christ in terms of the parts of the brain that need to be addressed in order for us to transcend into higher consciousness. Our thoughts create our reality. The two thieves, representing the right and left hemispheres of our brain, are constantly competing for our attention. An individual can only activate one hemisphere of the brain at a given time. It is a constant struggle of going back and forth between the two hemispheres of our brain that defines what is real for us. One hemisphere wants to keeps us here in the physical dimension and the other wants to transcend into the spiritual world. They both want to steal our

Inner G and conscience from which to create our reality. The question is which thief will you give your Inner G to in order to create your own reality?

The picture above is the Biblical interpretation of the crucifixion of Jesus Christ. Notice the two "thieves" on each side of him. They represent the right and left hemispheres of our brains that want to "steal" our time and Inner G from which we interpret ourselves and our reality.

Below are the lyrics to a song by Lauryn Hill called *Peace of Mind*. She is really talking about the internal struggle of her lower self versus her higher self. It is a constant battle of her ego, which represents her lower consciousness, and her spiritual self that represents her higher consciousness. This is a constant struggle in man; since one can never fully get rid of their ego, they can only contain it.

Peace of Mind

See, this is what that voice in your head says
When you try to get peace of mind...
I gotta find peace of mind, I gotta find peace of mind
He says it's impossible, but I know it's possible
He says there's no me without him, please help me forget about him
He takes all my energy, trapped in my memory
Constantly holding me, constantly holding me
I need to tell you all, all the pain he's caused, mmmm
I need to tell I'm, I'm undone because, mmmm
He says it's impossible, but I know it's possible
He says it's impossible without him, but I know it's possible
To finally be in love, and know the real meaning of
A lasting relationship, not based on ownership
I trust every part of you, cuz all that I... All that you say you do
You love me despite myself, sometimes I fight myself
I just can't believe that you, would have anything to do
With someone so insecure, someone so immature
Oh you inspire me, to be the higher me
You made my desire pure, you made my desire pure
Just tell me what to say, I can't find the words to say
Please don't be mad with me, I have no identity
All that I've known is gone, all I was building on
I don't wanna walk with you, how do I talk to you
Touch my mouth with your hands, touch my mouth with your hands
Oh I wanna understand, the meaning of your embrace
I know now I have to face, the temptations of my past
Please don't let me disgrace, where my devotion lays
Now that I know the truth, now that it's no excuse
Keeping me from your love, what was I thinking of?
Holding me from your love, what was I thinking of?
You are my peace of mind, that old me is left behind
You are my peace of mind, that old me is left behind
He says it's impossible, but I know it's possible
He says it's improbable, but I know it's tangible

He says it's not grabable, but I know it's haveable
Cuz anything's possible, oh anything is possible
Please come free my mind, please come meet my mind
Can you see my mind, oh
Won't you come free my mind?   —**Lauryn Hill**

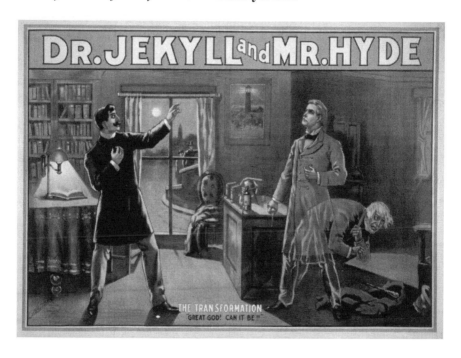

The characters of Dr. Jekyll and Mr. Hyde represent the twin qualities of all men. Man has a lower self (Mr. Hyde) from which to define himself and a higher self (Dr. Jekyll) from which to embrace. Every man is born of freewill, which he could use to choose the consciousness that he will embrace. Unfortunately, in today's system of white supremacy, we are forced to embrace our lower consciousness. Coincidently, his first name is Henry. Henry means "home ruler." The name refers to which consciousness will "rule" your home or how you define yourself.

Circle of Willis:

The circle of Willis (also called the cerebral arterial circle, arterial circle of Willis or Willis Polygon) is a circle of arteries *that supply blood to the* brain. *It is named after* Thomas Willis *(1621–1673), an* English physician.

Another part of the brain that our ancestors used as a symbol of Christ consciousness, but was later stolen to represent the Biblical character Jesus Christ, is called the Circle of Willis. This circle of arteries make up a figure that resembles a man with his arms outstretched, like he is being crucified. If one could lift the top of their skull to reveal their brain, they would see the Circle of Willis sitting on top of their brain. This group of arteries feed the brain the nutrients that it needs to function. See the illustration below. Our ancestors separated the lower self, the body, and the higher self, the brain. Man must rule his lower self, the body, before he can attain higher consciousness, the brain. The Circle of Willis represents the resurrection of man's higher consciousness. It signifies the nurturing and feeding of one's higher consciousness and not their lower selves represented by their bodies' wants and desires. The Circle of Willis represents the death of the individual being ruled by their lower self, the body and the transformation of the consciousness that dwells on top of the brain, which represents one's higher self.

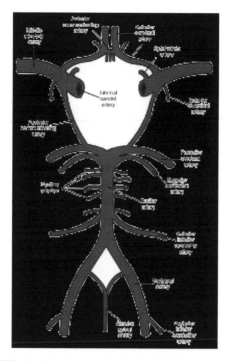

Circle of Willis is located on top of the brain and rules the body. It looks like a man on a cross. It represents Christ consciousness or man's ability to transcend, as in the crucifixion of Christ in the Bible.

Pavlov's Dog and Human Conditioning

Ivan Pavlov was a Russian physiologist who experimented on dogs in order to understand conditioning and behavior. He discovered that animals, as well as humans, can be trained to respond in a certain way given a particular stimulus (color, light or sound.) His research drew tremendous interests and paved the way for a more objective method of studying human behavior. He contrasted unconditioned reflex with conditioned reflex. Unconditioned reflex is behavior that comes naturally in humans when exposed to a given environment. For example, when a person hears a loud sound, they will automatically focus all their attention toward wherever the sound is coming from. Pavlov was able to instill conditioned reflex on his dogs. These are reflexes that are not natural and are taught by repetition and manipulation of the focus group. He taught them to salivate when he rang a bell. He previously conditioned them by feeding them right after they heard a bell. Later on, he was able to get the dogs to salivate profusely simply by ringing the bell, even with the absence of food not being introduced.

Black people in America, through the institution of slavery, have been conditioned to give a certain response when exposed to lower level frequencies and Inner G's. Black people do not realize the effect that four hundred years of conditioning, through slavery, has on how they perceive themselves, their environment and white people in general. The only way to overcome this "conditioned reflex" is to build new neural pathways in the brain. These new pathways are necessary in order for one to change any human behavior. If no new pathways are made, then changes in behavior cannot be accomplished. The Caucasian has implemented a conditioned response in Black people to promote conditioned reflex that gives white people the upper hand in all facets of society. This conditioned reflex has evolved into a natural state of permanent slave mentality and brainwashing. People of Afrikan descent still carry these neural pathways in their brains. They have been passed down from generation to generation through their common DNA, from the time their ancestors were stolen from Afrika to the present.

As stated previously, the only way to overcome these genetic, conditioned neural pathways is to create new ones. One does this by changing their thought process, which changes their behavior. The descendants of slaves have never been treated for this conditioning and behavior of post-traumatic slavery syndrome. If one still maintains the thought process that their oppressor has given them, they will always be his slave, no matter if he sets them free. There will be no need for physical chains because the psychological chains will always keep him in mental bondage. Black people will always be conditioned to respond to the stimulus or environment their masters put before them. In this way, Caucasians will always be able to predict the conditioned response of Black people in order to predict their behavior. It is hard for Black people to fight oppression if their enemy knows every move they will make before even they do. The answer to Black people's freedom is very simple. Change one's thought process and you change one's reality. This book was designed with this purpose in mind. Free the mind and the body will follow.

Chapter Nine: "As above, so below"

"The physical act of looking up to the heavens activates your higher consciousness. This is why your eyes roll to the back of your head during an orgasm. This is where you will find me. Avoid looking or bowing down with the eyes. That triggers the activation of your lower self." — Nekhebet

Kemet, which is present day Egypt, had a saying that was part of their universal philosophy, "As above, so below." Through countless generations of the study of the stars, they realized certain truths that always remained constant in their observations.

They realized truths, such as the changing of the seasons, astrological events and the calendar. They also applied this science to their everyday life. From this knowledge came the science of Astrology. I will cover some of the basics of this science that has been ridiculed and demeaned to a level of almost a hocus pocus ideology. The true foundations of Astrology were very exact and correct in their interpretation of the relationship to man and the Universe. Here are some of the basics:

The Kemetic goddess Nut & her brother Tefnut. Nut representing the sky above and her brother below her representing the Earth. They both reflect each other and their principles of Inner G.

The Astrological Wheel is the basic understanding of the Zodiacs and how they interact with each other. All life energies and expressions travel in cycles or waves. A simple observation of the wheel reveals the sign that is the direct opposite of your sign on the wheel, which is potentially your ideal mate, hence the phrase, "Opposites attract."

Next, you have the Cardinal Signs. These four signs represent the beginning of each season. These signs are the initiators. They are known as the life of the party. They are always looking to get things started. They bring in the seasons.

They are:

Aries (spring) Masculine Sign (+) Element FIRE Principle "I am." Red. Ruled by the head. Number is 1.

Cancer (summer) Feminine Sign (-) Element WATER Principle "I feel." Green. Number 4. Ruled by breasts & stomach.

Libra (fall) Masculine Sign (+) Element AIR Principle "I balance." Lavender. Number 7. Ruled by buttocks & lower back.

Capricorn (winter) Feminine Sign Element Earth Principle "I use."#10. Dark green. Ruled by knees.

A masculine sign means that you primarily or instinctively give out energy. This is when you are most satisfied.

A feminine sign means that you naturally receive energy. This is when you are at your best.

The element that each sign has represents the laws or principles that they adhere to, such as water flows and is adaptable, whereas fire needs a certain environment to burn at its brightest.

We will also discuss the next set of Zodiac signs called Mutable or Fixed Signs.

The next four signs on our Astrological Wheel are called Fixed Signs. These signs fall exactly in the middle of the season they represent. These people are hard to change because, to them, the season they live in is at its peak. Why change if you are in the epitome of the season? They like to supervise or manage people to reach the perfection of the goal that the group is trying to reach. These signs are:

Taurus- Feminine (-) Earth. Principle "I have." #2. Dark blue. Neck & throat.

Leo- Masculine (+) Fire. Principle "I will." #5. Orange. Spine & heart.

Scorpio- Feminine (-) Water. Principle "I desire." #8. Burgundy. Sexual organs.

Aquarius- Masculine (+) Air. Principle "I know." #11. Blue. Shins & ankles.

The last group of Astrological Signs is called, Mutable Signs. These signs are very flexible and able to adapt well. They are versatile people who can change courses without crashing. They are able to adapt to any situation. These signs are located towards the end of one season and the beginning of the next one. This is why they are so versatile. Their nature lets them change with the seasons. They are:

Gemini- Masculine (+) Air. Principle "I think." #3. Yellow. Arms, hands, shoulders.

Virgo- Feminine (-) Earth. Principle "I analyze." #6. Navy blue. Nervous system & intestines.

Sagittarius- Masculine (+) Fire. Principle "I see." #9. Purple. Hips & thighs.

Pisces- Feminine (-) Water. Principle "I believe." #12. Aqua. Feet.

Properties of the Elements:

AIR: [Libra, Aquarius & Gemini]

-Wants to be free

-Does not want to be contained

-Air will always find a way to escape containment

-Wants to express freewill.

-When under pressure, air gets stronger.

-Very adaptable in any environment.

-When agitated, air rises to the top and expands

-When cold, it gets depressed and sinks to the bottom.

-Wants to be in the background or behind the scenes

-Lets work speak for itself.

-Strong-willed and even-tempered.

-Can be destructive or uplifting, depending on its mood.

[Air Signs Relationship with Earth Signs]

Earth Signs: Capricorn, Taurus & Virgo

- Air wants to dominate Earth.
- Always wants to be on top of Earth.
- Wants to be the decision-maker for Earth.

- In confrontation with each other, Air will toss Earth and scatter it all over the place.
- Air always has to have the last word.
- Air will try to get under earth's skin.

Air Signs Relationship with Water

[Water Signs: Cancer, Scorpio & Pisces]

- Air will try to dominate water.
- Air will agitate water's surface but cannot penetrate water's depth.
- Air will be frustrated with water because water always protects its true self.
- Air refuses to submit to water.
- Air always has to have the last word.
- Air can move water to do awesome things.
- Once Air moves water, water's momentum cannot be contained by Air.
- Air can manipulate water only on a superficial level.

Air Signs Relationship with Fire

[Fire Signs: Aries, Leo & Sagittarius]

- Air feeds fire.
- Air helps fire to grow.
- Air is fire's inspiration and sustenance.
- Too much Air puts out fire.
- Air must trust fire to have its best interests.
- Air must let fire consume itself unconditionally.
- Air needs to be subservient unto fire.

EARTH: [Capricorn, Taurus & Virgo]

- Always grounded. Down to earth.
- Even keel and level-headed.
- Practical, safe and consistent.
- Highs are not too high and lows are not too low.
- Stable, reliable and accountable.
- Not easily angered.
- Very steadfast and in control.
- When angered, whole world shakes.
- Point of no return, uncontrollable.

[Earth Signs Relationship to Air]

- No problem being submissive to air.
- Earth cannot contain air for long periods of time.
- Earth will close itself off to air when hurt or threatened.
- Earth will let air express itself at its own expense.
- Has a high tolerance for air's personality.
- Earth complements air.
- Earth will be confused in confrontation with air and will need time alone to gather itself.
- Earth will lose itself if air tries to dominate it.
- Earth will allow air to see itself at its own expense.

[Earth Signs Relationship to Water]

- Earth is naturally accepting of water.
- Earth needs water to thrive and give life.
- In confrontation, Earth becomes lost and confused.
- Earth needs water to manifest its life's purpose.

- Earth needs water to regulate itself or Earth will ignore it.
- Once Earth has too much water, Earth will neglect water's needs.
- Earth shuts down if water is overbearing.
- Earth will treat water like a stranger if water continues to barrage Earth with its selfish intentions.
- Earth wants water to pay attention to its needs.
- Earth is very attentive to water's needs.

[Earth Signs Relationship to Fire]

- Earth puts out fire.
- Earth smothers fire's personality.
- Earth has to give too much of itself for fire to thrive.
- If Earth gives itself to fire, then it will initially cause pain, but in the end, it will be beneficial.
- Earth may lose patience before it sees the benefits of fire's personality.
- Earth is the opposite of fire, not water.
- Earth needs fire to help it manifest and create its will.
- Earth needs to feel fire's harshness to move it to greatness.

WATER: [Cancer, Scorpio & Pisces]

- Water is very adaptable.
- Water goes with the flow.
- Water is very self-sufficient.
- It is cohesive and attracted to itself.

- Water has the capacity to transcend to a higher form.
- Water is the source of life.
- Water purifies & cleanses.
- Water never dies; it just changes form.
- If water meets a frigid energy, it will be impenetrable, hard and stern.
- If water meets a heated energy, it will want to escape.
- Water cannot be contained for long periods of time.
- Water searches for the lowest common denominator and will attempt to raise it.

Use these Astrological numbers, mottos, Inner G genders, seasons, colors & specific areas of the body to stimulate your partner of this particular sign. Be scientific when you choose and commit to a relationship with a partner.

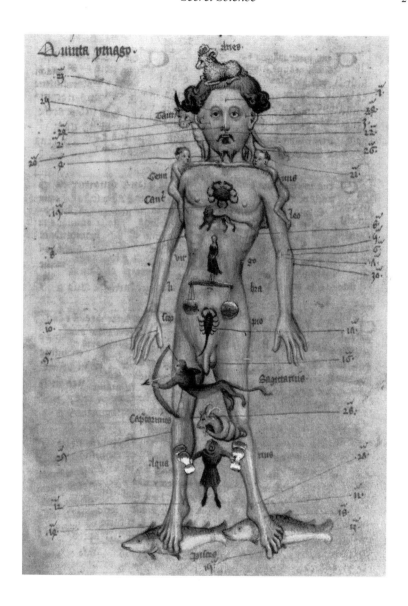

1) **Aries rules the Head. Color: Red, Oil: Musk**

2) **Taurus rules the Neck & Throat. Color: Indigo, Oil: Patchouli**

3) **Gemini rules the arms, hands & shoulders. Color: Yellow, Oil: Vetiver**

4)   **Cancer rules the stomach. Color: Light Green, Oil: Sandalwood**

5)   **Leo rules the Back, Spine & Heart. Color: Orange, Oil: Rose**

6)   **Virgo rules the Nervous System & Intestines. Color: Aqua, Oil: Frankincense**

7)   **Libra rules the Lower Back & Buttocks. Color: Violet, Oil: Orange**

8)   **Scorpio rules the Sexual Organs. Color: Maroon, Oil: Cinnamon**

9)   **Sagittarius rules the Hips & Thighs. Color: Purple, Oil: Clove**

10) **Capricorn rules the Knees. Color: Green, Oil: Myrrh**

11) **Aquarius rules the Shins & Ankles. Color: Light Blue, Oil: Violet**

12) **Pisces rules the Feet. Color: Turquoise, Oil: Amber**

For example, if I wanted to satisfy an Aries, then I would take into consideration the number one, the head region, the color red, the scent of musk and the element of fire. Aries is stimulated by the first touch, the first kiss, the first stroke, etc... Aries is highly stimulated by anything dealing with the number one or the first of anything. I would also wear and have in my environment things with the color red and the scent of musk. I would also concentrate on massaging, kissing and stroking her head region. This area is highly sensual for an Aries. Brushing her hair would probably be very stimulating to her. Finally, I would have a fireplace burning, or some type of candles around, to tap into the inner core of this fire sign.

Humans are made up of over 80% water. If this is true, then we should move, feel, think and act like water does in its natural state. Water responds to the moon at night. The moon controls water through its gravitational pull. The moon represents the light in the darkness of man. The moon represents the consciousness or light in the unseen world. In other words, it represents the consciousness of the spirit. Your Sun sign represents yourself on the outside in this physical dimension. The sun represents the external you. The moon represents the spirit of man or true self in the unseen world. The moon is the inner you or your true spirit. This is what creates currents in the ocean's ebb and flow. If this is true, then we should be conscious of the cycles of the moon and how it affects our daily lives. If the moon affects water and humans are made up of over 80% water, then the moon affects man's consciousness and behavior according to its cycle. Know your moon sign. Learn your Sun sign. Understand your rising sign. Know your zodiac chart. It is the blueprint to understanding why your spirit chose this particular place and time to have a human experience.

Study the Astrological charts of both yourself and your partner. Pay attention to the male and female Inner G's in both of your charts in relation to yours. One will discover that a balance of masculine and female Inner G is the key to having a balanced and healthy relationship. If one's chart is dominated by female Inner G, their partner's chart should be dominated by male Inner G in order to create a balance when the two form a union with each other.

"Can you bind the sweet influences of the Pleiades or loose the bonds of Orion? Can you bring forth the Mazzaroth (the Zodiac) in their seasons? Or can you guide Arcturus with his sons? Do you know the principles of the heavens? Can you set their dominion over the earth?"-Job 38:31-33

We are living in very special times. All of our spirits chose to incarnate into our physical bodies at this exact particular place and time for a particular reason. We all agreed to come here to fulfill our destiny in order to transcend in the spiritual realm once our physical bodies become deceased. . We are exiting the Age of Pisces (0BCE to 2,000AD), which is the Age of "I believe," into the Age of Aquarius (2,000AD to 4,000AD), which is the Age of "I know." That means we are leaving a lower state of consciousness in order to transition into a higher state of awareness. The beliefs and practices of our parents that went unchallenged for two thousand years are now suddenly under scrutiny. The "Do as I say, not as I do" motto does not satisfy our consciousness anymore. Our spirits are rejecting the old "business as usual" matrix. That's because, in the Age of Pisces, our parents believed what they were told without any thought or second guessing. As we transition into the Age of Aquarius, the consciousness of "knowing," we are now aware of the difference in believing in something and knowing something to be true. Old paradigms do not satisfy our new conscience, which is based on knowing truth and not believing in something or wishing it was true. All aspects of life are now open season and open to new interpretations.

In my dealings with single, Black women there seems to be a common theme as to what type of relationship they yearn for. The majority always seems to refer to their grandparent's marriage. They admire the commitment, dedication, strength and love that their grandparents seem to display for over 30, 40, and 50 years or more. I do not fault my sisters for wanting this type of relationship, as they all wholeheartedly deserve to experience love on this level. What I want our Black women to understand is that, with the changing of consciousness, comes a change in our reality and how we relate to each other. Be open to breaking the parameters of what we "think" will give us satisfaction, and let the new Age dictate and define how your happiness will be revealed in the future. I am specifically talking about polygamy. When our ancestors were operating at their highest level of consciousness in Kemet, polygamy was the practice of the time. Don't get me wrong; polygamy is not the solution to the Black male and female problem; raising our consciousness first, in order to be in a position to practice polygamy, just might be. All I want my sisters to be aware of is: do not put your definition of what you think will make you happy before you allow the universe to work its magic in its destiny to guide you to true happiness, despite your preconceived notions of what your lower consciousness desires.

"One must first embrace the darkness before they can be fully appreciated and bask in the light." —Nekehbet

Chapter Ten:
Chakras: Levels of Sexual Consciousness

"Love is a state of mind, not a feeling. One must rise in love; it is impossible to fall in it." – Nekhebet

The Chakra system was established in ancient Kemet, which is presently known as Egypt. This system was in place thousands of years before the birth of Christ. They believed that man could attain "God consciousness" if he was willing and able to devote himself and do the work. God consciousness could be defined as the "state of knowing." Man could become one with the Universe, and thus communicate and master the laws and principles of nature. This is why the Pharaohs and Queens of Kemet were considered "godlike". It wasn't so much that they were considered Gods, but they were reflections or representatives of what God would do if He was manifested in the physical form. In the following articles, we will explore and try to understand this system that has been lost. This system was taught to the ancient people of India, who have made their own version of this Afrikan system.

Chakras are Inner G centers in the body. They allow us to navigate the connection between the spirit and matter, mind and body, God consciousness and man. Chakras lay out the system of consciousness in the form of Inner G within the body. They are a way of measuring man's consciousness through enlightenment and recognition of one's self. Chakras are the stepping stones into reaching higher/God consciousness.

There are seven chakras aligned vertically throughout the body, along the spinal cord. Kundalini is masculine and feminine Inner G that connects the chakras to higher consciousness.

Chakras can be defined as spinning Inner G centers of Melanin in the body, along the spinal column. These 7 Inner G points in the body are located in strategic areas and are assigned a certain color and geometric pattern that promotes a specific Inner G or consciousness. There is also a component of this Inner G, called Kundalini. Kundalini is represented by two snakes intertwined with each other, traveling up a pole. This is the same symbol the medical profession uses. [See illustration.]

The two snakes represent the masculine and feminine principles of consciousness. The staff in the middle represents the spinal column. The ball on top of the staff represents what is called your "first eye" or Pineal gland. Once the Kundalini Inner G reaches your first eye, then the wings of your consciousness will fly and your understanding of yourself, reality and God will be greatly enlightened. Coincidently, this gland produces a chemical called Melanin, which is responsible for "God Consciousness," among other things.

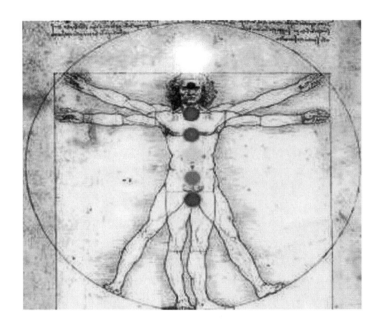

The first Chakra is called the "Root Chakra." It is located at the base of the spine or tail bone. This is the lowest Chakra which symbolizes our connection to this world as an animal. This Chakra is red in color and symbolizes all our survival instincts. One who embraces this Chakra is only interested in pleasing and sustaining himself. He is ruled by his carnal urges; his motivation is survival of the fittest. This Chakra's purpose is "To Have." Its element is Earth and its principle is to survive. The Root Chakra being the first is where all humans start out. It is up to our freewill as to whether we raise our consciousness.

First: Red Chakra

Location: Base of the spine

Element: Earth

Principle: Gravity

Characteristic: Survival; Physical

Purpose: To Have

Survival & Procreation:

This is the first and lowest level of sexual consciousness. This level represents the animal or beast in the human species. It is man as a mammal. This level is relegated to man's basic instinct for survival. Its sole and only purpose is to procreate. Man is born with the innate desire for self-preservation and the survival of his species. Man has a natural desire to keep his genetic legacy alive. This is the lowest form of sexual intercourse: Sex that is driven by the simple desire to preserve one's life. Sex is a selfish act. Motto: "Survival of the fittest."

The second Chakra is located in the abdominal region. It also entails the sexual organs. This Chakra is orange. Its element is water. Characteristics of this Chakra are emotions and sexuality. The purpose of this Chakra is pleasure and rhythm. Its only principle is attraction to the opposite sex. People who dwell in this Chakra make all their decisions based on their emotions. These people let their emotions control them instead of vice-versa. These people also define their reality by superficial things that actually get in the way of their best interests. They are easily angered and let foolish pride control their lives. They define struggle or a challenge as an obstacle that needs to be avoided at all costs. Sex is used as a pacifier. The statement, "No pain, no gain," does not make sense to the people who embrace this level of consciousness.

Second: Orange

Location: Abdomen; Hips

Element: Water

Characteristic: Sexuality/Emotions

Purpose: Pleasure, Rhythm

Principle: Attraction of Opposites

Lust & Addiction:

This level of sexual consciousness is driven by man's animalistic desires. Sexual intercourse at this level of consciousness represents man's submission to the needs and wants of his lower self. Man is controlled by the yearning and desires of the body. Man willfully submits and is a slave to the body. His actions are dictated and controlled by the will of the lower self. He has no concept of character, integrity, loyalty or discipline. Age has nothing to do with this level of sexual consciousness. Whether a man is 2 or 90 years of age, he can reside at this level for the rest of his life, if he chooses. His motto is, "How low can you go?"

The third Chakra is located in the Solar Plexus area of the body. It is represented by the color yellow. This Chakra is responsible for holding all your fire, passion and desires. Its element is fire, thus the Solar Plexus location. Characteristics of this Chakra are desire, will and passion. The purpose of this Chakra is to act and its characteristics are combustion and will power. People who operate at this level are very passionate people. They have dreams and desires, which nobody can convince them that they cannot attain. They are very passionate about anything they partake in and will not make excuses for being so. These people need to learn to balance their passions and desires with the other Chakras in the body.

Third: Yellow

Location: Solar Plexus

Element: Fire

Characteristic: Desire, Will

Purpose: To Act

Principle: Combustion

Desires & Passions:

This level is driven by man's desires and passions. It operates on the basis of raw emotions. It is fueled by man's deepest and rawest form of emotions. It dwells in the place where a man's tears and dreams are born. It exposes a man's hidden strengths, as well as his weaknesses at the same time. It does not discriminate. It cannot hide or deceive. It finds strength in its vulnerabilities. It is an uncontrollable fire that cannot be extinguished. This is what motivates a man to pursue his deepest dreams, thoughts and desires. It is the spark or catalyst to his physical existence. It is his reason for living when he cannot find any. This is the spark that a woman needs to fuel and sustain her. This is the thing that every woman wants her man to confide in her. If this level was represented by a lock, trust would be the key to unlocking it. Sexual intercourse at this level of consciousness can be extremely pleasurable and rewarding. It can come in the form of a one-night stand, booty call or a 30-year marriage. Levels of desire and passion do not need time for them to be justified and displayed. They are just in their rawest form. It can be mutually displayed no matter how long you've known your partner. Consequently, sexual intercourse, at this level, is often confused with love. This level of sexual intercourse is the last level of lower consciousness. After one masters and overcomes this level, love is the next step and the beginning of higher consciousness. Here, the motto is: "Come on, baby, light my fire!"

The fourth Chakra is located in a person's heart. This Chakra is green in color. Its element is air and its characteristics are acceptance and compassion. The principle of this Chakra is equilibrium. The object to obtain here is to think with your heart and feel with your mind. In other words, this ideology is the exact opposite of the motto, "It's just business, don't take it personally." This Chakra expresses that everything you do is personal. One cannot separate what one does from who one is, no matter what their intentions are. This Chakra doesn't change hats according to the task at hand. This Chakra only wears one hat.

> *Fourth: Green*
>
> *Location: Heart*
>
> *Element: Air*
>
> *Characteristic: Acceptance, Compassion*
>
> *Purpose: To Love*
>
> *Principle: Equilibrium*

Love.

This level is the first level of higher consciousness. Congratulations! This is where life begins. To achieve this level, man has to overcome all his fears, face all his insecurities, embrace humiliation and shame and sacrifice himself for a cause greater than himself. A piece of cake, right? This may seem like a daunting task, but don't fret. Simply put, man must overcome and "kill his ego." Man's ego has switched places with his true self. It has tricked and confused the individual to define themselves and their reality based on the ego's perception, which manipulates and controls our true self through fear. We voluntarily give up our true selves in favor of this imposter, who wants to keep us functioning at a lower level for its survival at the expense of our demise. How can we "keep it real" if one has no knowledge of their "real" selves? Man must learn to love "true" self first, before he can love anybody else. Man needs to be reintroduced to his real self. Rise in love; don't fall in it.

The fifth Chakra is located in the throat region. It is represented by the color blue. Its element is sound and its characteristic is communication. The purpose of this Chakra is to communicate. Mind you, the simplest form of communication is to speak. We communicate with each other on so many different levels that we do ourselves a disservice when we talk too much. On the other hand, be careful of the words you use to speak, because words are very powerful. Remember, the Bible teaches us that God created the Universe by speaking it into existence. When we express ourselves through words, we are creating "spells" to whoever we are communicating with. Choose your spells wisely. The principle of this Chakra is sympathetic vibrations.

> *Fifth: Blue*
>
> *Location: Throat*
>
> *Element: Sound*
>
> *Characteristic: Communication*
>
> *Purpose: To Speak*
>
> *Principle: Sympathetic Vibrations*

Spiritual Communication:

This level of sexual consciousness represents the unveiling of both partners' true spirits. One must overcome and master the physical body, in order for the spiritual self to manifest fully. This level reveals the true self of the individual engaged in sexual intercourse. I like to refer to this level as, "Soul Recess." Imagine that, while your physical bodies are engaged in sexual intercourse, your two spirits are swirling above you. They are playing in the spiritual plane, making the bond or connection with that person more intense and more intimate. The union of the spirits. The immersion of the souls. Total access to each other's true self. Not being able to decipher where one begins and the other ends. An experience that is not bound to the laws of the physical dimension. It is like having an "All Access" pass to that person's true self. Their soul. The motto is: "Riding the wave of ecstasy!"

This is the sixth Chakra located on the forehead between the eyes. This Chakra is represented by the color Indigo. This Chakra is known as the "Third Eye." It is represented by the element light and its characteristic is intuition. This Chakra's purpose is to see and its principles are perception and projection. Sometimes, we have to close our eyes in order to really see the truth. Remember, we only decipher 10% of Inner G that we call reality through our five senses. There is 90% of reality that we cannot decipher by seeing, touching, smelling, tasting or hearing. So this tells me that the real truth is something our senses cannot tell us. One must rely on their intuition and projection to fully understand what is so-called real. One must raise his consciousness in order to decipher what is considered real.

Sixth: Indigo

Location: Forehead, First-eye

Element: Light

Characteristic: Intuition

Purpose: To See

Principle: Perception & Projection

Clairvoyance & Manifestation:

This level of sexual consciousness specifically relates to the darker people of the world. There is a chemical called Melanin, which is in abundance in darker skinned people. It is manufactured in the Pineal gland, which is located in the center of your brain. Another name for it is called the third or first eye, because it allows you to see in the spiritual world. I labeled

Melanin, "the fruit of the gods." Without this chemical functioning properly in the body, one cannot transcend into the spiritual world. In other words, people who are classified as European, because of their lack of Melanin, cannot experience the same quality of sexual consciousness experiences that we can. "Once you go Black, never go back." Sexual experiences in this realm are timeless and have no boundaries in the spiritual world. The feeling of euphoria comes to mind. In the book, "The Secret," they gave hints to this principle. But because it came from a European perspective, it sadly missed its mark. Basically, with Melanin, you and your partner can manifest the same thoughts and energies and make them appear in the physical realm. This is a powerful tool that we have access to. It is a sad state of affairs that we have never been explained or exposed to this. For good reason, the powers that be want us to keep focusing and giving life to their dreams and not to our own. Melanin is the key to accessing the spiritual realm. The soul is the driver of the body. With that access, the physical realm is unlocked. We will cover the divine properties of Melanin in a later chapter. The motto is: "I see you for the first time."

The last Chakra in the body is located on the top of the head. It is also known as the Crown Chakra, the seventh Chakra. It is represented by the color purple. That is why royalty wore crowns and were only allowed to wear purple. This Chakra's element is thought. Its characteristic is the concept of understanding and its purpose is to know. The Crown Chakra's principle is consciousness. Once one has reached this level, one is able to have an out-of-body experience. Although this Chakra is located on the top of the head, it shoots up straight above the body. Mastering the other Chakras is the only path to obtain access to the Crown Chakra.

Seventh: Purple

Location: Top of the Head

(Crown)

Element: Thought

Characteristic: Understanding

Purpose: To Know

Principle: Consciousness

There you have it, the journey to enlightenment. The object is simply balance. We need all the Chakras in order to live a balanced life. One must learn to master each Chakra in order to properly displace it in the situation that calls for it. Do not get locked into one level, but be able to use your Kundalini Inner G according to the task at hand. The sky is the limit!

Astroprojection:

This is the level where one can, presumably, leave their body during sexual intercourse and astro-project themselves anywhere in the universe. In other words, during sex, when you see your partner's eyes roll up into the back of the head, then they have left the building! The eyes will automatically retreat back up inside your head so that they will not be distracted by the physical dimension. For one to truly see in the unseen world, the eyes need to eliminate the physical dimension. True sight comes from the Pineal gland or what's called the "first eye." This is how we are able to visualize dreams without the aid of our eyes. This is where true consciousness or sight dwells. For us to truly "see" on a spiritual level, our eyes have to be eliminated from the equation. If one can master this technique, then one would be able to manifest whatever they desire from the spiritual realm to the physical realm. Also, mysteries of questions you had can be solved in this state of mind. Healing ailments of the body, in this state, is also possible. Depending on the level of consciousness, the man will dictate the limitless boundaries that a couple could manifest during this state of sexual intercourse.

There was an expression in ancient Kemet which said, "He who does not have a boat, cannot cross the river." That boat is the Pineal gland and the river is the Melanin it produces. The motto is: "Come fly with me!"

From the Chakra system, I came up with seven levels of Sexual Consciousness. Like the Chakra system, my system also has the basic seven levels of consciousness. It basically parallels the Chakra system but incorporates sexual intercourse as its main focus.

As I alluded to earlier in the book, when a man and woman engage in sexual activity, it is the man's level of consciousness that dominates the experience. A woman can rise no higher than the level of the man's consciousness. This is a very clear concept that can be seen during sexual intercourse. The man usually "gets his" before the woman. It does not matter how enlightened the woman is or what level of consciousness she has achieved. The man, being the spark or the fuel to the woman's vehicle, is the driving force into how far she will travel during sexual intercourse. Remember, in sexual intercourse, the woman reflects the man's Inner G.

The good thing about this relationship can be seen if you flip the roles. If a woman has a lower level of consciousness and the man is several levels higher than her consciousness, she can ascend to the level of consciousness that the man has attained during sexual intercourse. This is only manifested during the time of their sexual engagement. Women, choose your men wisely. You want to connect with a man who has enough Inner G to not only sustain you, but to move you to heights that are beyond what you see in yourself. Just like the Sun can sustain the Earth. Women, choose a man who will inspire and guide you to your higher self, for if you do not, you will be stuck in a mundane existence of mediocrity.

Here is a breakdown of this theory shown in the following graphs.

The V-shaped lines represent each male & female's individual state of consciousness. The higher the line on the graph, the higher the state of consciousness. The shaded area represents the shared consciousness of both male & female during sexual intercourse.

In the first graph, the shaded area represents the combined level of consciousness achieved if the male consciousness is higher than the female, during sexual intercourse. The dotted line represents the added consciousness level that the woman can attain, just by connecting to a man with a higher consciousness than hers.

Levels of Sexual Consciousness

1) **Selfishness & Procreation**
2) **Lust & Addiction**
3) **Desires & Passion**
4) **Love**
5) **Spiritual Communication**
6) **Clairvoyance & Manifestation**
7) **Astro-projection**

MAN AT A HIGHER CONSCIOUSNESS THAN A WOMAN DURING SEX

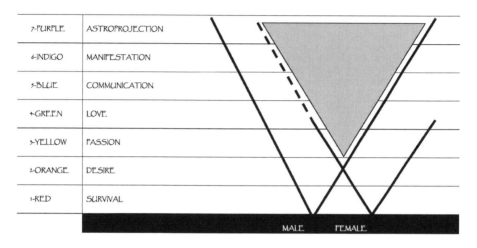

7-PURPLE	ASTROPROJECTION
6-INDIGO	MANIFESTATION
5-BLUE	COMMUNICATION
4-GREEN	LOVE
3-YELLOW	PASSION
2-ORANGE	DESIRE
1-RED	SURVIVAL

MALE   FEMALE

The second graph shows the result of a male with a lower consciousness and a female with a higher consciousness. As one can see, the female can only share or achieve a level of consciousness relative to the male's level. The woman's higher conscious state never becomes recognized, because the male cannot reach or communicate with her on that level.

MAN AT A LOWER CONSCIOUSNESS THAN A WOMAN DURING SEX

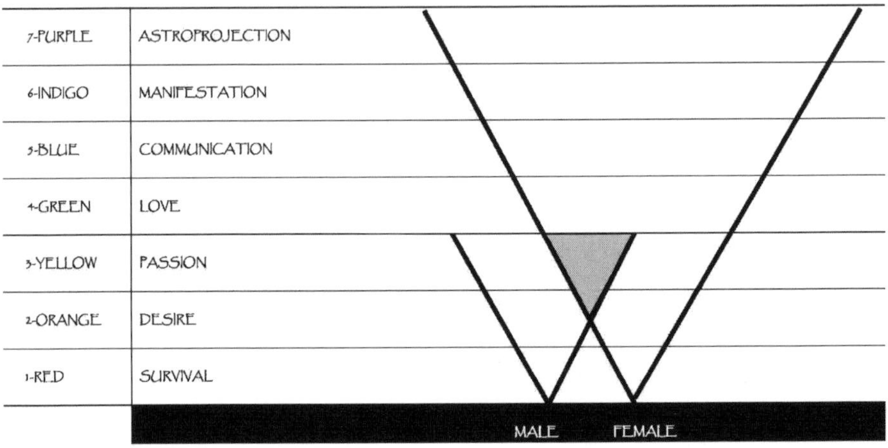

7-PURPLE	ASTROPROJECTION
6-INDIGO	MANIFESTATION
5-BLUE	COMMUNICATION
4-GREEN	LOVE
3-YELLOW	PASSION
2-ORANGE	DESIRE
1-RED	SURVIVAL

MALE   FEMALE

In conclusion, I want the reader to understand that there are different Inner G levels within one's body and consciousness. As we have covered in this chapter, we have seven Inner G levels in the body that we have access to. Sex does not necessarily have to always be at the highest Inner G level in a person, just as sex should not always be considered lower level behavior. Sex, however, should be an expression of the whole self and not just locked into the lower levels of consciousness that a man maintains. The act of sex should be used with purpose and intent, according to the needs and wants of the participants. This should be discussed before the act takes place. Sex should be emancipating and be explored to discover all realms of the Inner G levels that reside in the participants. Sex should not limit you to just one

Inner G level. I, for example, relate sex to a heart monitor. We have all seen the green blip of light going across the screen of the monitor. This blip represents the heart rate of the patient. The blip will either go up or down, depending on the heart rate of the patient. When the blip "flat lines" that individual is medically pronounced as dead. During sex, let your Inner G be the green blip on the heart rate monitor. Let your blip or Inner G fluctuate between the different levels of the chakras. Start at a lower level with the intention of reaching the higher levels of your Inner G sources. When you are at a higher level, drop down to a lower Inner G source to enhance and appreciate the higher level Inner G. As you fluctuate between different Inner G levels in the body, you can compare and contrast the different and unique Inner G's you hold within yourself and your partner. Sex is life. Life is experience. I urge you to have sex as if your life depended on it, because it actually does. Don't be afraid to be that green blip on the heart monitor machine. For if that blip is not moving upward or downward, you, my friend, are already dead and don't even know it.

Telltale signs that your significant other is "comfortable" operating at one level of lower consciousness:

- "Jesus Freak" or heavily involved in their religion, whatever it may be. They define themselves by their religion and not their individuality.
- Chronically overweight or underweight and has a weight problem.
- Have addictions, including: smoking, drinking, gambling, shoes, sports teams, clothes, brand names, internet, tattoos and even exercise.
- Likes to argue. Never admits they are wrong. Always has to "win" the argument.
- Cannot stop gossiping.
- Is good at playing the dozens or recognizing and exploiting other people's flaws.
- Cannot leave the house until hair, makeup and clothes are perfect.

- Couch potato that never leaves the house or never wants to be at home.
- Keeps a messy house. Is content living in filth or is disorganized and untidy.
- Watches sports, soap operas, talk shows or plays video games all day.
- Does not think they are responsible for their own happiness. Plays the victim role.
- Is egotistic & superficial.
- This person has their own space or room where they go into and do not want to be bothered.
- Will not be inconvenienced if they are preoccupied and others need help or a favor.
- Works a lot of overtime.
- Does not work.
- Does not take care of their children; —that includes just sending child support payments without fatherly participation.
- They're in love with their car, sports team or other material objects.
- Defines themselves through their job title.
- Stubborn to a fault.
- Must have the latest electronic gadgets or fashions, such as cell phones, iPods, video games, computer equipment or clothing, shoes, bags or jewelry.
- Had plastic or weight reduction surgery, wears body suit girdles, wigs, hair pieces, fake eyelashes, contact lenses, penis enlargements, breast implants, fake nails or dye their hair frequently.
- They are not goal-orientated. Satisfied with their mundane existence.
- Puts their career first over all other facets in their life.

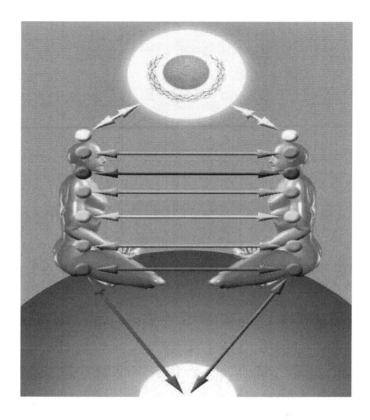

We are in a constant state of communication with others by attracting the same Inner G frequencies and repelling different levels of Inner G's than our own. This is the reason why we are comfortable with others the first time we meet them, while other people we meet we dislike them immediately and for no reason.

Chapter Eleven: Science of the Heart

"The best way to protect the heart is to open it, leaving it exposed and vulnerable." – Nekhebet

I used to believe that we were all alone from the moment of our conception to our birth, but my spiritual guide, Nekhebet, has led me to think otherwise. We were not so isolated in our incubation stage of taking on this human form at the moment of conception. Let's start at the very moment of our conception and work our way towards our birth. In the miracle of creation, our father's sperm must fight through a hostile environment and compete with billions of other sperm in its effort to be the first one on the scene to fertilize the egg of our mother. What gives our father's sperm the motivation and will to complete such a daunting task? Coincidently, what keeps our mother's egg waiting patiently for days on end, still and silent in the darkness, in its effort to create life, from the arrival of said sperm? I believe there is one important factor that science has ignored altogether in the act of conception and the creation of life. That common factor is the role of the heart.

The heart contains the rhythm, vibration and frequency of life. The rhythm of the heart is what sets the process of creation in motion. The heart is the life force, navigator and catalyst for creation.

Our father's heart rate must be above a certain rate per minute, in order for him to initially release his sperm in an effort to procreate. A man cannot ejaculate unless his heart rate is elevated to a certain level. This is why the drug Viagra has a warning label saying that the user of the drug must have a strong and healthy heart in order to use the drug safely. I personally know of several Black men, who have either died or have had heart attacks because they used the drug in order to participate in sexual activities. Their hearts were not strong enough to handle the heart rate needed for them to have an orgasm. The heart is the trigger for the man to ejaculate and release his sperm in order to procreate. It is the catalyst that starts the spark of creation.

The same can be said for the female. I am not insinuating that the woman's heart rate must be at a certain level for her to release her egg. What I am alluding to is that, in order for a woman to have an orgasm, her heart rate must be elevated to a certain level. The orgasm triggers or activates the egg to receive the sperm in order to create life. I understand that, unfortunately, more women than not get pregnant without achieving an orgasm. What I am saying is the "quality" of the child and the birth process is enhanced exponentially by the vibration of the heart that the woman achieves during her orgasm. It makes sense. If a man must achieve a certain heart rate or frequency to create life, then the woman must also achieve that same heart rate or frequency to enhance the life that she will bring into this physical dimension. The heart is the main principle in the creation of life and is necessary for life at its inception. Women must understand the importance of the role that her orgasm has in her ability to create and nurture life. Creating life without the woman having an orgasm creates a void or lack of direction for the child to develop. The orgasm of the woman opens up many more variables of her egg that the life frequency can attach to in the process of developing and guiding the new life into a healthy existence.

So now, the sperm of our father has penetrated the egg of our mother in her womb. Now the woman's heart takes over the creation process by itself. What initiates the fertilized egg to start replicating and duplicating itself to reach the form of a Zygote? The mother's heart is the key. Now the rhythm and beat of our mother's heart communicates with us and directs our growth. The Afrikan still uses the drum today because it is the best form of communication. Why? Because it speaks directly to one's heart. The woman's heartbeat initiates the cellular activity of the Zygote by sending messages through the vibration, rhythm and frequencies in its beats and rates, similar to the Afrikan drum. This triggers the replication of the cells of the newly fertilized egg. So we are never alone. The main focus has been shifted from our shared mother and father's heart rates to solely our mother's for the next nine months. We were never alone. We were always directed and guided by the heart in our mother's womb. The heart's rhythm, frequency and vibration have always been present from the day we were conceived. Our life essence was always orchestrated and nurtured by the heart in the participation of the creation process.

You may ask, if this is the case, then artificially inseminated births and "test tube" babies could never live outside the womb. But as we have witnessed, there have been many successful artificial births that go on to live healthy, productive lives. Or do they? There is no apparent heart frequency or rhythm found in the laboratory or Petri dish. So how can they mature and grow into healthy babies? I believe that the heart, as our ancient ancestors said, is the "Seat of the Soul." Christians will attest that Jesus lives in one's heart. In fact, Christianity stole this concept from our ancient Kemetic ancestors. The heart introduces the body to the soul. The heart's frequency infuses the amniotic fluid with the intent of the soul, and thus, it is received by the Zygote. The Zygote, of course, is one of our earliest stages of development, just before becoming an embryo, and later on, a fetus. The Zygote is now matched with a soul that has a particular life destiny or frequency that it must embrace in order to evolve into a higher realm of consciousness when it returns to the spiritual dimension. In other words, souls are matched to particular genetically coded bodies by the rhythm and frequency of the heart. This match is based on the particular mix or combination of the mother and father's DNA, which has been introduced into the Zygote. This genetic pattern or map is now recognized by the infused soul as a blueprint to learn his "life lesson" in the physical dimension, so that he can transcend to higher consciousness in the spiritual realm when he passes on and leaves his physical body behind.

For example, if a particular soul reincarnates into a physical body, it must learn a specific life lesson of being self-sufficient and independent in order to transcend into a higher spiritual dimension; the potential DNA of its parents is taken into consideration. The soul will look for a mother and father with a specific genetic makeup that is programmed to promote the opposite of what he needs to transcend. Thus, the soul will be forced into a physical condition that he must overcome in order to learn his most valuable life lesson. The soul's DNA of his physical body may give him a predisposition of addiction, obesity or dependence. The soul must learn to master these genetic "flaws" in order to gain access to higher spiritual realms when he passes on from his physical body. If the soul does not complete these tasks of being self-sufficient and independent, then he will simply be reincarnated into another physical body until he learns this valuable life lesson. So the heart matches the soul to the best genetically predisposed body that will give the soul the best opportunity to learn his life lesson in the physical dimension. In other words, before our spirits incarnate into our physical bodies, they select their parents and use their hearts' frequencies as the bridge to reincarnate into our physical bodies.

This means that the physical dimension is the lowest level the spirit can incarnate into and experience. The physical dimension is the concept of "Hell" referred to in the Bible. This is why they speak of Hell as being eternal damnation and a pit of fire. The spirit must descend or fall in order to enter the physical dimension. Albert Einstein defined insanity as such, "Doing the same thing over and over again and expecting different results." We dwell or go to "Hell" because we choose not to change our thinking and behavior into one that will let us transcend into higher, spiritual realms. Thus, we come back to this physical realm over and over again, because we choose not to learn our life lessons. We have all agreed, as spirits, to come down to the physical dimension in order to learn our life lesson that keeps us from transcending into higher spiritual realms. The only problem is, we lose all sense of our spiritual purpose once we take on and define ourselves by our physical bodies. It is up to us to listen to and get reacquainted with our heart's destiny in this life, in order to achieve higher spiritual consciousness. We blame our environment and everything around us before we look within our hearts for solutions to our problems. Hell is a mindset or state of consciousness and not necessarily a physical place. It is a level of consciousness that we choose to call our reality. Our purpose is to raise our consciousness; that is the only way to escape eternal damnation. Listen to your heart and not your minds!

Artificially inseminated or test tube babies are not infused with a soul. Everything has a "Spirit" but not all things have a soul. There is a difference, as our ancestors called the spirit "the Ba" and the soul "the Ka". I believe test tube babies that are conceived outside the womb, with no heart to infuse the amniotic fluid with the intent of the soul, are lacking life purpose and direction. I believe they are easily influenced and generally operate at a depressed state. I could find no research on the subject, so my findings are strictly the results of my spiritual guide, Nekhebet. If I am wrong, I will humbly apologize and find out the truth. But as for now, my journey of seeking knowledge and truth has led me to this conclusion. Mind you, my quest for truth is never ending. To be continued.

As we mature and grow into a fetus, we can be seen on the doctor's ultrasound machine, smiling, sucking our thumb, kicking and turning. It looks like we are having a real good time in there. We also respond to outside light and touch on our mother's womb. I believe we are communicating with the rhythm of our mother's heart. We are at play, displaying behavior as if we are in tune with another entity in the womb. I believe that entity is our mother's heart. We are being taught and prepared by the heart for the world we are about to be born into. We are shown the blueprint of our life's destiny if we choose to follow it. The heart is our first teacher. The heart is the "seat of the soul" that initiates your spirit into your body. The heart is the key that gives the frequency to the spirit to enter the physical body. The heart infuses the amniotic fluid with its vibrations and the frequencies that communicate the principles and laws that we need to know in order to survive outside our mother's womb and reach our destiny. Sound or vibration travels four times faster through water than through air. If this is true, then our mother's heart teaches us at a rate of four times faster in the womb than outside of it. In other words, in the nine month gestation period that we are in the womb, we have learned approximately 36 months worth of information compared to a student outside the womb in an isolated class, who is being taught twenty-four hours a day, seven days a week! This is an incredible concept and tribute to the importance the heart plays in our consciousness and general well-being before we are born. After birth, the first thing the doctor does to relieve our anxiety from this traumatic experience, is to lay us on our mother's chest. Once we feel and hear our mother's heartbeat, we usually calm down immediately and fall fast asleep in peace.

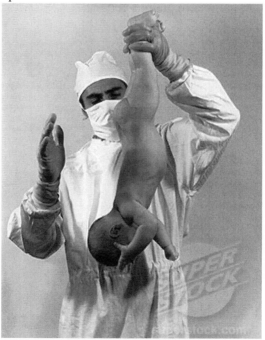

At birth, we were conditioned to ignore our hearts that guided our spirits and we are forced to be motivated by fear and pain. This is represented by the picture above. First, the doctor, who represents the white man's system, turns our world upside down, and then he spanks us to get our attention focused on the pain he just inflicted as a means of psychological control. The result is that our hearts are neglected and ignored in the process and our main motivation in life is fear and to avoid pain and discomfort.

What is tragic is that almost immediately after we transition into the physical realm through birth, we forget or neglect our own hearts altogether. Our hearts are taken for granted. We don't acknowledge them anymore. We don't take care of them and we surely don't learn or listen to them. Subconsciously, we still look to the heart when we need to heal and comfort our physical bodies. One of the first places a doctor checks when we receive a physical exam is the heart. When we have a sprained ankle, knee or general injury to our limbs, the first thing the doctor tells us to do is raise our injured limb above our hearts. When we hurt our finger, wrist, hand or arm, we instinctively raise it and place it close to our hearts. When we see a doctor for this injury, he gives us a sling to keep the arm close to our heart. When someone is physically under attack and is emotionally overwhelmed, they will ball up in a fetal position and tuck all their limbs, torso and head close to their hearts. The fetal position, referring to the position we were in when we were in the womb, is close to our mother's heart. This is the same position we get into if we are having a nervous breakdown, stressed or suffering from different ailments. So as you can see, we rely on our hearts for protection, healing, guidance and comfort. We do all this without being conscious of it. In Asian cultures, one seems to bow in the presence of another as a sign of respect. In actuality, the person lowers his head to fix his gaze towards the heart of the other person, so that person knows this is the level of consciousness he is operating on. He thinks with his heart and feels with his mind. The heart chakra is the first level of higher consciousness.

Life begins and ends with the heart. In order to live a fulfilling life, it is important to pay attention and listen to the heart. Our hearts should be our guides in all decisions in our lives. This is why the fourth chakra, representing the heart, is Love. This is where true love is defined, in the heart. If this is true, then people who have heart attacks have neglected their hearts or the concept of true love. What atrocities and neglect does one have to reach a point where the heart gives out on them? The heart, of all organs, is the one that always believes in the best of you. It must take major punishment being constantly inflicted on it, in order for the heart to want to give up on you. This is a tragic scene of hopelessness that the heart must feel. So heart attacks are more spiritual than physical. This makes sense, because if you knew how important the heart was on a spiritual level, you wouldn't physically abuse or neglect it. What is a heart murmur? Definition of "murmur"- *A murmur is a low indistinct whisper or confidential complaint.* So a heart murmur is your heart trying to communicate with you, in a subtle way that something is not right in your life, according to reaching your life's destiny.

We need to start listening and paying attention to our hearts. We need to let go of logic and embrace our heart's decisions. Any decision based on the heart will put you in a better situation than you were before you made that decision. It may seem outside your comfort zone or be temporarily uncomfortable, but in the end, you will be better off. We have been conditioned into believing that hardship or being uncomfortable is somehow bad for us. You see, we have been tricked into listening to things that are outside of ourselves so that we will continuously be subjected to other people's will. People who do not have our best interests at heart. We have voluntarily given up the very thing that would find us true happiness: our hearts. When you give up yourself to the heart, you immediately begin your life's purpose and destiny. What may be revealed to you may make you uncomfortable, but it will always be what's best for you. Trust in the heart and it will never fail you. Give it the opportunity to work for you. True freedom and happiness comes from within. This is where the heart resides. The heart our ancestors believed was where the soul resides.

The heart sends more messages to the brain, than the brain does to the heart. — Dr. Leonard Horowitz

Fear and love hold the same frequency. Our heart pounds at the same rate when we experience both these emotions. This is the frequency of life. The heart holds within it all frequencies that are needed for communication on a spiritual level. In order to give life to ideas, thoughts or people, the heart must reach a particular vibration or frequency. This is the same frequency that one experiences when they have an orgasm, whether they are male or female. It is a rapid beat that must be reached for a man to ejaculate and for a woman to have an orgasm. It is the same heart rate. Coincidently, this frequency is also the same frequency of what we interpret as fear. We only interpret our heart's response to fear as something that should be avoided because we have been trained to operate according to the left hemisphere of our brains. If we were interpreting our reality through our right hemisphere of the brain, we would see that this frequency should be embraced and not avoided. Once we embrace this frequency or heart rate, we master fear and are able to produce the outcome we wish. Fear has now become the threshold to being able to manifest miracles. But in reality, fear is nothing but an illusion from which to control and manipulate human behavior. It keeps you away from manifesting your miracles. This rapid heart rate or frequency is the vibration that gives life from that which the individual can perceive. If we embrace this frequency, we can create miracles. If we run from or avoid this frequency, we block our path to manifesting miracles.

Birth defects are caused by our parent's hearts not being in the "right place" during the time of conception or when we are in our mother's womb. — Nekhebet

The Science behind Heartbreak

One of life's most trying experiences is the pain of a broken heart. Although I have experienced many different types of pain in my life, nothing compares to a broken heart. The old adage, "Sticks and stones may break my bones but words can never hurt me," is a false assumption. The breaking of a bone heals in time. The bone can actually become stronger than it was before it was injured. Although your brain may be reluctant to use that part of the body that was injured, over time, the individual overcomes the stigmatism and resumes normal activities. Words, on the other hand, can scar your heart and soul for life. Although they may heal, the scar will always be eternal. So it is with heartbreak or heartache. It is a pain that runs deep into the core of your being. It shakes the foundation to its very roots. It pierces the soul and exposes your wound for all to see and judge. It turns you inside out and chews you up as it devours you, then proceeds to spit you out. Many songs have been written about it. Many poems have been inspired. Many people have gotten terminally ill and some have lost or even taken their own lives because of it. It is no joke. It can bring the strongest man to his knees and make the softest woman as hard as steel. "It is better to have loved and lost than to never have loved at all." This attests to the greatness of love. To experience love first hand, is the greatest human experience man could ever know. It is one of life's ultimate achievements. So the rewards of the experience of love negate any effects one might suffer from its loss. In other words, it is better for a spirit to come down and have a human experience than to stay in the spiritual realm and never know the pain, hurt, agony, despair, joy, bliss, ecstasy and all emotions and experience that love brings with it. We are all better people for the experience of love if we embrace and learn from all its experiences. Such is the spirit's ultimate destiny in the physical plane: to know and experience love firsthand.

"To cry all our cries. To know the pain of too much love."Kahil Gibran, "The Prophet."

Let us break down the science of heartbreak in terms of the feminine principle or perspective. Since the woman is built to receive Inner G, her experience is going to be interpreted differently than a man's experience. Neither sex experiences heartache deeper or more intensely than the other. What is different is the two genders' opposite perspectives and interpretation of the same experience.

Remember our analogy of the atom. The woman, being negative, revolves around her center or nucleus, the proton or male principle. She orbits around him because his energy reflects the best in her. She voluntarily revolves around him because she benefits from his energy shining on her. She, in turn, uses his energy to manifest their reality. This beautiful balance in nature is what makes the world go round. This formula is the building block of all creation. This is God's blueprint to the physical dimension. So what happens when the proton or male principle decides to leave the electron, female principle, without a mutual agreement or understanding? The answer is immediate chaos. The male has pulled his light or Inner G away from the female counterpart. She has been involuntarily pushed away from her life source without her consent. She was in a position of being closest to him, and now, she is relegated to a position as far away from him as possible. This is a violent and a tremendously stressful situation for the female or feminine principle of Inner G. Her whole world has literally been turned upside down. She is left to try to pull herself together and collect all her thousands of pieces that have been scattered all over the universe by his absence with no light to guide her. The female's denial of this action further plunges her into chaos as she tries to hold on to the sun that no longer wants to invest his Inner G in her reflection.

This is a very traumatic experience on a scientific level, let alone on an emotional and spiritual plane. Since the woman has been pushed out against her will, she no longer has the light or Inner G from which to sustain her. Her world is now plunged into darkness, into a lonely, cold abyss. She will wander out in the deepest regions of space, searching for another light to sustain her. For the time being, she has to make do with no light to sustain her or her Inner G to keep her balanced. A piece of her will feel like it has died every day that she goes without her Sun. The sooner she acknowledges the situation, then the sooner she can overcome it. If she holds on to a sun that no longer wants to shine on her, she will continue to suffer in spite of herself. The sooner she lets go of her sun, then the sooner she will start to heal. One of two things will happen. The sun that does not look to her for his reflection will realize his loss and will want her back, or she will attract another sun in the cosmos that will accept her for who she is and the reflection she can give him. Ladies, be careful. Do not continue to revolve around a Sun that does not appreciate the reflection you give them. You will be better off attracting a sun that appreciates you for who you are and not what you can do for them at the moment.

Male Heartbreak

The male's reality or experience of heartache is defining the opposite side of the spectrum of the same experience of the female's heartbreak. Scientifically speaking, the male represents the nucleus of the atom, which contains the protons and neutrons that the electrons of the atom revolve around. The electron is the scientific representation of the female. So scientifically speaking, what happens when the electron, representing the female, leaves the atom's nucleus against the proton's wishes for her to stay with him? The male has invested his time and Inner G in the female in order for her to reflect back to him his understanding of himself and the environment around him. The female holds the reflection of how a man defines himself and his reality. She holds the key to how he sees himself and how he relates to the world around him. Without her there to reflect back to him, he cannot define who he is or where his place belongs in his reality. The male will lose all sense of self and self-worth. He will go through a phase of confusion, uncertainty and depression until he can find another woman to substantiate his knowledge of self and his place in his environment. The male will be lost in his own pity and confusion. He will start to question his self-worth and understanding of himself as a man. The male will yearn to get the female back because he has convinced himself that only she holds his reflection and no one else. He will pursue her to get her back, as if his life depended on it. It is only after he finds his reflection in another female that he will lose interest in his original female, who left him in the first place. Coincidently, once a man is allowed to see his reflection in a female, he will always be attracted to her, no matter what the circumstances are between them.

What is Love?

360
To know, appreciate and celebrate the totality of a person.
To know the heights they have the ability to ascend to, as well as the depths they may fall.
To embrace, the all, unconditionally.
To fully internalize the definitions of their existence.
To travel through the gates of hell to save them and wait at the gates of heaven for them to arrive.
No matter if it takes an eternity.
To spend all your tears and pay all your laughs until you have emptied your heart.
To never look back.
To never have doubt or second guess.
To never fear.
This is how I love you. –TC

TELL HIM

Let me be patient, let me be kind
Make me unselfish without bein' blind
Though I may suffer, I'll envy it not
And endure what comes, 'cause he's all that I got and tell him

Tell him I need him
Tell him I love him
And it'll be alright

And tell him
Tell him I need him
Tell him I love him
It'll be alright

Now I may have faith, to make mountains fall
But if I lack love, then I am nothin' at all
I can give away, everything I possess
But I'm without love then I have no happiness
I know I'm imperfect and not without sin
But now that I'm older all childish things end and tell him

Tell him I need him
Tell him I love him
It'll be alright

Tell him
Tell him I need him
Tell him I love him
It'll be alright

I'll never be jealous
And I won't be too proud
'Cause love is not boastful
Ooh and love is not loud

Tell him I need him
Tell him I love him
Everything is gonna, is gonna be alright
Ooh, ooh, yeah yeah, oh yeah

Now I may have wisdom and knowledge on earth
But if I speak wrong, ooh, then what is it worth?
See what we now know is nothing compared
To the love that was shown when our lives were spared and tell him

Tell him I need him
Tell him I love him
It'll be alright

Tell him
Tell him I need him
Tell him I love him
It'll be alright. – Lauryn Hill

If I speak in the tongues of men and of angels, but not have love, I am only a resounding gong or a clanging symbol. If I have the gift of prophecy and can fathom all mysteries and all knowledge, and if I have faith that can move mountains, but have not love, I am nothing. If I give all my possessions to the poor and surrender my body to the flames, but have not love, I gain nothing. Love is patient, love is kind. It does not envy, it does not boast, it is not proud. It is not rude, it is not self-seeking, it is not easily angered, it keeps no records of wrongs. Love does not delight in evil but rejoices with the truth. It always protects, always trusts, always hopes, always perseveres. Love never fails. But where there are prophecies, they will cease; where there are tongues, they will be stilled. Where there is knowledge, it will pass away. For we know in part, and we prophesy in part, but when perfection comes, the imperfect disappears; When I was a child, I talked like a child, I thought like a child, I reasoned like a child. When I became a man, I put childish ways behind me. Now we see but a poor reflection as in a mirror; then we shall see face to face. Now I know in part; Then I shall know fully, even as I am fully known. And now these three remain: faith, hope and love. But the greatest of these is love. — 1 Corinthians 13:1-13

When love beckons to you, follow him, though his ways are hard and steep. And when his wings enfold you yield to him, though the sword hidden among his pinions may wound you. And when he speaks to you believe in him, though his voice may shatter your dreams as the north wind lays waste the garden.

For even as love crowns you so shall he crucify you. Even as he ascends to your height and caresses your tenderest branches that quiver in the sun, so shall he descend to your roots and shake them in their clinging to the earth. Like sheaves of corn he gathers you unto himself. He threshes you to make you naked. He sifts you to free you from your husks. He grinds you to whiteness. He kneads you until you are pliant. And then he assigns you to the sacred fire, that you may become sacred bread for God's feast.

All these things shall love do unto you that you may know the secrets of your heart, and in that knowledge become a fragment of Life's heart. But if in your fear you would seek only love's peace and love's pleasure, then it is better for you that you cover your nakedness and pass out of loves threshing floor, into the seasonless world where you shall laugh but not all of your laughter, and weep but not all of your tears. Love gives naught but itself and takes naught but of itself. Love possesses not nor would it be possessed

For love is sufficient unto love. When you love you should not say, "God is in my heart," but rather, "I am in the heart of God." And think not you can direct the course of love, for love, if it finds you worthy, directs your course. Love has no other desire but to fulfill itself. But if you love and must needs have desires, let these be your desires; To melt and be like a running brook that sings its melody to the night. To know the pain of too much tenderness. To be wounded by your own understanding of love;

And to bleed willingly and joyfully. To wake at dawn with a winged heart and give thanks for another day of loving; To rest at the noon hour and meditate love's ecstasy; To return home at eventide with gratitude; And then to sleep with a prayer upon your lips.

And in Marriage, let there be spaces in your togetherness, and let the winds of the heavens dance between you. Love one another, but make not a bond of love: Let it rather be a moving sea between the shores of your souls. Fill each other's cup

But drink not from one cup. Give one another of your bread but eat not from the same loaf. Sing and dance together and be joyous, but let each one of you be alone, even as the strings of a lute are alone though they quiver with the same music. Give your hearts, but not into each other's keeping. For only the hand of Life can contain your hearts. And stand together yet not too near together: For the pillars of the temple stand apart, and the oak tree and the cypress grow not in each other's shadow.
—Kahlil Gibran

"The Prophet"

What Love is Not:

Down Here in Hell

I love it when we make mistakes.
Because once again,
it gives me a reason to complain,
I love the battled lines,
the battled lines we draw when crossing the mud
I love it when we fight,
standing on the verge of breaking up or making love

What would I do if we were perfect,
where would I go for disappointment.
Love without pain would leave me wondering why I stayed.

I think of saving myself,
but with nothing to complain about up in heaven,
what will I do
I think of saving myself,
but I really want to work it out
down here in hell with you

See I want to make you feel the fire,
while I burn you with my bad days,
Oh want to be unsatisfied, (sure)
you can feel the heat comin' from me...baby.

What would I do if we were perfect,
where would I go for disappointment,
words without hate would leave me nothin' else to say.

I think of saving myself,
but with nothing to complain about in heaven,
what will I do
I think of saving myself,
but I really wanta work it out
down here in hell with you

I think of saving myself,
but with nothing to complain about up in heaven,
I think of saving myself,
but I really wanna work it out
down here in hell with you
(hook). —Van Hunt

It Kills Me.

Oh yeah I've got trouble with my friends
Trouble in my life
Problems when you don't come home at night
But when you do you always start a fight
But I can't be alone , I need you to come on home
I know you messin' around, but who the hell else is gonna hold me down
Ooooh I gotta be out my mind to think it's gonna work this time
A part of me wants to leave, but the other side still believes
And it kills me to know how much I really love you
So much I wanna ooh hoo ohh to you hoo hoo
Should I grab his cell, call this chick up
Start some shhhh then hang up
Or I should I be a lady
Oohh maybe cuz I wanna have his babies
Ohh yah yahh cuz I don't wanna be alone
I dont need to be on my own

But I love this man

But some things I can't stand ohhhh

I've gotta be out my mind

To think it's gonna work this time

A part of me wants to leave but the other half still believes

and it kills me to know how much I really love you

So much I wanna oohh hoo ohhh, to you hoo hooo.

                          — Melanie Fiona

Relationships that we call Love, which are based on passionate confirmations of outer displays of affection (gifts, hugs, sex, relations, etc.) are in reality not love but a hypocritical relationship in which two immature people (driven by Ego), are afraid that if they let go of the passionate confirmations their mate will not want them any longer.

                 "Egyptian Tantric Yoga"

                 - Dr. Muata Ashby

Chapter Twelve:
The Orgasm: The Gateway to Heaven!

"Through my womb, life begins, and through my heart, life will return." — Nekhebet

Humans are made up of over 80% water. If this is true, then we should move, feel, think and act like water does in its natural state. Water responds to the moon at night. The moon controls water through its gravitational pull. The moon represents the light in the darkness of man. The moon represents the consciousness or light in the unseen world. In other words, it represents the consciousness of your spirit. Your Sun sign represents yourself on the outside in this physical dimension. The Sun represents the external you. The moon represents the spirit of man or true self in the unseen world. The moon is the inner you or your true spirit. This is what creates the currents in the ocean's ebb and flow. If this is true, then we should be conscious of the cycles of the moon and how it affects our daily lives. If the moon affects water and humans are made up of over 80% water, then the moon affects man's consciousness and behavior according to its cycle.

There have been studies that suggest holy water, or water that has been prayed over or consecrated, has healing properties that normal water does not possess. This is because water contains, in its vibration, the intent of the Inner G that has been infused in it. The same can be said of the female's fluid that she produces when she is sexually aroused. Women must be very careful and particular of the men they choose to engage in sex with. Remember, if the man's intentions are of a lower level, the woman will internalize and give life to those intentions. However, if the man and woman's intentions are synchronized and maintained at a higher vibration or level, then they have the ability to manifest what we call miracles in the physical dimension.

This is what is behind the ancient Afrikan tradition of pouring libation or the calling on the ancestors. First, the person doing the ritual carries a gourd or container of water. This container represents the womb or the female principle of Inner G. The group's intent (masculine principle of Inner G), is then infused into the water. This happens by the group saying the names of their ancestors to call them into existence to share with them the event at this particular moment in time. Every name carries a unique vibration or sound that infuses in the water. The water receives the vibration in its structural memory code and manifests the vibration or name into the physical dimension. The water is then poured out of the container, symbolizing the birth of the intent of the water. The water is either poured on the earth or into a plant so that the water's intentions can be manifested in the physical dimension. When completed, the names or the vibrations that were collected by the water are brought forth to be with the group.

This is also the theory behind holy water. Prayer over the water equals man's intent spoken into existence. That's why prayer over water or holy water works. One infuses the water with the intention of the one who is doing the ritual through prayer. Prayer equals vibrational intent and nothing else. Water is the vessel for the manifestation of thoughts in the physical dimension.

Water is the only element to express itself as solid, liquid and gas. It also is the only element that expands when it gets cold and contracts when it gets hot.

The water or the fluid that Black men and women produce during sex has structural memory. The water or fluid takes a picture of all that is in its environment. It records all our thoughts, actions, feelings and intent.

Remember, over 90% of what we call reality is unseen. The water or fluid can recognize and record this unseen Inner G. You may see the ripples in a glass of water when it is exposed to music. These ripples are the footprints of the unseen Inner G that the water is receiving and recording. One cannot lie to water or fluid. Your partner's state of mind, along with yours, will be infused together during sex to create a frequency that you two will share and give life to. This frequency of Inner G will permeate through you and your aura. The level of the vibration of the frequency will affect the level of your reality. Low frequencies manifest low-level realities. Higher frequencies manifest high-level realities. We can control our reality by the people and environment we wish to share our Inner G with. Remember, only a man can raise the frequency of a woman but a woman cannot raise the frequencies in the men they choose to share their life with. Women, do not waste your time with men who choose to live at a lower frequency than you. You will be disappointed and heartbroken time and time again. A man must be willing to raise his own frequency on his own accord. That is the only way it can happen. A woman is a reflection of the man's Inner G; she cannot be the catalyst for him to raise it.

Rhythm is the result of the consciousness of the water or fluid's particular frequency. Just like the waves in the ocean. You can work with the wave and have it carry you to places you would have never been able to go. Or if you go against the wave, you can wind up fighting against your own best interests and wind up drowning yourself. Because of the white man's lack of Melanin, his rhythm is dysfunctional. This is why the white man always seems to be in conflict, in one form or another. Conflict is going against the natural order and rhythm of the universe. With no rhythm to guide you, especially in sex, opening the gateway is virtually impossible. This is why the Afrikan used the drum to communicate since the beginning of time. The drum is the best form of communication because it speaks directly to your heart. Your heart keeps the rhythm of life. So the object during sex is to catch the Inner G wave of your partner. Do not tense up and go against the flow of their Inner G. Leave the ego out of the bedroom. Catch the wave by trusting your partner and see how far one can travel.

Our actions, thoughts, emotions and words that we express travel like water to resonate in the physical realm. The vibration will find similar frequencies and naturally align or attract one another. Remember, water is cohesive. It does not want to separate from itself. Water or fluid unites men and women with the same frequencies. Use this science to your advantage. Raise your frequency and you raise your quality of life by changing the environment around you.

Be aware that if you choose to have people of lower frequencies in your circle, then your vibration will have to drop to their level in order for you to communicate with them. It doesn't work the other way around. One has to be willing to do the work to raise their consciousness. A person cannot just hang around people of higher frequencies and somehow expect it to rub off on them. Remember, "One bad apple can spoil the whole bunch." This person's toxic Inner G can poison your water. This poison can accumulate and infiltrate your water at different levels. Your fluid or water has memory. This toxic person can literally store its lower level Inner G within your water. If this process were to continue for a significant amount of time, that person who is storing the toxic Inner G, infused by their partner, can literally lose their mind or sense of self. They can lose all identity of who they were before this person entered their life. We all have had a friend or family member who we don't recognize anymore because their willingness to put up with or internalize another person's low level Inner G.

But all is not lost. Water or our fluid is endowed with a capacity to purify itself. This occurs at the moment of phase transmission. Water, just like the Black man and woman, has the ability to raise its consciousness. Water, when infused by the Sun, just like the Black man and woman, has the ability to receive instruction and consciousness to raise its vibration. Water, when exposed to the Sun's rays, immediately starts to transform as vapor. The process called evaporation starts to take place. Just like Black people can receive Inner G from the Sun to guide our Melanin to a higher vibration. When water evaporates, it literally changes from a liquid to a vapor. The water is basically the same; it is just expressed at a higher frequency. The water leaves behind the toxins and poisons on the ground as it raises its vibration and transcends into the air.

The Black man and woman also have the ability to leave things that are toxic and poisonous to their well-being by transcending to higher consciousness. Once the water completes its vaporization, it will condense to form a cloud in the sky, and then fall back to Earth as purified rain. Another way the water purifies itself is by freezing. This isolates the toxins into one concentrated area. The water will then melt away and distance itself from the once self-contained poisons. The water does this process over and over again to preserve its basic structure. It is like the snake that sheds its dead skin so that a new and improved layer of skin can take its place. So it is with the Black man and woman. We must be able to raise our vibration continuously in order to transcend to a higher frequency. If we do not constantly maintain this cycle, then we are doomed to be contaminated by a system that bombards us with lower level Inner G. This is the program for life. This is the Creator's gift to you.

JUST LIKE WATER

Moving down the streams of my lifetime
Pulls the fascination in my sleeve
Cooling off the fire of my longing
Boiling off my cold within his heat
Melting down the walls of inhibition
Evaporating all of my fears

Baptizing me into complete submission
Dissolving my condition with his tears
He's just like the water
And moving me around and around. — Lauryn Hill

Japanese scientists have experimented with the concept of water carrying or holding intent. They did an experiment where water was placed into two containers. The first container of water was given to one group and the other container of water was given to another group. The first group gathered around the water and meditated at a higher vibration of thought. This means that they complimented the water in terms of love, grace, appreciation, goodwill, compliments, etc. The second group took the other container of water and meditated over it. They meditated at a lower vibration. They focused on hate, fear, anger, jealousy, insecurity, malice, etc. They proceeded to freeze both containers of water. The water that was inscribed with the words of Love developed a crystal shaped like a hexagon.

Remember that the six-pointed star represents the "Gateway," otherwise known as the Seal of Solomon or the Star of David. It is represented by two pyramids overlapping each other. It is one upside-down triangle pointing downward and one right-side-up triangle pointing upward, as both triangles overlap each other. The upside-down pyramid or triangle represents the feminine principle of energy and the right-side-up pyramid represents the masculine principle of Inner G. When both Inner G's come together, they create an electro-magnetic vortex called the "Gateway." This gateway is the six-pointed star that you see in the crystallized water. It is the portal of the unseen or spiritual world to materialize in the seen or physical dimension. In other words, the "gateway" is the bridge from the spiritual world to the physical dimension. This is the secret science of Black male and female sex.

"The more relaxed the muscles are, the more energy can flow through
the body. Using muscular tensions to try to 'do' the punch, or attempting to
use brute force to knock someone over, will only work to opposite effect."
— Bruce Lee

This symbol may look very familiar to you. It is known by different
names. Some call it the Seal of Solomon. The Jews hijacked it from Afrika
and call it the Star of David. They use the symbol on their national flag. The
Kemetic or Afrikan name for it is called Sephedet. It represents the male and
female principles of Inner G coming together. This is illustrated on the cover
of the book. Female Inner G is always shown on the top and the male Inner
G is always displayed on the bottom.

As we stated in a previous chapter, God embracing her feminine
principle, which is magnetic, collected the material in the spiritual plane to
make a physical body. You will see that the upside-down pyramid is wider
at the top and then condenses to a point at the bottom. This illustrates the

gathering of the materials in the ethers, which gradually becomes denser as it gets smaller. Just as a rain cloud gathers moisture in the atmosphere and then, when it becomes too heavy, it falls to the Earth as rain. So was the first manifestation of God in the physical plane. Once the feminine principle of God becomes too dense or heavy to stay in the ethers, the feminine principle of God fell to the Earth. Once the feminine principle got to Earth, she gathered the materials from the earth from her magnetism to create her counterpart, the making of the masculine principle of the one God, man. As you can see in the illustration, the right-side-up pyramid is wider at the bottom, and as it becomes denser, comes to a point on the top. Just like children making a sandcastle at the beach. Thus, the feminine principle of God, being magnetic, gathered up the earth and the materials that it needed to create its masculine counterpart. So the materials became denser as they were solidified into human form. This, as you probably recognized, is the story of the creation of Adam in the Bible. But the Adam they are referring to is really spelled Atum or Atom, which of course, is the basic building block of the physical dimension.

Remember, God separated him/herself in the physical dimension so that He/She could appreciate both his and her qualities. The coming together of the male and female represents the physical reunion of the one God coming together in the physical dimension.

In the illustrations below, we see the ancient symbol for the woman on the left, represented by the upside-down triangle coming down from the heavens and the ancient symbol for the man, on the right, represented by coming up from the earth. When these two symbols come together during sexual intercourse, they create the Sephedet or six-pointed star that creates a hexagon in the middle of it. It is through this hexagon that I call the "Gateway" where the couple can manifest their thoughts and ideas into the physical dimension. One will also notice the male and female reproductive organs are mirror images of each other. This suggests the "oneness" of man and woman as reflections of the same entity.

There are five geometric shapes that have faces, edges and angles that are congruent. Revered by the Greek philosopher, <u>Pythagoras</u>, each of these Platonic Solids produces specific energetic effects. The pyramid is one of these shapes.

Female & male sexual organs are reflections of each other.

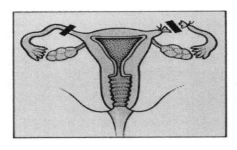 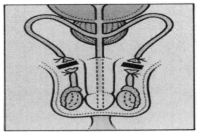

FEMALE Body Part		**MALE Body Part**
Clitoris	=	Head of Penis
Ovaries	=	Tesicles
Vagina	=	Shaft of Penis
Fallopian Tubes	=	Vas Deferens

Each part of the male has a direct counterpart in the female. And each part of the female has a direct counterpart in the male. We are literally reflections of each other or different expressions of the same thing.

Since the male is masculine, electric and positive in nature, he is made to produce or give out Inner G. Thus, his sexual organs are located externally or outside of the body.

The female is feminine, magnetic and negative in nature. She is made to internalize or receive Inner G. Thus, her sexual organs are located internally or inside the body.

So the act of sex to our ancestors was the most sacred act that a man and woman could ever be a part of on this earth. It was the opening of the Gateway to be used for the manifestation of the unseen world into the seen world. In other words, sex was used to open the portal or bridge from the spirit dimension to the physical plane. With this knowledge, our ancestors could create "miracles." They could manipulate this Inner G and science to will their dreams and ideologies into existence. This was a very powerful tool. In order to use it properly, one had to master himself to cross the threshold into the unseen world.

As we stated in previous chapters, the woman possesses this power innately. She is the Gateway because she is magnetic. The only problem is that she cannot access this power without her male counterpart, who holds the key to the gate. So the pressure is on the male to raise his consciousness high enough in order to have access to the Gateway. This is why the goddess Auset is symbolized by having a throne perched on top of her head. She is the Gateway. The kingdom lies within her. It is up to the man to prove himself worthy of sitting on her throne in order to be privy to the kingdom. So it is with sex. Our ancestors' version of sexual intercourse was the woman on top. This meant that the woman was in control. It was then up to the man to be able to sustain himself physically, in order for the woman to reach the entrance of

the Gateway. The entrance to the "Gateway" is described here as her orgasm.
If the man fell short of the woman reaching her peak, because he had not
mastered his body and was not strong enough to hold his seed, then she knew
that he was not worthy of the kingdom because he did not have the fortitude to
reach the steps of the Gateway. So as a test to see if a man was worthy, he had
to maintain enough control over his bodily functions in order for the woman to
reach an orgasm, i.e. control premature ejaculation.

You will notice in the symbol of the Sephedet, that a hexagon is formed
in the center of it. The hexagon, of course, is a six-sided shape. Hex, which
means six, is also equivalent to sex, as in sextuplets. They both mean or
equal six! Six is the number of man or the manifestation of God in the
lowest dimension, which is the physical plane. So how does the spiritual
dimension manifest into the lower physical plane? Through the Gateway!
The Gateway is the coming together of the male and female Inner G's to
create life in the physical dimension. The Gateway is the hexagon created by
man and woman engaged in sexual intercourse, which can also be defined as
the coming together of God on the physical dimension.

Tetrahedron is the Sephedet. The key of life is the complex dance between positive and negative Inner G that creates an electro-magnetic field to bring the spiritual realm into the physical dimension.

It is interesting to note that, when drawn over one another, each of the 24 letters in the ancient language of Hebrew together form the Star Tetrahedron.

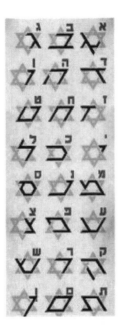

***The Star Tetrahedron is the electric balance to magnetism. This is
how data is stored so efficiently within a computer. It is this geometric
shape that provides memory.***

As pointed out in the previous chapter on the chakras, in order for man
to reach higher consciousness, he must master his lower self or his physical
body. This is why many religions fast, practice celibacy or go into seclusion or
isolation called deep meditation. It is all about mastering your physical body in
order to reach higher levels of consciousness. Our Afrikan ancestors believed
that this is what separates man from the beast.   They believed that this was
man's sacred purpose and duty in life. Man was born with the purpose of
overcoming his lower physical body so that, when he died, he would transcend
to higher, spiritual consciousness. With this knowledge, the white man turned
the tables of the Black man's world upside down. The Caucasian has tricked the
world into following his dysfunctional behavior and view of reality. Instead of
people of color yearning and working to reach their higher selves, we are now
forced, manipulated, encouraged and rewarded to ignore our higher

consciousness and embrace our lower selves. This is why the Black man dominates the fields of professional sports, the entertainment industry and the prison population. These are the industries that define man by their lower selves. Consequently, he is only "allowed" to participate and succeed in these areas in his life. In ancient Afrika, the Black man defined his manhood by trying to achieve "god consciousness." In today's racist system, the Black man is coerced to define his manhood by his lower, animalistic consciousness. There is a saying among white men that they don't really become men until they sleep with a Black woman. They still pay homage to the Black woman having the access to the Gateway, which they cannot open.

This concept or mindset is also displayed in how the Caucasian interprets and defines his role in sexual intercourse. The white man egotistically and selfishly places himself in the position of being on top of the woman so that he can dominate and oppress her and her offspring. This goes against the sacred science of our ancestors and their understanding of the synergy between masculine and feminine principles in nature. Coincidently, the man-on-top sexual position is called the "missionary position." *Missionary can be defined as imposing your will on another and having that person believe in your ideologies, as if they came up with them themselves.* In this position, the white man was not required to master his lower self because the focus was on fulfilling his animalistic desires and not raising his vibration to serve and please his woman. Instead of raising his consciousness to a level that the woman demanded and would measure her man, he now subjected her under "his" rule. In doing so, he admitted to himself and the world that because of the lack of melanin, he could not attain the level of consciousness to manifest the spiritual plane into the material world. Because of his lack of Melanin or higher consciousness, he would have to subjugate the darker or melanated people of the world to manifest his reality for him. This is the mindset that drives the behavior of white supremacy and racism. The white man asks himself, "Why take on the difficult task of trying to elevate one's consciousness without Melanin, when it is easier to embrace your lower consciousness and oppress the world in an effort to get the people you conquer to serve you?" The white man has mastered this ideology, and with the ruthless passion and fervor of a cold-blooded killer, now rules the world because of it. The European has now tricked people of color into adopting his ideology, rather than pursuing their higher consciousness. Black people have now become more dependent on a system that celebrates their lower selves and don't realize that their participation in it supports their own demise and purpose in life.

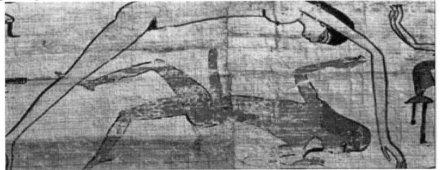

The goddess Nut illustrated on top and the god Tefnut on the bottom. The feminine principle is represented by the heavens and the masculine principle is represented by the Earth.

There is a legend that most Bible and religious scholars know about but choose to keep a secret. It is the story of Lilith. She was Adam's female mate before Eve came on the scene in the Garden of Eden. Lilith considered herself just a strong and important as Adam and refused to submit to him sexually. She did not want to lay under him during sexual intercourse because she felt that she was being degraded. Lilith wanted to be on top of Adam where she believed God intended for her to be. Because of her stubbornness and unwillingness to submit, Adam went to God to complain about his unruly mate. God banned Lilith from the Garden of Eden and Eve was created later to satisfy Adam's requests.

The picture above is of the Hindu gods Shiva and Shakti. You will notice that Shiva, the female, is always represented as being on top of her male counterpart, Shakti.

Water is infinitely flexible. It can be seen through, and yet at other times, it can obscure things from sight. It can split and go around things, rejoining on the other side, or it can crash through things. It can erode the hardest rocks by gently lapping away at them or it can flow past the tiniest pebble. "Empty your mind, be formless, shapeless — like water. Now you put water into a cup, it becomes the cup; you put water into a bottle, it becomes the bottle; you put it in a teapot, it becomes the teapot. Now water can flow or it can crash. Be water, my friend." — Bruce Lee

The Gateway

During sexual arousal, the woman produces water or fluid in order to receive the man's Inner G. She will then allow her fluid to be infused with the man's fluid, which contains his electrical intent, in order to manifest his ideas into reality on the physical plane. This is the science of Black male & female sex. Coincidently, ***the definition of the woman's Clitoris has a Greek origin that means, the key or to close a door.*** The Clitoris has a hood over it when it is not aroused. It is similar to the foreskin of the male penis. When aroused, the Clitoris is engorged with blood and becomes very sensitive. Its hood is then pulled back, exposing the Clitoris to external stimulation. In order for the male to "open" the Gateway, he must "open the door" by unlocking the "key" of the Clitoris. In other words, the man must bring the woman to an orgasmic state in order for the Gateway to be opened and utilized.

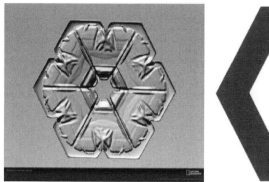

The Hexagon. The shape of manifestation from the spiritual dimension to the physical realm. Otherwise known as the "Gateway."

Atoms are made up of 99.999999% space. It is up to us to fill that space in order to manifest our reality.

The fluid or liquid that the woman produces has divine properties:

Sound, vibration, Inner G or intent travels through water or her fluid four times faster than through air. If this is true, then the child in the womb, surrounded by the mother's amniotic fluid, is receiving information, Inner G and consciousness four times faster than a child who has already been born! That means that the first nine months of a child's life in the womb is equivalent to the first 36 months of the child's life after he has been born! Be very careful what Inner G you expose your child to while the mother is pregnant. The mother, being the "Gateway" to the child who is manifesting in the physical dimension, must be conscious of her thoughts, actions and deeds, while she is with child.

The fluid has consciousness. It can carry the intent of the female and male, who are engaged in sex. Being that the woman is magnetic and the man is electric, they produce a vortex of electro-magnetic energy when they are engaged in sexual intercourse. This vortex is illuminated! If you were able to take a picture of the inside of the womb during sexual intercourse, it would be glowing because of the electro-magnetic Inner G being produced.

Coincidently, the two X chromosomes of a woman create the gateway symbol in the middle where the X's come together, the six-sided hexagon or tetrahedron, otherwise known as the "Gateway."

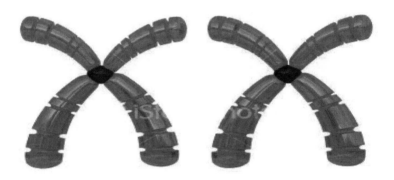

The figure below shows the woman's Inner G, always on top, being magnetic; it circulates in a counterclockwise motion. The male Inner G, always on the bottom, circulates clockwise in motion. When the two Inner G's come together in sexual intercourse, illustrated in the center, both Inner G's align themselves in one continuous motion. This is the creation of an electro-magnetic field being displayed in its vortex. The "Gateway" is illustrated by the line of arrows lining up in the center, going in the same direction. Just like two gears going the opposite way of each other, but when they are both engaged with one another, they are in unison in one fluid motion and direction. This "opening of the ways" is what I call "The Gateway."

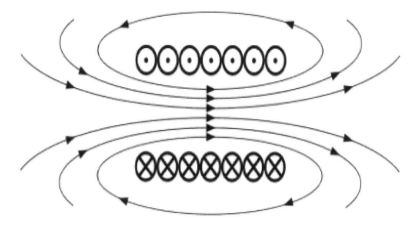

The liquid is the carrier of life and is sparked by the electro-magnetic field produced by the couple. This is why the woman's water "breaks" before she is about to give birth to a new life.

Water or her fluid is cohesive. Have you ever seen a drop of water on your glass shower door? When it rolls down, it will automatically attach itself to other water droplets during its descent. Water wants to bind with water in an effort to lose itself and create a larger entity. This is exemplified in the woman's ability to create life. She loses herself in her man so that life can attach to her, and then she creates a new life form that will eventually separate from her. Water or a woman's fluid never wants to separate from itself. Its main personality is to bind together to create new life. This is why a woman wants and needs to attach herself to her man. She is like water. Women provide the gateway for life's consciousness. Electricity is also like water. It has a current and it flows. The man supplies the woman with his electric Inner G. This act initiates her magnetic flow during sexual intercourse. The woman, in turn, receives the man's current, which initiates his spark, otherwise known as ejaculation. Once the man ejaculates, the woman is triggered to start the process of creating life. That "life creation" does not have to be just a baby. A woman is needed to give life to ideas, thoughts and also dreams. She possesses the "Gateway" to bring the unseen or spiritual world into the physical dimension. A man must have a woman in his life in order to fulfill his desires and dreams, and the woman needs a man for her to initiate her "life creation" process. Otherwise, the manifestation process cannot take place. **The word *memory* takes its origins from the ancient Hebrew words *mem*, which means Water, and *ohr*, which means** <u>**Spirit.**</u> Our ancestors always made a direct correlation between the spirit and the element of water. This is further proof of the scientific concept that water contains the thought or memory of the entity that gives it intent. Use the concept of sex to retrieve and communicate with the spirit that manifests in physical objects.

"No one can enter the kingdom of God unless he is born of Water and the Spirit... You must be born again." John 3:5-7

JUST LIKE WATER

Moving down the streams of my lifetime
Pulls the fascination in my sleeve
Cooling off the fire of my longing
Boiling off my cold within his heat
Melting down the walls of inhibition
Evaporating all of my fears
Baptizing me into complete submission
Dissolving my condition with his tears
He's just like the water
And moving me around and around. – Lauryn Hill

The Ankh is one of those ancient symbols that hold all the secrets of life. Our ancestors called it the "key of life." It is directly related to the masculine & feminine principles of Inner G. As we covered in previous chapters, sex is life and life is sex. Sex is the synergy of feminine and masculine Inner G and the expression it uniquely manifests. The top of the ankh looks like an omega sign, the 24th letter in the Greek alphabet. The top part represents feminine Inner G. Remember, feminine Inner G needs to be on top or first to fully appreciate and manifests its full potential. The Greeks, dissecting the ankh, used this part to represent the last, the end or the ultimate limit of Inner G. Remember, feminine Inner G is stronger than masculine Inner G. The Greeks also made it the 24th and last letter in their alphabet. Twenty-four in numerology represents the number 6. This is the number of the spirit at its lowest level of vibration, which is the physical form. All life in the spiritual world must use feminine Inner G to enter the physical dimension. The number 6 symbolizes God or the 1, which has become impregnated to produce life in the physical dimension. The omega sign represents a negatively charged elementary particle. Remember, feminine Inner G is negative. The word "omega" literally means a large "O." This is the symbol of the gateway or the womb that one must pass through in order to enter into the physical realm. Omega also has a value of 800. Eight in numerology represents infinity or that which is eternal. *In genomics, omega sign is used as a measure of evolution at the protein level. This suggests the concept of the life force always transcending or correcting itself. In astronomy, the omega sign represents the ranking of a star's brightness. Brightness can be defined as Inner G or measurement of life force. So the feminine principle, represented on top of the ankh, is the 360 degrees that one potentially has the ability to access, if one can raise their consciousness.*

Put the Omega symbol over the Alpha symbol, or the woman over the
man, and you get the key to life, the Ankh.

The bottom part of the ankh, of course, represents the masculine
principle of Inner G. Remember, the masculine principle of Inner G is
always displayed on the bottom of the feminine principle of Inner G. It is
usually represented by a T- or A-shape. The T-shape represents the male
phallus. When you put the two shapes together, they represent the union and
balance of feminine and masculine Inner G coming together as one. This

principle is the key of life. The T is the 20^(th) letter in the alphabet. In numerology, this number represents division or separation. This is how man came into existence. Remember, the Creator needed the feminine principle of the One to be able to manifest in the physical plane. So man, the masculine principle of the One, divided or separated itself from the feminine principle, to become man. The concept of all men must come through the woman in order to be born. Man is part of the woman that separated herself. All men's skin is made up of the endometrine of his mother. Our mothers separated or divided herself so that we may have life. That separation is called man. The other symbol the ankh uses to represent this principle is the A. In the Greek alphabet, it is called the Alpha. Alpha is the first letter in the alphabet. The European wanted to make his woman last and himself first, so he made the order of his alphabet to put himself first and his woman last. We are all familiar with the term "alpha male." Alpha is also the Phoenician word for ox. The horns of the ox represent the erection or power that man has at his disposal. Ox is spelled with the letter "O" first. The "O" is the womb or gateway that represents feminine Inner G. The letter "X" next to it is the 24^(th) letter of the English alphabet. Remember, this number is the number of man or the spirit represented in the physical plane. One needs the feminine principle to manifests in the physical. The letter "X" also symbolizes the resurrection of man, as worn by the Kemetic god Ausar. We now understand that for man to resurrect himself, he needs the feminine principle of Inner G.

Each arm in the ankh represents the balance of these two concepts. The right arm of the ankh represents the masculine principle of Inner G. This is man's logical, moral, ethical, lower and physical side. The left arm represents man's intuitive, spiritual, creative, higher and imaginative side. To live a well-balanced life, one must weigh both arms in congruence with each other. One must master their lower self, the right arm of the ankh, in order to gain access to his higher self, the left arm of the ankh. Once this is achieved, man can access the 360 degrees that is located in his higher self by recognizing the feminine principle, the womb, of his God consciousness. When one sees the Metu Neter, or what they call hieroglyphs today, you will see our ancestors holding the ankh by putting their fingers through the circle of the ankh. This act symbolizes sex, which accesses this Inner G. They usually are also holding it with their left hand, unless they are reflecting another character in the scene. Remember, the left side is your higher, spiritual side.

I have taken the science of the ankh and transferred it as an interpretation of Ohm's Law:

Ohm's Law I= V/R[a] [b]   *the equation when inverted, coincidently* **resembles the Ankh. I= R/V**

Ohm's law states that the current **through a conductor between two points is directly** proportional **to the** potential difference **or** voltage **across the two points, and inversely proportional to the** resistance **between them.**

The law was named after the German physicist Georg Ohm**, who, in a treatise published in 1827, described measurements of applied voltage and current through simple electrical circuits containing various lengths of wire.**

Ohm's Law defines the relationships between (P) power, (E) voltage, (I) current, and (R) resistance. One ohm is the resistance value through which one volt will maintain a current of one ampere.

(I) Current **is what flows on a wire or conductor like water flowing down a river. Current flows from negative to positive on the surface of a conductor. Current is measured in (A) amperes or amps.**

(E) Voltage **is the difference in electrical potential between two points in a circuit. It's the push or pressure behind current flow through a circuit, and is measured in (V) volts.**

(R) <u>Resistance</u> *determines how much current will flow through a component.* <u>Resistors</u> *are used to control voltage and current levels. A very high resistance allows a small amount of current to flow. A very low resistance allows a large amount of current to flow. Resistance is measured in Ωohms.*

(P) <u>Power</u> *is the amount of current times the voltage level at a given point measured in wattage or watts.*

Let us break down the science of this law in terms of male and female relationships in layman's terms. We have four concepts that are taking place. The first concept that we will break down is Voltage. Instead of talking about the characteristics of electricity, we will call it Inner G. Since all Inner G moves in waves or cycles, we will relate our Inner G to water. Voltage represents man or the masculine principle of Inner G. Man has a limited amount of Inner G, according to what he was born with. Man cannot create more Inner G or lose Inner G after he is born. Man is born with a set capacity or threshold of Inner G that he can access. Some men have the capacity to hold more Inner G than others, just like some Suns in the universe burn brighter than others. All men are not created equal. Voltage represents man's ability to release his Inner G as opposed to the potential amount of Inner G he has access to. Relating this concept to water, man may have a 1,000 gallon tank of water, but can only release so much at a time, because of his level of consciousness. In other words, a man may have 1,000 gallons of water in his possession but his nozzle, because of his lower level consciousness, can only release or have access to say only one cup of water at a time. The higher the consciousness of man, the bigger the nozzle he possesses, and the more he can access or utilize his water or Inner G. This is a very important point that women should take into account when choosing a man. Ladies, do not fall in love with a man's potential. What you see is what you get. If he is not displaying behavior that exemplifies the best in him, then chances are, he will never achieve his potential. This does not necessarily have to do with finances, as a man can provide a woman with so much more valuable commodities than just money. On the other hand, ladies, do not think that you can build the man you want from a man who you consider has potential. A man is born with a certain "star power" or Inner G that he will maintain throughout his life. You cannot dress him up or prop him up to be the man you desire. You will only wind up hurt, disappointed and frustrated in your quest to make the man you want.

The next concept that we will discuss in the equation is called Current. The measurement for current is called the Ohm. This is represented by the Omega symbol, which is represented by the top part of the ankh, which represents the feminine principle of Inner G or the womb. The Current or the womb measures the intensity, volume or quantity of the water or Inner G flow. Current is the quality or grade of the water or Inner G flow from the male to be received by the female. It is determined by the Voltage or the man's consciousness within the water or Inner G. In other words, the female has the capacity to measure the consciousness or quality of the male's Inner G when it is exposed to her womb. Women, trust your intuition. Your man is giving you his Inner G, which you cannot decipher with your five senses. It is only through your intuition that communicates with your spirit the quality of the man that you are engaged with. Intuition is your greatest and strongest sense. Your man may look the part, act the part and possess all the qualities that you think will make you happy in a relationship. But if your intuition tells you that something is not right, be willing to walk away without any further thought or actions. Your quality of life depends on it.

The next concept is called Resistance. It measures the flow of the water or Inner G. The higher the consciousness of the man, the more Inner G flows or comes out. The lower the consciousness of the man, the less water or Inner G flows or comes out. So, ladies, if you are receiving from your man all the intangible things you need to make you happy and he has the capacity to sustain, inspire and heal you, then you have the man you need. Also, his Inner G will always lead and support you to be the very best that you can be. There will be no limits to the things that he can help you become. It will not be temporary, as his Inner G will be inexhaustible to you. You will always sustain the capacity to manifest infinite possibilities. He will be able to do this just by being himself. He will not have to try. It will be second nature to him because that is who he is. Be leery of men who try too hard to please you.

The last concept we will break down in regards to relationships is Power. It is scientifically the measurement of Current times the Voltage level at a given point. My translation of Power, as it pertains to male and female relationships, can be interpreted as: The measurement of the amount of feminine Inner G times its exposure to a specific masculine Inner G level, at a specific point in a relationship. In other words, it is the measurement of the synergy of the male and female in the relationship. The power will be displayed by asking the question: Are you two good for each other? Do people notice that you seem to be happier, healthier and seem to be doing better since you met one another? Or do people see you as miserable, stressful, sickly or downright depressed since this person has come into your life? I challenge each person who reads this to look at their relationship in terms of Ohm's law. What is the Current, Voltage, Resistance and Power level in your relationship?

Chapter Thirteen:
The Final Solution

"Black Love is a performance art. It requires discipline, determination, devotion, dedication-and practice, practice, practice. It is painted on the canvas of our actions, illustrated by our fidelity to our best selves, framed by our willingness to sacrifice for the good of our children and our future, and exhibited by an investment in what is best and beautiful about our people."— Adisa Ajamu

One thing that has not been consistently addressed in the Black community is the psychological trauma that was systematically perpetrated on kidnapped Afrikan people, who were forcefully bred and brutalized through the institution of slavery, for over 400 years, here in America. Because of white guilt and fear of retaliation and reparations, white Americans have swept this holocaust under the rug. Also, because of the hurt, pain, suffering and trauma that the remembrance of this time stirs up, Black people are reluctant to fully embrace and dissect the issues and legacy of this horrific period in the history of the world. Any victim of a traumatic experience will try to avoid revisiting their life-changing, devastating catastrophe at all costs. Victims of molestation, rape, murder, torture, kidnapping, and physical, psychological and sexual abuse, have a difficult time addressing these events in their tortured past. All these traumatic experiences were part of slave history, which Black people had to endure for over 400 years. We are not talking about one traumatic event in our lives, but an economic, political and social institution that lawfully and unequivocally supported this behavior and ideology for four centuries!

Did I miss the class on this subject in my elementary, middle, high school or college education? I may have remembered a paragraph or two in all my formal education, outside of the Black studies courses in college. These classes should be mandatory for all Americans, let alone Afrikan Americans. What happened to the mandatory counseling sessions for all descendants of the victims of the most devastating and horrific period in the history of the world? When did society fully address the psychological trauma and dysfunctional behavior that was inherited by the descendants of victims of America, who were thoroughly and systematically broken, stripped and beaten down to the point where they gave up their cultural definitions of reality and submitted to the definition that their masters forced fed to them? To the point where they believed they came up with that definition themselves?

Here we are, 400 years later, and we are still waiting for our masters to give us the answers to the problems in our community. How tragically ironic that we automatically and unassumingly turn to our masters for the solutions to the problems that he created for us in the first place! This mindset is the product of institutionalized slavery. This is the mindset of a slave, whose master took off his physical chains, but kept his psychological chains firmly reinforced, locked and secured, as Master Teacher Carter G. Woodson, in his book, "The Miseducation of the Negro," thoroughly and eloquently expounds on.

This is where the solution to Black male and female relationships must be addressed. There is a symbol and a saying from the Akan people in West Afrika called, Sankofa. It means: "One must return to their past, in order to move forward." Or the literal translation is to "go back and fetch it." This is where the solution to Black people's problems lies. We need to go back to Afrika in a mental sense, before we were brainwashed by Caucasians, and recapture the knowledge and culture that had us operating at the highest level of civilization the world has ever known. The Caucasian wants us to believe that our history began with the Middle Passage, otherwise known as the

Triangular Slave Trade. One can witness that the so-called Black History Month in February only observes and acknowledges Black people's accomplishments AFTER slavery. This is also an elegant tactic to keep Black people operating at a low level. Remember, we are only allowed to honor Black folks who have achieved and accomplished goals in the face of a racist institution and environment after slavery. This subtlety suggests that Black people's only goal is to be "just as good" as white folks, to be acknowledged as a success story and tribute to their race. In other words, Caucasians "set the bar" for Black people economically, socially, politically, and in regards to intelligence, beauty, health and nutrition. This paradigm sets the parameter for Black people to follow.

If one can control "the box" in which one lives, breathes and thinks in, then one doesn't have to worry about Black folks wanting to "escape" from it. Black folks are like a fish in an aquarium. A fish will bump its nose on the four sides of its aquarium. It will then instinctively know how far it can travel before pain or discomfort is inevitable. Once the fish internalizes its limits in the aquarium, it will not even attempt to travel outside his perceived barriers. One can even transfer the same fish and release him out into the vast ocean. The fish will instinctively swim around in the same small area, as if he was still in the aquarium. This is the same programmed behavior that Black people have been conditioned to accept. We were not only trained to think inside the parameters that our oppressor had established for us, but also, only focus on the paradigm of how far we have come since the advent of slavery. We are not allowed to focus on how far we have fallen when compared to our illustrious history before the white man invaded and colonized Afrika.

We need to return to Afrocentric ideology to retrieve the solutions to our problems that have been created by the same masters that still profit from our dysfunctional behavior, hurt, pain, suffering, low self-esteem, despair, disenfranchisement, ignorance and low-level behavior. It is still not in the

Caucasians' best interests for Black folks to be free, mentally, physically and spiritually. Caucasians need us to look up to them for approval of our worth in a reality that he has created and continues to profit from. Caucasians need us to blindly participate in a system that keeps him running the world. If we, one day, refused to participate in his system, his world would collapse over night. So the Caucasian's ultimate fear is the reawakening of Black people throughout the world. Especially Black people here in America. Because what Black people do in America, the world will follow! We are the trendsetters that the rest of the world looks up to for the latest fads in language, music, sports, fashion and entertainment.

There is a method to the madness, called the Black community. Miseducation is a strategy. Unemployment is a tactical deployment. Guns, gangs and drugs are a necessity. Substandard housing is deliberate. Police brutality and a racist court system is a conspiracy. Malnutrition and the absence of health care are blatant constants. Why do you think the Caucasian rewards the most ignorant, selfish and the lowest level of behavior of our people, by promoting them in the media, entertainment, sports and politics? Think about the most popular of our people. Think about how they made their fortunes and what keeps them popular? All of them are rewarded handsomely by promoting their master's agenda. One day, if they think of helping their people on a broad scale, then they will either suffer a tragedy themselves or their family or loved ones will. Look at the patterns and life of these so-called stars? One will begin to unravel a system that the more perceived wealth and power our Black elite acquire, the more of a slave to the system they become. If they want to keep their popularity and riches, then they must get with the program and never bite the hand that feeds them. So one can conclude that for Black folks to be free, and then one must think "outside of the box" that they created for us in the first place. This is where life, freedom and solutions dwell. As the character Morpheus told Neo in the movie, "TheMatrix" when he took the red pill, "Welcome to the real world."

I highly suggest for all Black people to read the Willie Lynch Letter. It can be found online, as well as in book form. Many of you are already familiar with it and some may even question the validity and authenticity of its author. Bottom line for me, authentic or not, it addresses the conditioning and state of the Black community as a direct result of our slave history. There is no question in anybody's mind that the issues of our community are a result of the institution of slavery. No one could ever argue that fact! It is real as real can be. Undeniably, unequivocally, undoubtedly and without question, we have been damaged by our slave history. Please read this literature. Please internalize it to the point where every thought and action amongst our people is based on the knowledge of this book. We need to be conscious and rethink all behavior that we deem as natural or ingrained. We need to recognize the repercussions of said thought and actions within our community. All Black people need to scrutinize all learned behavior that we accept as being second nature. Because if one goes back far enough in our lineage, one will discover that all behavior is learned. Our best teacher was and is the slave master.

I will paraphrase a passage from the Willie Lynch Letter: "You take the strongest and courageous Black male, the leader, of the group. You strip him down naked to humiliate him in front of his people. You beat him down to an inch of his life. You make sure all the women and children have the best view of what is taking place. You tie one of his arms to a horse. You tie the other arm to a different horse going the opposite direction. You do the same for each leg. You then proceed to whip each of the horses so that they will take off in opposite directions, as an attempt to pull this Black man's body apart. You then set his body on fire for all his people to witness.

The Black woman being traumatized by the experience will want to protect her sons. She will instinctively raise her sons to be docile and subservient, so he will not be perceived as a threat to the slave master. She will automatically let him hide behind her. She will teach him instinctively to lower his head and bow down. He will always accommodate his master and never go against him. She will then teach her daughter to be the opposite of her son. The mother will be tougher and harder on her daughter. She will teach her daughter to be hard, strong and independent. She will teach her daughter to be tough because she will not be able to rely on the Black man to protect and provide for her. The mother was coerced into raising her sons to be submissive and docile and her daughter will be tough, strong and independent."

Don't these Black male and female roles sound familiar today? No other race of people glorifies the strong, tough and independent character traits as their ideal definition in describing their women. But for the Black woman, this is her sole goal in life and the only definition that she needs to internalize in order to be considered a success in today's society. Enough is enough! What happened to the caring, nurturing, understanding, consoling, healing, life giving and gracious Black woman that found her strength in her femininity? We are still being bombarded with this "I don't need no man and I can take care of myself" definition of what a strong, Black woman is. Black women continue to emphasize that they are just as "hard" as men and define themselves by displaying this type of behavior. Sister, I am not your competition and you are not mine. You and I complement each other, not compete with each other. I was made to complete you and you were made to complete me.

Mothers are still raising their sons to be subservient and docile to authority figures for fear of their son's life. Why do you think our young, Black men rebel so much? Without the guidance of the father and the overprotective mother, our Black sons are relegated into displaying aggression in an unbalanced state. They have no self-control or discipline and display erratic and aggressive behavior when the situation does not warrant it. In young, Black men, aggression becomes a cry for help and not an appropriate response to the environment that they are faced with. Instead of our focus and definition of manhood being on fatherhood and protecting and providing for the Black woman, we are preoccupied with the issues of hurt, neglect and abandonment that run deep inside our genetic makeup. We refuse to believe that we have the capacity to put our own pain aside for the good of another human being, like our women or our innocent children. Black men have been conditioned to be motivated by fear and fear alone. Fear is the lowest vibration that one can live on, and they call it their reality. Fear is the opposite of love, not hate.

The chains have been taken off approximately 150 years ago, which is not that long ago. However, we still hold the same mentality which produces the same results that it did when it was first implemented. All is not lost. Thousands of years ago, our ancestors in Kemet were so brilliant that they foresaw a time in the future when Black people would be in a hopeless and dire position, stripped of all knowledge of self and no means or strategy to overcome its effects. Their hope would be dismal and they would hide their responsibility to overcome their plight by embracing ignorance. Our ancestors also knew that in order for a people to resurrect themselves to a higher consciousness, they must be put into the fire in order to eliminate the impurities and imperfections that they have acquired along the way. A diamond is a lump of coal that has withstood tremendous amounts of pressure over a long period of time. We have the potential to be that diamond, if we are willing to focus on transcending into our higher selves. This is the plight of the Black community. Let us use this opportunity to transcend to a higher consciousness and not dwell in a sea of inferiority and low self-esteem. Let us recreate our own reality through a system that has our best interests as its main objective. No one is going to do this for us. It is up to us to take the challenge and run with it, as if our life depended on it. As a reward for our diligence and faith, the kingdom of heaven here on Earth awaits us. We have done it before and we can do it again!

Black people of the Diaspora, and more specifically, here in America, are these chosen people. How can a people, who have been stripped of their mind, body and souls, become the undisputed leaders in the entertainment industry, such as music, dance, comedy, theatre, athletics and the arts? Whatever Black folks in America do, say, think or wear, the world runs behind them to try to emulate them and profit from their exploits. The only problem is, Black folks operate at such a low vibration that we in turn give the world nonsense, foolishness, materialism and buffoonery. We are the trend setters and the world follows our lead. Remember when the ghetto was an environment that one prided themselves on overcoming and escaping? Now the world is running to its culture to emulate, inspire and internalize.

Written on the temple walls in Kemet is the blueprint for the people of Afrikan descent to overcome this system of oppression they face today and assume their rightful place in the world as kings and queens. They have the potential to become rulers of their own dominion, operating at the highest level known to man. Just as the character of Jesus escaped to Kemet to avoid the wrath of King Herod, who was trying to kill him as a child, so must we return t Afrika, to receive the tools and keys to our resurrection. When you raise the Black man, you automatically raise the Black woman at his side. When one raises the Black woman, the child is never far behind, for the woman is the first teacher of the child. When you uplift the child, you automatically raise the family. When the family is raised, the community follows suit. This is because the family is the basic component or building block of the community. When you uplift the community, you build a strong nation. This is the science of our ancestors. This is where we must begin our resurrection.

Let us break down one of the most important stories that our ancestors wrote on the walls of their temples. Our ancestors wrote in symbols, known as Metu Neter, or what people call hieroglyphs today, because that is the best form of communication when speaking to the subconscious of the individual. They knew that they must bypass the conscious state of Black people in order for real change in behavior to incur. The story goes as follows:

In the beginning, there was a god named Ausar and his goddess wife named Auset. They were happily married. Ausar had a jealous brother named Set. Set was jealous because he did not have a beautiful wife of his own. Set's jealousy became uncontrollable to the point where he plotted to kill his brother so that he can have Auset for himself. Set secretly took Ausar's measurements and built an elaborate sarcophagus with gold and precious stones according to his brother's exact measurements. Set then held a party and invited his brother to come celebrate with him. At the party, Set showcased the beautiful sarcophagus he had built. Set announced that anyone who can fit in the coffin could have the sarcophagus for themselves. Of course, Ausar climbed into the coffin and it was a perfect match. Just then, Set slammed and nailed the sarcophagus shut, trapping Ausar inside as he whisked him away. Set murdered his brother and then proceeded to chop his brother's body into fourteen pieces and scattered them far and wide throughout the land of Kemet.

Set then approached Auset to force her hand in marriage. Auset adamantly refused his wishes and set out on a long journey to try to find the fourteen pieces of her late husband's body, that was scattered far and wide. Auset never gave up her quest of finding all the pieces of her late husband's body. She searched high and low and would go to great lengths to secure and gather all the pieces to her man. She was relentless and never gave up hope in putting him back together, piece by piece. Auset had found thirteen pieces of Ausar's body and was down to looking for the one last piece. Coincidently, that last piece was probably the most important out of all the pieces she had already collected, his penis. While searching in the depths of the Nile River, Auset finally found Ausar's last piece. Just as she was getting ready to retrieve it, a catfish came out of nowhere and swallowed it. This did not detour Auset's mission of putting her man back together. She reassembled the thirteen pieces she had found on a slab or table. She missed and wanted her husband with such passion she climbed on top of his reassembled body, in an effort to be with him one last time. In an instant, she turned into a hawk as she straddled her husband and vigorously started to flap her wings. Because of her dedication, faith, determination, will and perseverance, Ausar miraculously was resurrected! Auset also conceived a male child and named him Heru.

This was the original Immaculate Conception that other religions copied or stole from. When Heru was of age, he went after his uncle Set, to avenge his father's murder. Heru eventually overcame Set and was proclaimed the victor of their long battles.

In the picture below, notice that the three top points of the Sephedet are located on the Pineal glands and the bottom three points indicate their sexual organs and the physical dimension, the earth.

THE STAR OF DAVID IS SHARED BY RASTA'S, BUT I AM WILLING TO BET THEY TOO ARE UNAWARE OF ITS KEMETIC ORIGIN. THIS ICON'Z ORIGINAL NAME IS CALLED A SEPHEDET AND REPRESENTS THE UNION OF AUSAR AND ASET, KEMET'S FIRST FAMILY.

The above picture represents the original Trinity: The son, Heru on the left, the father Ausar, in the middle and the mother, Auset, on the right.

Let us break down this mythology and translate its meanings as it pertains to the predicament of the Black male and female relationship of today. As we discussed in earlier chapters of the book, in regards to decoding the Bible, we must administer and dissect the story according to the principles of universal law or metaphysics. Ausar represents the state of consciousness among Black men today. The Black man is mentally, spiritually and physically dead. He has lost his mind through the institution of slavery. His mind has been replaced with the mindset of someone who defines himself as less than a man. He is someone who will always play a subservient role and look to others to take care of him. He thinks of himself as anything but a man. He calls other Black men homeboys, playboys, pretty boys, players, ballers, pimps, macks, dawgs, cats, hogs, beasts, gangstas and niggas, to name a few. His spirituality is extinct. He makes no connection with himself and the unseen realm that he is innately connected to and where his true power lies. He doesn't realize his responsibility or connection to a higher power. He is disgusted, dissatisfied and does not care for the religion that he was made to practice when they first enslaved him four hundred years ago. Physically, he cannot even protect and provide for his woman or his children. He is sick and embraces his illness as a permanent state of his existence. He is the leader in all major categories when it comes to disease, addiction and illness, such as heart failure, high blood pressure, diabetes, arthritis, cancer, organ failure, impotency and many others. Mentally, he is operating at a level of retardation when compared to the beautiful mind of his past. He has an inferiority complex. It has become so ingrained in his psyche that he has given up any potential mental capacity that lies dormant in his DNA. He wants others to solve his problems for him. He will not search for or initiate solutions to his problems. He will embrace his problem and issues and define himself through them. He is the permanent victim and is comfortable with his victimization. He has convinced himself that he can't win a race that he hasn't even attempted to run.

These are the reasons why our Kemetic ancestors put our Black god, Ausar, into a coffin when they wrote the story on the temple walls in Kemet. Set, representing our oppression or white supremacy, tricked us into climbing in the coffin voluntarily, where he then proceeded to slam the lid and trap us in this state of existence. We are the living dead. We are the zombie or the undead. What is not brought to our attention is the means with which the European was able to kidnap so many Afrikans in Afrika and sell them in the slave trade. It was through his cunningness, manipulation, trickery, deceit, and use of the element of surprise and fear. We were tricked into this position just like Ausar was tricked into climbing in the coffin, presumably of his own freewill. Just as Set set up his brother Ausar, so did the European. When the European set foot in Afrika and conjured up the idea of the Triangular Slave Trade, he played the role of friend and confidant to the native Afrikan. He earned the head of the Afrikan tribe's trust by befriending them with gifts of gun powder, weapons, rum, trinkets and novelty items. Remember, the

Afrikan didn't use the sophisticated weaponry of guns at this time. He did
not know the ill effects of rum when you consume it. In fact, rum was like
crack cocaine to Afrikans during this time period. We have seen the ill
effects of the introduction of crack cocaine in our communities today. We
have still not recovered. The European also impressed the Afrikan with
simple glass beads, mirrors, magnifying glasses, music boxes and other
novelty items.

   This is the scam that started it all and is still the source of the
European's power over the darker peoples of the world. The more things
change, the more they stay the same. The white man would visit each
Afrikan tribe in the region that he set foot in. He would then show the leader
of that tribe his superior firepower that has never been witnessed in this
region before. The white man would then try to get into the chief's head. He
would tell him that if he acquired this advanced weaponry, his rule, kingdom
and his people's allegiance would be secured during his reign. No one would
dare go up against such a powerful chief as he. It would be considered utter
suicide for the fools that would even think about it. The white man would
tell all the chiefs in the region this same story. The only thing the white man
wanted in exchange for his weapons of mass destruction was the captives
that the chiefs had acquired during war time. One can imagine that if the
white man told every chief in the region this same story and supplied the
same weaponry, then war would instinctively resume. War was the
inevitable product of such an equation. Every chief's ego was exploited in
terms of the mentality of "keeping up with the Joneses." The act of doing
business with the Europeans became a matter of survival and necessity, and
not a luxury or an option that they were led to believe. Of course, with this
mindset firmly implanted in the Afrikan chief's reality, minor differences and
tensions, which were exploited between the tribes by the Europeans, were
now considered acts of war. Just for good measure, the Europeans
introduced rum into the equation to further seal the doom of hundreds of

millions of Afrikans. Afrikans, at the time, had no understanding of the potency of the consumption and consequences of this liquor. Rum was literally the liquid crack to Afrikans during this time period. The Europeans strategically introduced guns and drugs to the Afrikans, at the same time, in an effort to dismantle the culture and relationships among the tribes of the region. As a byproduct, the region became unstable. Sounds like the state of the Black community today. It is easier to steal from someone if their house is in chaos and disarray. War time is the best time to perform the biggest heists. The more things change, the more they remain the same.

As a result, the Afrikan chiefs of the region would instinctively do anything in their power to satisfy their addiction for guns and drugs. They even stooped so low as to invade neighboring villages to acquire captives to trade with the Europeans for more guns and drugs. When the chiefs could not obtain enough captives, he turned on his own people and condemned them to eternal servitude to the white man in exchange for more guns and drugs. This behavior weakened the Afrikan chief's kingdom. His army would become decimated by being overextended in its efforts to acquire captives from other villages in this perpetual time of war, instigated and manufactured by the white man. At the same time, the chief exchanged the strongest of his own people to the European because they fetched the most guns and rum. This made the chief highly vulnerable and susceptible to attack. The European would then step on the scene and finish the deal. The European would capture all that was left over and even enslaved the king, whom they had originally made the deal with in the first place. This was a timeless, flawless tactic that has been proven, tried and true, since the white man first came into contact with the indigenous people of the world to the present day. Look at the state of the Black community today and tell me that we have made progress. Black men are still killing each other to acquire guns, drugs, trinkets (bling) and novelty items (cars & clothes.) The Black man, like Ausar, has been tricked by his oppressor who befriended him.

Now he is trapped inside a coffin that has been built specifically for him, without him even knowing it. It was all a trap sprung on the unsuspecting Black god. The bait he used was the Black man's ego, which his oppressor fed with money, power and greed. The Black man has no clue how to get out of this trap. In fact, he doesn't even know it's a trap. The Black man is mentally, spiritually and physically dead and he doesn't even know that he is trapped in a coffin, specifically designed for him, according to his unique specifications that exploit his weaknesses.

For good measure, Set, representing white supremacy, scattered pieces of Ausar, who represents the Black man, all across the world. This was done so that there would be no way for anybody to put him back together. The pieces of Ausar, if they ever came together, wouldn't even recognize that they came from the same body. The pieces wouldn't acknowledge that they used to be one whole body at one time. The pieces would never be united, always separated. During slavery, the white man shipped the Afrikan all throughout the Diaspora. He shipped some to Brazil, Costa Rica, Panama, Belize, Cuba, Haiti, Jamaica, Nicaragua, Guyana, Trinidad & Tobago, Bahamas, United States, Columbia, Puerto Rico, Honduras, Mexico and many other foreign lands. This represents Set scattering Ausar's pieces all over the world. When men of Afrikan descent meet other men of Afrikan descent in each other's foreign land, they don't realize that they are pieces of the same body: The Afrikan body. Even though they speak different languages, dress differently, have different hair textures and skin shades, they are actually pieces of the one! Ausar's pieces have been apart for so long that they don't recognize that they were literally cut out from the same Afrikan body which is undeniable. Black men unite! Understand that we are the same. Our body has been scattered throughout the world in an effort to keep us apart. When we return to Afrika or Kemet, we make ourselves whole again. We become united. We are the one! This is the white man's fear. That one day the Black man will understand his plight and what has been done to him and work to put himself back together again.

Remember, the one piece of Ausar that Auset could not find was his penis. The penis, of course, represents Ausar's manhood. This was represented in Kemet by a tall phallic symbol called a Tekken. The Greeks named it the Obelisk. The Washington Monument in our nation's capital is an imitation of this Kemetic structure. Obelisk, by the way, means "meat cleaver" in Greek, because this is what the European has done to the unsuspecting Afrikan man: they castrated him. The basic motivation for the system of white supremacy is to destroy the Black man's manhood. This was needed in order to enslave him and his people. For without a means to protect and provide for his woman and children, the Black man was relegated to being less than a man. Protecting and providing for his woman and children defined the Black man's manhood before he was enslaved. This definition of manhood has now been replaced by swagger or street credibility, his car, his ego, violence, his clothes, haircut & jewelry, his bank account and how many women he can have sex with without being attached to them. Fatherhood and being a good husband are not even in the equation of being a man anymore! The one thing that Auset could not give us, or put back together, was our manhood. Black men are going to have to do that part for themselves. When this event takes place and the Black man becomes one again, the game is over!

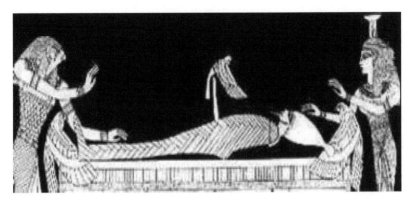

The Kemetic god Ausar is pictured above, lying down with an erection. His goddess wife, Auset, represented by the hawk, lands on Ausar's penis to resurrect him from the dead. Heru, on the left, is their son, who was conceived by their union. This is the first Immaculate Conception story known to man. Coincidently, the word "erection" comes from the word "resurrection."

Auset, in the story, represents the Black woman and the mission that she must assume to resurrect her man and her people. During slavery, the Black woman was willing to go to any lengths with her white slave master, in order to try to save and protect her family. By going along with her master, she was guilty, through her conspiracy of silence, of supporting the program. Because she wanted to protect her son's life from the slave owner, she told him to let his master use his physical labor, strength, power, ingenuity and knowledge for the benefit of the master's estate and not his own. She trained him to be docile and never outshine or threaten the master in any shape, form or fashion. She taught her son that master knew what was best for him and to never question master's intentions.

The Black woman also instilled in her daughter this docile mindset. She told her daughter to give up herself willingly, so that the master wouldn't be displeased or angry. She trained her daughter to separate her spirit from her body so that when the white man raped her, she would not be psychologically scarred for the rest of her life and still be functional. She taught her daughter that if she didn't fight her rape, then she wouldn't be beaten or tortured as much. She even told her daughter that there was an incentive, for her if the master was pleased with her, then she may receive some scrap material or food as reward for her submission to him.

The Black woman maintained this secret relationship with the white man throughout slavery in an effort to save her children from the pain, suffering and even death inflicted by her slave master. The Black woman saw no other alternative or means to protect her family from this despicable situation that she was forced to make sense out of. She understood that the more docile she and her children behaved, the more rewards, gifts and higher status she would receive on the plantation. All in all, the Black woman needed to make the sacrifices because in her reality, the only person who can protect and provide for her was the white man. She felt that she had no other choice but to offer herself and her children up to the white man so he can do what he pleases as a means of her family's survival.

Here we are in 2010. The Black woman is still going along with her slave master's program. The secret relationship between Black women and white men still exists and has been exposed. Because the Black man has been decimated by the white power structure and cannot protect and provide for her in his present state, the Black woman relies on the system that the white man has built at the expense of her man. Corporate America gives her what she needs to provide for her family with the absence of her man in the household. The Black woman has embraced the white man's system, at the expense of the Black man, and is being rewarded handsomely for it. The Black woman makes more money than her man. She is more educated than her man. She is in better health than him. She has better credit than him. This is the basis for the Black woman's complaint about the lack of quality Black men at her disposal. Instead of being rewarded with pieces of material, trinkets and food scrapes, as she was when she knew she was a slave, she is now compensated with designer clothes, shoes, jewelry and the finest restaurants. She supports her own lifestyle. She buys her own cars and homes. She listens to songs that glorify her independence and belief that she is somehow better off being by herself. She pays for her own vacations and travels the world. Because she can do these things, she is labeled a success, according to the white man's economic system.

But deep down inside, she is not happy. She is not complete. Her slave master hasn't really given her anything but the illusion of security, success and happiness. Her slave master can take these things from her at anytime. There is no man to stand up for her. So many sisters have given their lives to achieving their careers at the expense of their children and their man. They have achieved the titles, like the slave received higher status on the master's plantation. They have the prestige and are showered with all the accolades that her master can bestow on her. She acquires all of this at the expense of the Black man and her children. Her sons are confused and angry at the world for being neglected and forced to deal with life issues without any guidance. Her daughters are still served up to the slave master. They are prostituted in music videos, in fashion, in the movies, in the entertainment field and in corporate America. They are called bitches and hoes and nobody is there to stand up for them. They are mentally, physically, sexually, spiritually and emotionally abused, and everyone just goes along with the program. Since no one is there to love and protect her, she internalizes this lower level behavior and defines herself as such.

Remember our Kemetic story. Auset did not turn to her husband's murderer, Set, to try to make a life with him out of necessity or fear. She refused all his advances and attempts to manipulate her. She never gave up on being at her man's side, even after his perceived death. This is another key on resurrecting the Black male and female relationship. Auset wanted nothing to do with her husband's murderer. She did not make any deals with him, let alone support his system. She was never motivated by fear. She was always motivated by the love that she had for her husband. She never gave up on him. She never conceived defeat. She never envisioned life without him. She understood that she would never be happy unless her husband could experience life with her. She never left his side to do her and her master's agenda. It was always about doing "US!" Separation was not an option! Auset would not have it any other way. There was no reality or life without her man by her side. This is the key to Black male and female relationships. We both need to internalize what has been done to us. Instead of blaming each other, we should look at the system that made this reality for us. We both need to do whatever it takes to put the needs of our mate in front of our own personal needs and wants.

The Black god Ausar shown on the temple walls in Kemet with his erection to symbolize his being "Born Again." The Washington Monument in Washington D.C. is a plagiarized version of the Tekken or Obelisk representing "New Life" in the "New World," otherwise known as America.

Black man, find your manhood. Your woman can't give that back to you. Make an oath to define your manhood by your ability to protect and provide for your woman and your children. Get your right mind back. Embrace your spirituality that gives you the resources and insight to fight and define the system of white supremacy. Get your health back. How will you protect and provide for your community when you are weaker than your woman and children? Raise your consciousness so that you will be able to resist the temptations of lower level behavior. As long as your oppressor has you defining your reality at this level, he owns you because he can manipulate and control you. Raise your vibration and you raise your nation!

Black woman, put all your time, energy and resources in putting your man back together. Never make a decision based on fear or money, for they are both illusions that the white man has enslaved you with.

Hold your man to his highest standard. Let go of your fears and ego; let him be a man despite you wanting to take control of the situations. How is he supposed to be a man if you won't let him? You have done it your way and look where it has taken our community. Get out of the driver's seat; scoot your butt over and let a man drive to the Promised Land. For every hour your give your job or the system, you should give your man at least three hours. Your time and energy have been consumed building the white man's system of oppression and it has built the most powerful and richest country in the world. Imagine what you can do if you put all that time and energy in the Black man. If your man doesn't want the responsibility of being a man, then by all means let him go. But believe me, Black women, for every one that doesn't want to be a man, there are several that do. You won't even have to look to find them; they will find you. You probably have already overlooked them. For those Black women who are driven by ego and want a man only for themselves, I suggest you stick to your guns. But remember, Black women, when we were at our highest level of existence, in the history of all civilizations, the best, strongest and brightest leaders of our people had more than one wife. Believe me; a real man does not have to take Inner G from one entity in his life so that he can share it with another entity in his life. The Black man, being the Sun, can sustain more than one universal body if he has the capacity to sustain them. Not all Suns are created equal. Some burn brighter, stronger and more brilliant than others. Know the man you are dealing with. Know what he is capable of and not capable of, and act accordingly.

Black women, believe in your man as if your life depended on it and he has no choice but to rise to the occasion. You have been letting us off the hook by supporting our lower level, cowardly and dysfunctional behavior. You have the power to put us back together. You have the power to resurrect our nation. You have the power to achieve all the goals and dreams that you desire. Just remember, it all starts with you focusing and investing in the Black man first. You have tried to obtain the career, the house, the car and the clothes, and you have been successful. You thought that once you acquired those things, you could "plug in" the Black man as the final step in creating your fairytale ending. You have found out that it doesn't work that way. I offer you this strategy: Invest your time and Inner G into your man FIRST and all those other things you want in life will fall into place. Make sure you select that right man that practices righteousness, humility and embraces his higher consciousness; otherwise, you will be setting yourself up for failure later on.

The last character of this story is Heru. Heru is the potential in all of us. It is our true self that lays dormant in our entire DNA, waiting to assume its divine responsibility and destiny. Heru represents the future generations of the Black family. He is the savior in the midst of his people. Out of the yearning of our ancestors to be free, one will rise up from the ashes and lead his people to the Promised Land. Heru is that defining Inner G or spirit. Heru is where you get the word "Hero" from. We have all seen in the movies how the hero goes against all odds with no fear, reaches into the jaws of death and saves the world from destruction, when all hope seems lost. Heru represents our higher consciousness. Heru represents the infinite possibilities that we have access to, as long as we have the faith and determination to accomplish what we will. Heru never fails. Heru was born out of the union of his father, who was resurrected from the dead by his mother, who was relentless in putting her man back together.

The solution to the Black male and female relationship has been on the temple walls in Kemet for thousands of years. It has been hiding from us in plain sight. The knowledge has been waiting for us to achieve a level of consciousness before it can reveal its secrets to us. It was waiting for the right moment in time when we could fully internalize the knowledge so that we could use it properly. That time is now. We all came to Earth at this particular place, at this particular time, to witness and be a part of the resurrection of the Black man and the Black woman. Let us all take responsibility for giving up our responsibility to honor the Black man and the Black woman. You are here for a reason; you just forgot what it was. We have been preoccupied and led astray from our true destiny in life. Let us embrace the struggle, and in so doing, we embrace each other. They created the illusion of this reality because we did not want to be responsible for achieving higher consciousness. Our ancestors specifically wrote this blueprint for our resurrection for this particular time and place. Like they say in the movie Mission Impossible, "This is your mission in life, if you choose to accept it."

Black Love Topics & Issues

• Don't ask your mate for what they are not equipped to give you. Your expectations of them may exceed their capabilities in their present state.

• Don't select your mate based on their potential. Potential, with no work behind it, will always lead to disappointment. If they are lazy in their life's goals and dreams, then they will be lazy in your relationship with them. Love and accept them for who they are now and not what they can become.

• Treat your relationship like a Wall Street investment. If you do not make a profit off your investment, get rid of it and invest your time and Inner G into another stock. Never blame the stock for your losses or disappointments. Blame your poor judgment that initially invested in the stock in the first place.

• Boys like the chase, not the attachment. Men hate the chase, want the attachment. Women, if a man pursues you too hard to the point where it seems like harassment, then know that he is only interested in the hunt. The harder you put up a fight, the more intense his actions will be in capturing you. The goal for the man becomes the devouring of his prey, not protecting and providing for it once he has captured it. Women set themselves up by playing this game. Real women will be open to a man's Inner G if her intuition is operating from a higher frequency. She will know right away if his Inner G in conducive or destructive to her well-being. There will be no need to go back and forth in her communication with him that sends out mixed signals. A real man will let his Inner G stand on its own. There is no need to convince a woman how great you are by over-pursuing her. Men, let your light shine and it stands and attracts on its own. A real man does not have to chase the woman, only court her.

• Black women have the biggest egos. Because of her slave history and oppression, she has been forced to fend for herself. The Black man was taken from her and continues to be psychologically destroyed. For five hundred years, she has had to protect and provide for herself and her children on her own. The lowest level of consciousness is self-survival. This is the Black woman's state of mind. The ego thrives in this mindset and environment. Black women must acknowledge this lower level of consciousness and not define themselves by it. It is not a natural or healthy state of existence. Black women, remember one thing: "Humility kills the ego and opens the heart, which is the first level of higher consciousness." Humble yourselves. Do not define yourselves by your strength, but by your vulnerability.

• Courtship today is only focused on trust and not love. The Black community mistakes one for the other when they are two different entities unto themselves. Once trust is accomplished, the relationship is relatively over. The Black community is operating at such a low frequency that trust is something that has to be earned not unconditionally given. This goes against nature and our best interests as a people. Our community has become preoccupied with fear, so that love is virtually unattainable. The opposite of love is not hate; it is fear. So for love to happen, feelings of fear cannot take place. If one has fear in their heart, trust becomes the only issue they want to accomplish, not love. Since our community is preoccupied with only trusting one another and not unconditionally loving one another, trust becomes the main and only focal point in our relationships. Love is not in the equation; it's all about trust. So Black men are preoccupied with trying to convince women to trust them. While Black women are only concerned with the consequences of what will happen if they let their guard down and trust a man. So the Black man solely focuses on and works to gain the Black woman's trust and not her love. Once he has her trust, which is acknowledged by the Black woman having sex with him, the Black man's mission has been accomplished. All he wanted to do was gain her trust, which has nothing to do with his love. The Black woman's only goal was to see what happens after she gave the man her trust by having sex with him. When he doesn't show his feelings of love for her, she is hurt because she feels that she was led astray. She is confused because she set the parameters of the relationship, which were only focused on "trust" and not love. The woman will add this to her other experiences of disappointment and betrayal and put the same parameters on the next man she meets. The man will still compete to gain another woman's trust and not her love. The solution to this self-fulfilling prophecy in the Black community is to love first and trust second.

No one can Use you without Your Permission:

Let us put this concept into perspective. If one is operating according to their higher consciousness, they will understand that their behavior in their physical bodies has a direct correlation in regards to reaching and attaining higher spiritual consciousness, once they transcend from their physical bodies into the higher, spiritual realm. In other words, people of higher consciousness understand that their experiences and behavior in their physical bodies will dictate how far they will travel in the spiritual dimension. The physical dimension is the threshold or proving ground that the spirit must pass through in order to achieve higher, spiritual consciousness. So when we help other people by sacrificing ourselves and putting them first, we build collateral in the spiritual realm, which Christians call "Heaven." So when we give people money, when we take them in at our inconvenience and expense, when we give them resources or invest our time and Inner G into their upliftment in spite of ourselves, then do not look to that person for your reward. Their actions to your kindness have no bearing on what you will receive in the spiritual dimension. All you are doing is displaying your higher spiritual consciousness by exhibiting kindness, selflessness, humility and love. Those attributes are sufficient unto themselves and no one can take that away from you.

Recognize that it is our lower selves or lower consciousness that wants us to play the "victim" role. It wants us to lash out at the individual that "took advantage" of us. It wants us to operate in a defensive state, so as to never get "hurt" again. It wants us to define ourselves by the physical dimension inside our physical bodies. This is how we become "trapped" in the lowest dimension that the spirit can descend to. We should acknowledge and operate according to our higher selves, otherwise known as the "God" in us. As one knows, you can't use God. It's like trying to steal from a person whose heart is generous and would have given you what you stole, if you only asked for it. The burden and lower level karma will always be the taker and never the one who gives and continues to give, even when it seems like they have no more. When one operates at their higher or "God" consciousness, they become infused with infinite possibilities and inexhaustible resources. They will always manifest that which they need when it seems like they have given it all away. They will not want for anything and will always be looked after and taken care of. It is only when we operate according to our lower consciousness that things seem to dry up and become barren. In conclusion, thank the people you have given to, whether they were appreciative or not, for they gave you the opportunity to prove your worth in your efforts to achieve higher, spiritual consciousness in the spiritual dimension. Remember, we are only here in the physical dimension for what seems like the blink of an eye compared to the eternity we experience in the spiritual world. Focus on your higher, spiritual consciousness and not the illusion of the lower, physical dimension that we are trapped in.

A Sexual Ritual:

Be conscience and aware of all of the variables that your partner's zodiac sign is sensitive to. I came up with a generic ritual that one can do to raise the couple's consciousness during sex. Perform this ritual before sexual intercourse with your partner and you will be able to unlock the best in them, as well as bring out the best in yourself. The idea of this ritual is, first of all, to raise both of your vibrations to attain higher consciousness, and also to direct your sexual Inner G to manifest your desired purpose into physical existence.

1. Before the ritual, the couple should go on a 3-day, 7-day or 40-day fast. The longer the fast, the more powerful the ritual will be. The fast should include no meat or dairy products and nothing to drink but water with lemon.

2. While fasting, the couple should make a CD to be played during the ritual. I recommend Me'Shell Ndege'ocello; The Spirit Music Jamia: The Dance of the Infidel

3. In the place of the ritual, preferably the bedroom, burn sage and/or Frankincense and Myrrh incense an hour before the ritual takes place. This "cleanses" the room of lower level Inner G so that the couple's higher Inner G can be optimized. Keep the door closed at all times.

4. Include four objects that represent the four elements in your ritual. For example, obtain a rock representing the earth, massage oil representing water, a candle or fire place representing fire, and your breath, a feather or a fan to represent air.

5. Look at the zodiac chart mentioned above. Obtain colors, numbers and fragrances that resonate within your partner's particular zodiac

sign. Also, be aware of the region of the body that is ruled by their particular zodiac sign.

6. Include a libation, such as alcohol and chocolate. Each person should only take a sip and a small bite to give honor and tribute to the higher, spiritual forces who you want to communicate with to manifest your dreams in the physical dimension.

7. Both people should strip down naked and stand in front of each other, holding each other's hands. Each person will close their eyes and visualize their partner in their minds. Neither one should say a word. This act will allow you to see your partner on a spiritual level without the distraction of their physical bodies. Do this for at least 2 minutes.

8. Next, the couple should turn sideways towards a mirror, embracing each other. The woman should be looking over her left shoulder, facing the mirror, and the man should be looking over his left shoulder, looking away from the mirror. After two minutes, the couple should switch places while keeping their embrace. Now the man, still looking to his left, is now looking at the mirror, and the woman, still looking to her left, is now looking away from the mirror.

9. The woman always comes first. Lay her down on the bed on her stomach or face down. The back of our bodies represent our past. Have her focus on things she wants to leave behind that are keeping her from moving forward. Things that cause her fear, stress, hurt, abuse, relationships, worries and childhood traumas.

10. Have her write these things down on a paper and have her immediately burn them after the massage on her stomach.

11. Massage her from the head first, ending at the bottom of her feet. Make sure the man is pushing and pulling all that lower level Inner G down to her feet while he is touching her.

12. Make sure the one massaging is focusing on the part of the body that her sign rules. Always go back and touch that part of the body before and after you start a different region in the body.

13. Get rid of her lower level Inner G by having her write down these character traits that keep her from achieving her higher consciousness. According to her zodiac sign (fire, earth water or air), have her burn it, bury it, flush it or throw it to the wind.

14. Turn her over on her back and start to work on the front of her body. The front side of her body represents her future. This time, the both of you will reaffirm the things she wants to achieve in her future. Both of you should only be focused on the optimistic things that she wants to accomplish in her life. Focus on her infinite possibilities.

15. Now you will start the massage from the bottom of her feet to the top of her head. Make sure you incorporate all the props you acquired that resonate with her particular zodiac sign.

16. After the front massage, have her write down on another piece of paper the things she wants to accomplish in the future. Crumple up the paper and have her eat it.

17. Switch positions and repeat the same ritual with your male partner. Follow it by sexual intercourse focused on manifesting each other's needs and not your own.

18. Don't be afraid to use your imagination and incorporate concepts and ideas that you come up with on your own. The more creative and unique the couple's ritual is, the more powerful the ritual will become.

Sexual Healing:

Everyone is aware of the "sixty-nine" sexual position, but few are aware of its healing properties. This sexual position can be used to heal mental, spiritual and physical ailments in the body if implemented properly by the couple. First off, the man must always be positioned on the bottom and the woman is always on top. This position is similar to the two double-A batteries found in your television remote control. Although both batteries are laying side-by-side, they are positioned at opposite ends of each other. They are lined up so their positive or masculine end of the battery is positioned next to the negative or feminine end of the other battery. They must be in this position in order for the electricity or Inner G to flow in a continuous loop from one battery to the other. If they were not lined up in this position, the electricity or Inner G could not flow or otherwise be utilized. The same is true for the sixty-nine sexual position. Inner G flows from the positive or male principle to the negative or female principle. Once this Inner G is allowed to continuously flow through the male and female, it can be utilized for our individual healing purposes. You may ask yourself, "How can we utilize this Inner G?" Each person must meditate on the things their partner wants to heal mentally, spiritually and physically. You must concentrate and focus on your partner's needs and not your own. If each partner can engage in this position with their partner's needs over their own, then they can utilize this flow of Inner G to heal themselves. Also, the flow of Inner G must be maintained for as long as possible. Each person should suppress their orgasm as long as possible. If they don't, the flow of Inner G will be disrupted and the healing will cease. The best case scenario is for each partner to have an orgasm simultaneously after at least 30 minutes in this position. This position can be utilized as much as possible to keep a balanced and healthy mind, body and soul.

Stress and Relationships:

What people fail to understand is that stress is a natural human reaction. The characteristics of what we determine as stress are really the body's natural defensive reactions when it is exposed to danger. The symptoms we call stress are triggered by our reaction to "fight or flight" when we are in danger. Our body prepares for our response to danger. Our adrenaline and blood pressure goes up to a heightened state to either stand up and meet danger head-on or run away from it. We fall to a lower state of consciousness where self-survival is our only concern. In nature, these confrontations only last three-to-five minutes because our response to the danger is only meant to be sustained until the danger is no longer prevalent. Once we are safe, our bodies go back to their natural, non-stressful state of existence.

Unfortunately, under white supremacy, the Black community was designed for Black people to live in a constant state of stress or "fight or flight." The Black community is bombarded with constant attacks in relation to drugs, guns, alcohol, malnutrition, miseducation, unemployment, substandard housing, materialism and slave history & mentality. This leaves Black people only two solutions to their controlled environment. One can either constantly fight the system that was meant to destroy them or try to escape the neighborhood. Either choice results in an imbalance of the person's mind, body and soul. Stress now becomes a way of life and not a temporary response to danger. The Black man and woman are so strong that they now accept their stressful condition as a way of life and adopt it as their reality. This is where we get the term, "Ghetto Mentality." It represents the lower level response of a person who is constantly living in a state of "fight or flight." They become greedy, self-serving, defensive, cold, hardened, resourceful, conniving, ruthless and deceitful. All these attributes are necessary when one feels that they are constantly in danger and under attack. As a result, any relationship that a person tries to have with this mind set will not be healthy. When it is all said and done, each person in the relationship will only be interested in their own self-survival and well-being, even at the expense of the one they say they love.

Trust, which is the foundation of any healthy relationship, cannot not be displayed or acquired in this lower level environment. These two people are doomed to fail before they even start their relationship. This reminds me of the flight attendant's speech about putting on your own oxygen mask before you put it on your child, in the case of an emergency. If the adult passes out, the child will suffer and probably die. So it is important for the parent to make sure they are out of danger so that they are there to help the child. If the parent passes out before the helpless child, for lack of oxygen, then both of them will perish. In relationships, make sure you are doing the work on yourself first before you try to participate in any relationship. If you don't have it together, none of your relationships will have it together. Love starts at home before you can give it to anyone else. Make sure you understand the things that are causing you stress in your everyday lives. Try to eliminate these variables before you bring another person into your reality. Your relationship will thank you for it.

Why Women Love So Hard:

Oxytocin is best known for its roles in female reproduction: 1) it is released in large amounts after distension of the **cervix** and **vagina** during labor, and 2) after stimulation of the **nipples**, facilitating **birth** and **breastfeeding**, respectively. Recent studies have begun to investigate Oxytocin's role in various behaviors, including **orgasm**, social recognition, **pair bonding**, **anxiety**, trust, **love**, and maternal behaviors.

This chemical is released when the woman has an orgasm or when her breasts are stimulated. It connects the woman to the other body that is doing the stimulation. This chemical, as well as a spiritual connection, creates the bond, whether she wants it or not. This can be confusing for a woman who wants to leave a man alone, but for the life of her, cannot seem to let go. You are not crazy, weak or sprung. It is nature doing what nature intended. Women, be aware of this chemical reaction and act accordingly.

What is being unfaithful?

We are comprised of three components that make the whole of a person: the mind, the body & the spirit. The white man has taught us to only focus on the body because he has a hard time deciphering and recognizing the other two components. The Bible says that if you have a thought about sin, you are guilty of it. Let me explain. True love exists on a plane where lower level thoughts cannot dwell. Love is incapable of fear or being subjected to the ego, which causes one to justify his lower level behavior. You can cheat with your mind and/or spirit and it carries the same value or impact as cheating physically. Does this make one a bad person and should they tell their mate? Of course not, one should be aware that if these lower level thoughts do creep into their minds, they are not as far along in love as they think they are. Remember, love is a state of mind, not a feeling that someone gives you outside of yourself. Getting to and staying in love is a constant struggle because man is made of imperfect material. Love is the first level of higher consciousness. One must rise in love; one can never fall in it.

We are constantly bombarded with lower level Inner G that is designed to keep us prisoners of our lower selves. Understand what is being done to you and strategize accordingly. Don't accept these thoughts as a normal function in your reality, for they weigh as equally as one who has physically had sex with another person. Coincidently, one can physically be faithful for fifty years of their marriage, but cheat on them every day with their thoughts and their spirit. But the white man has taught us that this is a healthy and a successful marriage because it only concentrates on the physical aspect of marriage. I disagree and reject that type of relationship. In fact, the spiritual realm is really 90% of what we call reality. So for me, this is the worst possible case of being unfaithful. I would rather have my wife sleep with another man than to mentally and spiritually be unfaithful to me. Do not be so focused on the physical dimension, for it is only 10% of what we call reality. Remember, there are three aspects that make up a human being. Just because one has never physically had sex with someone outside their marriage doesn't make them faithful or a good spouse. On the other hand, the investment of our time and Inner G, whether physical, mental or spiritual, is the key to understanding whether you have been faithful to your significant other. If your time and Inner G is more invested outside of your relationship and not in the nurturing of it, then you have already broken up with that person without you or them even acknowledging it. Remember, love starts within before it can be expressed in a relationship with another person. One must hold themselves to the higher standard of love if they want their partner to reciprocate it. Love has always been an internal or personal journey. Remember, we attract that which we put out. Our mate is our reflection.

Long-distance Relationships:

These relationships are really modes of survival until the couple can reconnect with one another. Don't fool yourself into believing that it is anything more than what it is. Your relationship will not grow stronger and your heart will not grow fonder. Men need their women to reflect them in their immediate geographical location. Just as women need the Inner G from their men to give them inspiration and direction. If you eliminate the opportunity for this science to take place, they will naturally drift apart and find other entities to take their place. Please do not be fooled. Long-distance relationships are never done by choice. Both parties are literally in survival mode until they can share each other's Inner G.

Remember, self-survival is the lowest level of consciousness.

Food for Thought:

I like to relate the concept of having sex as making and consuming a batch of homemade, hot-out-of-the oven, chocolate chip cookies. First, the man or the woman has to gather all the ingredients out of the kitchen and lay them out on the kitchen counter. This act can be related to the man or woman handling their mate with care and taking time to acknowledge all of their attributes individually and not as a whole. Take time to recognize all the characteristics of your mate before you engage in the act. Acknowledge their personality traits that you adore, as well as visiting their physical features. To appreciate the chocolate chip cookie that you are about to consume, pay homage to the ingredients that go into making the recipe. To make chocolate chip cookies, one needs eggs, milk, butter, flour, sugar and chocolate. The totality of your mate consists of individual ingredients as well. Take the time to acknowledge, pay homage and explore these attributes that your mate possesses. When you are honoring your mate for having a specific attribute that you love, verbally tell them why you admire that part of their body or personality. Pay homage to each individual ingredient before you combine them altogether in your mixing bowl.

The next step of the recipe is to take your time and carefully blend all the ingredients together. This is where you should connect all the individual attributes of your mate into a single entity. Let them know how the sum of the individual parts makes a greater whole. Love and appreciate the whole person and not just stay in one particular area for a longer period of time than another area. A good way to get this point across to your partner is to look at them directly in their eyes and tell them how beautiful they are and how fortunate you are that they chose you to be with them in such an intimate way. Thank them for believing and trusting you for exposing their most vulnerable part of themselves for you to appreciate.

Now you want to shape the dough and put it on a cookie sheet that was oiled with butter, so the cookies won't stick. Make sure the oven was preheated before you put them in the oven. So now, we are about to engage in the act. We want to make sure our partner is thoroughly prepared and ready to be placed in the oven. Preheating the oven is a must, especially for the Black woman. Always check the oven first before inserting the cookies. For the cookies to be ready for consumption, they need to be exposed to a certain amount of heat for a particular length of time. If the heat or time is too short, the cookies will also suffer. Coincidently, if the temperature and time is too high or long, the cookies will burn. Making excellent cookies requires the best ingredients exposed to the perfect amount of time and temperature. Now your cookies are ready for consumption. Be mindful when you are eating them; be aware of the time and Inner G it took to make them, as well as the quality of the ingredients that made them. Don't be afraid to verbally express to each other how good the cookies taste. Sound effects are greatly encouraged. It makes the cookies taste better.

Picked from the Vine:

In all of life's experiences, timing is everything. If one was to pick a tomato off the vine too soon, it would be green and bitter to the taste. The tomato would be ruined. You cannot make up for your hasty decision by trying to put the tomato back on the vine. It doesn't work that way. Once the tomato is picked, it contains all the potential that it has and cannot grow anymore. The tomato's life was cut short. Think about this when we are first trying to court in a relationship. Understand that timing is everything. Sometimes, it is okay to sleep with someone on the first date; other times, it is not. If one has sex or picks the tomato too soon, then the relationship will not have a chance to grow. The relationship will always be underdeveloped. But, if both people are right for the picking, the tomato can be the sweetest and juiciest they have ever eaten. Be mindful of the space you and your partner are in when you meet. Pick your tomato accordingly.

Oral Sex:

This is the best way to fully understand and communicate with the most intimate and sacred part of a person's spirit. The Inner G in the throat magnifies and intensifies all Inner G that it comes in contact with. This is why babies are always putting things in their mouths. They are trying to figure out what these new objects in this physical dimension are supposed to be about. Remember, they have just crossed over from the spiritual dimension. This reality is brand new to them, so they use their mouths to communicate with the spirit of objects around them. The throat absorbs the unseen Inner G of a person, place or thing. It is the ultimate receptor for all Inner G. When a man performs oral sex on a woman, he is receiving her pure and sacred Inner G source. This Inner G is coming straight from her power source, the womb. This is the gateway to heaven. When she achieves orgasm, he is consuming the vortex that transfers Inner G from the spiritual world to the physical dimension. This is empowering. This Inner G, when accessed and directed appropriately, can be used to heal, manifest and enhance whatever the man is focused on. It is an undiluted, pure source of feminine Inner G that holds the power to manifest miracles.

When a woman performs oral sex on a man and he ejaculates, then his Inner G is not as pure as the woman's. The man's sperm takes about seventy days to mature. In these seventy days, a man passes along in his semen all his thoughts, actions, stress, and lower level Inner G that he has experienced during this time, as well as his higher level Inner G. All this Inner G is ingested in the woman as well. A woman is powerful enough to consume all Inner G and filter out the lower level variety. If a woman wants to ingest a man's pure and sacred Inner G, she needs to continue to perform oral sex after the man has fully ejaculated. A man has the ability to have multiple orgasms after he has ejaculated, according to the level of consciousness he has attained. For these men, they can continue to have five or six orgasms after ejaculation. The man will still ejaculate spiritually, even though no semen is produced. The feeling will even be the same as if there were semen produced. A woman doesn't have to do anything but leave her mouth on him during this time. She will still feel the muscles contract, just like a regular orgasm. Although no semen is produced, pure spiritual and sacred Inner G of the man is released. This is where the true essence of the man lies. This is where women can communicate more spiritually and more intensely with their man. You can literally see his heart whether he wants you to or not.

Premature Ejaculation:

Premature ejaculation is not a physical problem; it is a mental and spiritual deficiency in the man. If a man suffers from this trait, he has become comfortable and content in embracing his lower consciousness. This type of man defines himself by his lower, physical self and not by his higher spiritual consciousness. In the animal kingdom, there is no such thing as premature ejaculation. In fact, the faster they ejaculate, the better off they will be in their ongoing task of survival of the fittest. Man has an animalistic characteristic as well as a higher spiritual aspect. So this condition is a precursor to understanding what level of consciousness the man operates from. Coincidently, man's spiritual self controls his physical, lower self. If this is the case, then in order for man to overcome any physical deficiency, like premature ejaculation, he must first embrace his higher self, which will reign over his body. There is no pill, physical technique or exercise that will cure a man from this condition. The only way for him to overcome this ailment is to raise his consciousness. The first step that the man must take is to show humility and kill his ego. The second step is not to define himself or his reality by his physical body, or take stock in this physical dimension over the spiritual realm. Only he can do this for himself; no one can do it for him. He must make this decision for himself.

If a woman wants to help her man overcome this condition, she must raise the bar in regards to what she expects from him sexually. Women do themselves a disservice by either accepting her man in his present state or by belittling him for his unsatisfactory performance. A woman must walk the fine line between holding her man accountable to his higher self, while at the same time being nurturing and supportive of his condition that he is trying to overcome. A simple way for a woman to help her man is to speak to him during sex. She has the capacity to empower her man, if the man is willing to accept her guidance and demands. This is why the man must overcome his ego. He must be open or accessible to taking directions from his woman. Feminine Inner G is more powerful than masculine Inner G. In order for a man to be stronger and more powerful, he must embrace his feminine principle. This is very difficult to achieve because Black men have been brainwashed into thinking that embracing their feminine principle makes them a "Bitch" or "Punk." That is because they have been miseducated on what the feminine principle really stands for. It represents their spiritual, higher consciousness that masters their physical bodies when they embrace it. Men, embrace your feminine principle in order to be stronger, mentally, physically and spiritually.

Masturbation:

Let us begin with the female act of masturbation. A popular form of masturbation for the Black female is the use of a vibrator or dildo. When a woman introduces a foreign element or object inside her vagina, her mind, body and spirit must adapt and conform to the introduction of this foreign, unnatural invader. Since the body doesn't recognize this artificial material, it must decode the plastic, glass, metal or rubber on a molecular and spiritual level. Her essence adapts and reconfigures its metaphysical aura to accept the inorganic material. The body then conforms to this unnatural state, in order to communicate with it. The woman must now receive unnatural stimulation from the foreign object in order to be satisfied.

The manufacturer of these products may design these products to look similar to a penis, but that's where the similarities end. The penis was made to communicate with the vagina spiritually, physically and on the mental plane. Remember, unseen Inner G, or what we call the spiritual dimension, makes up 95% of what we call reality. The woman does not keep this in mind when she is engaged in this activity. She unknowingly changes her natural energy and aura to accommodate this foreign object in order to have an orgasm. She must communicate with the object that she has introduced inside her most sacred place. This act unwittingly changes her frequency. When a natural object or male penis enters the body of a woman who practices this form of masturbation, the body initially does not recognize it as such. This makes communication with the penis, otherwise known as an orgasm, harder or impossible to achieve without artificial stimulation. In other words, the woman sets herself up for disappointment and frustration because she has changed her aura, or natural energy, to recognize artificial stimulation, and thus, rejects the natural penis, which the Creator has designed for her only.

Now these vibrators also come in all kinds of shapes and sizes, and with many accessories. The more complicated the appliances, the further away the woman's body loses its connection to nature or God. The female body now responds to artificial vibrations, Inner G's and frequencies to make her satisfied. The female body has now adapted herself to absorb, receive and attach herself to artificial stimulation. The Black female will even go as far as to give it a name! The female body now doesn't recognize the physiology and energy of the natural male. So the woman cannot open herself to absorb, embrace and reflect male energy in its natural state.

Women, be conscious of introducing foreign or unnatural objects into your most sacred place. Be aware of the change of frequency or vibration that you are forcing your body to accept. Understand the benefits as well as the consequences of this behavior.

Clitoral Stimulation:

Remember, the female counterpart to the penis is the clitoris. The same rules apply to both sexes in regards to this form of masturbation. The clitoris is highly sensitive to touch because of the high concentration of Melanin and the high number of nerve endings, just like the male penis. Thus, the clitoral orgasm can be more intense than a vaginal orgasm. Just like the penis, the clitoris can become very sore from too much direct contact. Also, the sensitivity of the clitoris can be diminished from too much direct contact, similar to the penis. Of course, this takes away from the pleasures and sensations of sex.

Too much stimulation of the clitoris also de-feminizes the woman. The woman is now partaking in masculine behavior that does not enhance a woman's feminine principle. Remember, the woman in her natural state is closer to God when she is receiving Inner G, as the male in his natural state is closer to God when he is giving out Inner G. So this form of masturbation is mimicking the male act of "jacking off." The male performs this act because he wants to "give out" Inner G or ejaculate because this gives him great satisfaction in his natural state. Too much of this activity keeps the woman out of her natural state of "receiving Inner G" by imitating the male principle of "giving out" Inner G. Too much of this type of masturbation takes away from a woman's feminine principle and embraces her masculine side. As a direct result, it is harder for her to reach climax through the penetration of the vagina in sexual intercourse.

Male Masturbation:

First off, there are different levels or degrees of masturbation for men, as well as for women. While the woman's primary focus, while she masturbates, is on her feelings of wanting to be attached, recognized and appreciated, the man's primary focus is on releasing or giving out his Inner G source. The man does not have to "feel" or be in the mood to masturbate, as the woman does. He basically can masturbate on command. It is not a personal issue but more of a self-expression and exercise of empowerment. So for men, the act of masturbating does not specifically make him satisfied. It is the ejaculation or end result that is achieved; whereas, the woman enjoys the journey as well as the destination. Men just want to get to the destination. If a man is preoccupied with masturbating, this is a sure sign that he has embraced his lower level consciousness. This is a very slippery slope that men can fall victim to. This happens very fast and can consume a man's thoughts, Inner G and actions. A man does not plan for this to happen but he usually finds himself in this position and doesn't realize how he got there. He must refocus his Inner G to climb out of this abyss.

Why Men Cheat:

Primates live in groups of 15 to 150, made up of a few males, many females and their offspring. Let's look further into this concept of cheating to see what we are really talking about. Man and woman are comprised of three components which represent self: the physical realm, the mental realm and the spiritual realm. The physical realm makes up only 10% of all Inner G. This Inner G can be deciphered through our five senses (touch, taste, sight, smell and hearing). We will call this "Seen Inner G." The other 90% of Inner G is deciphered through the mind and the spirit. This realm we will call "Unseen Inner G."

Did you know that a man can have passionate sex with a woman that he just met and come home and love his wife as if nothing happened? The only thing that would bother his conscience is the betrayal of trust, which he broke with his wife. The physical part of the sexual act with the other woman does not affect his psyche. If he had an agreement with his wife to have an "open" relationship, he wouldn't have a guilty conscience. This would actually enhance his relationship with his woman. Let me explain. A man is made to feel guilty for acknowledging and expressing his attraction to other women. This is a natural occurrence and needs to be understood. Males are built to give Inner G, while females are made to receive Inner G. A male is made to feel guilty if he wants to express this natural state when he finds a woman he is attracted to. He is only feeling and acting as nature intended. The part of cheating that makes the man feel guilty is not the actual sexual, act but the betrayal to his wife.

A man has sex to see his own reflection. He wants to witness, first hand, his power, strength, brilliance and divinity, especially the Black man. The Black man is limited in his avenues to express his divinity, in the system of white supremacy. These are the only avenues of expression a Black man is allowed to excel in without restraint or ridicule in the system of white supremacy. The only avenues where he can absolutely, unequivocally, without remorse exhibit his divine, masculine, positive energy. That is why it is hard for men in these professions to retire. It's not just because of the addiction to the limelight, fame and fortune. The root of it is because they get to be masters of their own destinies. By exhibiting their god-given talents and abilities, they are allowed to be their natural selves. They are allowed to be gods. If he is not a sports star, singer, dancer, musician or artist, he is perceived as irrelevant in today's society. The Black man will express his divinity through lower level or animalistic behavior. He will adopt roles such as: pimps, players, gangsters, drug dealers, thugs or hustlers. In every other "legit" occupation, the Black man has to give up too much of his essence and adopt the roles and behavior that his oppressor wants him to play. These "legit" avenues of expression are: doctors, lawyers, policemen, firemen, teachers and CEO's. For him to qualify for these avenues of masculine expression, the Black man needs to be qualified in these limited avenues of masculine expression. The Black man needs to be "domesticated." The definition of being domesticated is to learn behavior in speech, writing, dress and mannerisms.

Coincidently, because these men are allowed to manifest their divine power and energy, white supremacy will not allow them to be men. One may ask, "How can you be a god in one sense and less than a man in another?" Simple, gods just are while men have responsibilities. Gods are brilliant in their natural state. They are divine in their essence. They do not have to work hard at it. Man's purpose is to overcome his lower self to be a god. A man must work, while gods are self-serving. So these Black men, in order for them to be gods, must give up their manhood in return. They are only allowed to display their power, strength, courage and character while they are participating in their occupations. Off the field, court or stage, they are relegated to being less than a man. In other words, they are not allowed to make a significant effort to help their communities. This ideology is displayed in the comic book hero named Superman. He is the mild-mannered Clark Kent, who is a fearful bumbling fool, but once he puts on the suit and cape, he becomes a god! They are simply encouraged to be children. They play with their toys in the form of fast cars, shiny jewelry, wearing costumes and live in cribs. Some are even given an allowance to spend on frivolous things, while other men handle their finances and responsibilities for them. These men's only objective in life is to Play. They play a game designed for children. They play musical instruments. They "act out" in plays on stages. Life for them is one big recess. It is not about growing up. It is not about maturing. It is to simply play until you can't play no more. Then he must take his ball or instrument and go back home to mama.

Women, remember this if you deal with this type of man. Understand what you are getting. He will not change for you or anybody else. He believes that he was born to live like this. He believes this is his life's purpose and everything else in his life is secondary. Understand that he doesn't want to be held accountable for anything else in life, except displaying his god-given talent.

This is why the system of white supremacy props these men up as so-called leaders in the community. Off the court, these men might as well be castrated. Their power is deceiving. They are just props. They are impotent outside of their genre. This is the relationship they have with their owners. This is the world they participate in. They are virtually high-priced slaves. All this takes place without thought or remorse. It is a culture and conspiracy of silent slavery.

Ladies, I know it is hard for you to comprehend the idea that a man can have passionate sex with a stranger and come home and love you as if nothing has transpired. You do not understand because, like the saying goes, "it's a man thang." This is not a cop-out. This is not an excuse. Men are made to give out Inner G, not receive and own it like women do. Every experience of Inner G that a woman encounters or receives stays with her whether she likes it or not. This is why it is inconceivable for women to fathom sleeping with somebody else and not carrying that Inner G home to their mate. Their experience actually becomes a part of their DNA. When her man cheats on her, she can't help but internalize his behavior as disrespecting and hurting her intentionally. She will exclaim to him, "How can you do this to me?" The man's response will be, "But baby, I still love you. She has nothing to do with us." Do you understand the miscommunication? She internalizes the act of sex with another woman as a blatant attempt to hurt her, while he views sex as just an experience outside of their relationship. Ladies, please look at this concept through the eyes of an objective scientist, not through the ego of a woman scorned.

Women, being magnetic and absorbers of all Inner G, know when something is not right with a man. They can sense it in their aura or presence. Women, use your intuition and believe in it more than if you saw it with your own eyes. Acknowledge and understand the signs all around you. Do not make excuses, question or disregard any signs that may show you a reality that you do not want to acknowledge. If you choose to do this, the pain, suffering, neglect and misery you suffer, in the future, will all fall back on you and your conspiracy of silence and ignorance. In other words, you have no one to blame but yourself.

If man does not receive 100 percent of his reflection in his woman, he will seek other avenues to make up for what is missing. His woman may be reflecting 50% of his reflection, so he will be motivated, if he knows it or not, to seek the other 50% outside of his relationship.

Dating Outside Your Race

Because this book is specifically written for the Black man and woman, our focus will be on Black men and women choosing to marry white folks. We have a very unique and peculiar history that must be addressed. Because of this, people outside of the race cannot fully comprehend the complexity of the problem.

Specifically, why do brothers date and choose white women for their wives? Black men marry white women because white girls take the burden of being responsible for their communities off their shoulders. White girls "lick the wounds" of the Black man's traumatized psyche. Understand, the Black man is born with generations of hurt, anger and despair infused in his DNA, because of his slave history. He may not be able to articulate or understand the complexity of the stress, but I guarantee you, he feels it every day. Combine that with a system that has declared war on him and his community, without him even recognizing that he is at war. This produces a male who is angry, but doesn't know where his anger stems from. He is frustrated and confused and doesn't know the root cause. He embraces the lowest of himself and displays deviant behavior and doesn't know why his self- esteem is so low.

The white woman eases the mental anguish of the Black man and also eases her guilt at the same time. By allowing her to do this, the Black man now distances himself from his responsibility to protect and provide for his community. In exchange, he is now excused from his responsibilities as a Black man. A high percentage of Black athletes choose to follow this lifestyle. Remember, they are exceptionally gifted at their chosen profession. They have internalized this feeling of being "exceptional." Because they are the "exception to the rule," they feel they are not obligated to abide by the same rules that "normal" people have to follow. Consequently, they do not feel obligated to uplift their own communities from which they came. This is a very selfish mindset. These men really believe that they are special and shouldn't be held accountable for responsibilities assumed by "lesser" or normal men.

The majority of these men are really good men at heart. They, just like all Black men, have been damaged by images that their oppressor has forced upon them. They are otherwise victims of white supremacy. Not victims like Malcolm X or Huey P. Newton, but victims nonetheless.

Secret Relationship between White Men & Black Women:

Black women also turn to white men for similar reasons. Let's get this straight first. Since the days of slavery, Black women have had a secret, dysfunctional relationship and agreement with white men. In slavery times, the Black woman made an agreement with the white man. Whether it was implied or formally addressed, the agreement stated that if the Black woman raised her son to be docile and complacent, he would not kill him. One hundred and fifty years later, the agreement has evolved. It now states that since your man is now docile and complacent, he is not equipped to protect and provide for you. So if you leave him out of your family equation, I will supply you with a job, housing, health care and food. I will give you everything you need. The Black woman has accepted this agreement, whether she knows it or not. Because she is left alone to fend for herself, she believes that she had no alternative than to make a deal with the devil. I can empathize with her. But truth be known, she now has the career, the house, the education and the car, but is still not happy. She is still lacking the most important aspect of the equation. The one thing she is missing is the one thing that she should have never compromised on: her Black man.

So like the Black male, who runs into the arms of the white woman to escape his tortured past and his inherited responsibilities, the Black woman also runs into the arms of the white man because she wants to be loved, without the added burden of nurturing the Black man back to his right mind. It's like two people who have been in an accident together. They both have severe injuries. Both of them have equally fatal issues. There is no one else around to help them, so they must help each other. Both are ill-equipped to help one another because they are both wounded and in pain. Both cannot put aside their own fatal trauma to help the other. Also, neither one of them is willing to give their lives so that the other may heal. Because of their conditioning, which has lowered their self-esteem over hundreds of years, each partner does not see the worth in saving the other. In both cases, both Black men and women are displaying selfish, ruthless, egotistical behavior. A people will always perish when individuals of that said group put themselves ahead of the greater good of the whole. This is the master plan. This you can never escape. In both cases, they will never find true happiness. You cannot run away or hide from the responsibilities the Creator has bestowed upon you. You will not find happiness or peace. Just ask the brothers who are not taking care of their children. He is suffering even when you don't see his pain. He must do right by them or live a lifetime of unfulfillment. You must correct that which is unbalanced. You cannot run from yourself.

There are other types of Black men and women who come from different backgrounds. They may be of mixed heritages or lived in all-white communities. Because of their circumstances, they have attached themselves and their definitions of who they are according to the popular white culture, which bombards us on a daily basis. They do not relate to Black folks in general, because they have internalized "white" culture as their own. We have all witnessed brothers and sisters who are better representatives of white men and women than white folks themselves. In an act of survival, they have adopted white culture and behaviors in order to function in white society. This is all they have known as their reality. Again, this is another tragic result of white supremacy. It is equivalent to kidnapping a lion cub, taken from the wild, and throwing him into a family of monkeys to be raised. The lion will adopt and internalize the ways of the monkey. He will embrace the culture and lifestyle of the monkey and have no true knowledge of who he really is. This is what has been done to Black people for hundreds of years. This is the result of being raised in captivity.

Daddy's Little Girl:

Much attention and studies have been placed on the issues of sons being raised without their fathers. What about the daughter who did not have the father in her house? These girls grow up to be women, just as the boys grow up to be men. Both still carry issues stemming from their childhoods. The father, being the first relationship a girl has with a man, is never acknowledged or experienced. So the woman grows up not knowing how a man is supposed to treat her and how she is supposed to submit to his Inner G to fully appreciate the relationship. These women now have an ideology or preconceived view of how a man should treat them. Their definition usually comes up short because they think that they can "plug him in" to their reality as a missing piece of their puzzle. This does not work and they wind up frustrated, bitter and alone. Ladies, be willing to let go of the fear that you carry that you think is protecting the lil' girl in you. It is an illusion, for it is actually inhibiting your growth, power and happiness. Your power lies within the little girl in you. It is in her innocence, femininity, unconditional love, courage and trust that give you your power. Let a man see that part in you that is void of the hurt, pain and anger you carry to protect her. You will be surprised at her ability to discriminate good men from bad men. Hold her hand, for she will lead you to where you want to go. Set her free, for she does not need your protection. In fact, she is waiting to protect you, if you just let her. Give her a chance to find the love she never had. She knows what to look for, more than you.

Anal Sex:

The word "Orifice" comes from a Latin word meaning mouth. The anus is one of the body's orifices, or mouths. All orifices possess both masculine Inner G and feminine Inner G. The body orifices are the mouth, ears, nose, urethra, vagina in the female and the anus. That means that all orifices can receive Inner G, as well as give out Inner G. Inserting an object in any of these orifices triggers a feminine type of Inner G sensation. I have seen people clean their ears with a Q-Tip, rub their eyes and even pick their nose, and look like they were pleasuring themselves in a sexual nature. Some orifices are made to gravitate more towards feminine (receiving) Inner G or masculine (giving out) Inner G. The anus is no exception. Understand that embracing the feminine or masculine Inner G of any orifice will affect the overall balance of Inner G of the total body. As a man, I choose to embrace my masculine Inner G as the foundation of who I define myself as a male. Women embrace their feminine Inner G as their foundation that defines themselves as a female. Understand the balance of both Inner G's in the body when one chooses to participate in anal sex. In nature, men were made to give out Inner G and women were made to receive Inner G. But whether a man or woman, we both have the capacity to embrace either Inner G as it pertains to our body's orifices. Just be consciousness of the imbalance in the body that will occur, if one participates and embraces an Inner G that goes against their natural foundation.

Orgies & Ménage a Trois:

Let us break down the synergy of what is happening during group sex. Remember, there is a delicate balance of masculine and feminine Inner G that holds the universe together. Masculine Inner G has the capacity to hold and satisfy several entities that house feminine Inner G. Feminine Inner G, in its natural state, can only reflect a single masculine Inner G at one time. It is both of these scenarios that keep the world going round and around. If there is an imbalance of masculine and feminine Inner G, the result is a dysfunctional display or form of sexual Inner G. Let's take a look at the sexual act of Ménage a Trois: one man vs. two women. This equation expresses sex in its natural state. One man can satisfy two women in a sense that one proton, which represents masculine Inner G, can sustain two electrons, which represent feminine Inner G at the same time. It is the display of this Inner G that duplicates nature on an atomic level. The only problem is picking a man who has enough Inner G to sustain the two women. If the man is not strong enough, the two women, like the electrons, will avert their attention elsewhere. This type of sexual act will promote higher consciousness or behavior. Feelings that will be supported in this sexual act would be nurturing, sharing, encouragement, selflessness and unity.

We will now visit the other Ménage a Trois: one woman vs. two men. This sexual relationship goes against the natural order of things in the universe, in relation to sexual Inner G. The two males, which represent masculine Inner G, will now compete with each other for the attention of the female, who represents feminine Inner G. Competition is a byproduct of lower level consciousness. This type of Inner G will permeate this sexual expression. The sex will go against nature; thus, the act will promote the worst in all the participants engaged in the act. It will enhance feelings of greed, fear, jealousy, hate and ego in the participants that engage in this sexual act.

The sexual act of orgies is just a wider example of the synergy of the ménage a trois. All orgies are really many ménage a trios' happening at the same time, in close proximity to one another, when one breaks them down. If you choose to participate in these sexual encounters, whether you are a male or female, be very aware of the ratio of men to women in your vicinity. Remember, when the women outnumber the men, you are promoting sex in its natural state in the cosmos. This synergy will promote higher consciousness and behavior when explored in higher consciousness. But, if the men outnumber the women, be aware of the promotion and nurturing of lower level behavior, thoughts, and consciousness. Choose wisely on what Inner G you want to expose yourself to and the byproduct of the Inner G that you will internalize by participating in such practices.

Sexual Positions:

I have included this chart of sexual positions to reawaken that part of your brain that has been dormant and underutilized. The best rituals, positions, ideas and concepts are the ones that a couple comes up with on their own. I want to leave that part up to your own imagination and interpretation. I will include keys to direct your Inner G, but where you go and what you experience, I will leave up to you.

The left side of your body houses your feminine, spiritual and negative side. It is open to higher consciousness as well as being more equipped to receive Inner G. Be conscious of these attributes when engaged in sex. The right side of your body houses your masculine, physical, positive side. It is made to give out Inner G and experience Inner G on a physical basis. Be conscious of the attributes of this side of your body during sex. Learn how to manipulate, enhance or suppress certain Inner G's by the different positions that one engages in during sex. Know that the woman is magnetic in nature, as well as recognize a man's electrical tendencies.

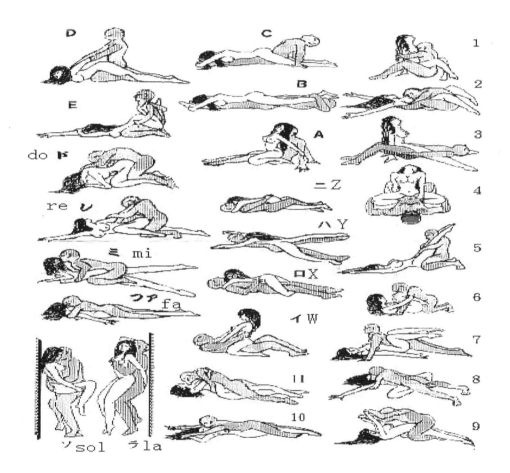

Sexual Positions Study Guide — EBook Download

0 comments 8:07 AM Posted by pralinson EBook | PDF | 171 pages | English | 1.12MB

All parts of one's body correspond directly to the whole body. For instance, reflexology shows a direct correlation between a person's feet, hands and ears with organs and other parts of the body as a whole. For example, a person's left pinkie toe is connected to their sinuses. Or one's right index finger is connected to their mouth. Also, the middle part of your earlobe is connected to one's eyes. I suggest you obtain these reflexology charts, study them and do your own research. The body is an amazing organism by itself, but once you add the other half of God into the equation, heaven awaits!

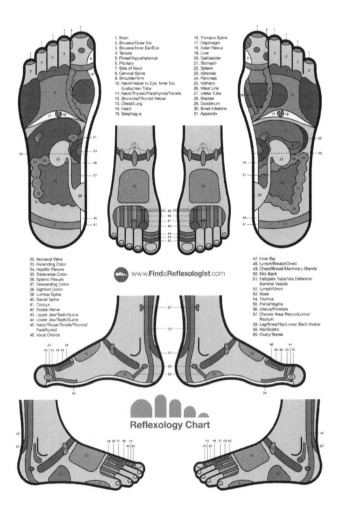

Reflexology Chart

Remember, there are no right and wrong ways to experience sex. Do not limit yourself by sex guides or how-to books that can become methodical and robotic. Go with the flow. Open yourself up to the Inner G you create and trust it with all your heart. Have no preconceived notions or limitations to the experiences that one can obtain. When engaged in sex, always put your partner's feelings and pleasure ahead of your own. I can guarantee the Inner G you put out will be reciprocated. If it is not, think about changing to partners who are on the same conscious, Inner G level as you. Remember sisters in your dealings with men. A woman cannot raise a man's sexual consciousness up to her level. She can only rise and function according to the lower level he is on. Only a man can raise a woman's sexual consciousness to the higher level from which he resides.

Sexual Positions: Kemetic Practices & the Manipulation of Sexual Inner G.

In Kemet, all sexual positions have to do with unlocking a specific sexual Inner G that was used for a specific condition or reason. Sex is the single Universal Inner G that permeates all life forces. Once one understands how to use this Inner G, they have unlocked the key to life as we know it. Listed below are deliberate reasons our ancestor locked when they engaged in sexual intercourse:

- *Making the connection & bringing sexual healing to one's physical body through the spirit world.*
- *Overcoming psychological trauma & fears.*
- *Being able to control the lower self instead of it controlling you.*
- *Connecting the heart to the thought process while connecting the brain to feelings. Think with your heart and feel with your mind.*
- *Being able to have an orgasm without ejaculating. This promotes health, vision & higher consciousness.*
- *Transforming sexual energy to be used to heal the entire body.*

- *Using sex as the "gateway" to connect with the Divine.*
- *The merging of the feminine principle with the masculine principle to become the One, together.*
- *To be able to manifest the spiritual body through mastery and control of the physical body.*
- *To achieve "God consciousness," and experience a glimpse of Heaven here on Earth.*
- *To procreate and give birth to God representatives here on Earth.*

Talk to your partner before you engage in sex. Ask them what is going on in their lives at this particular time. Ask them what you can do for them. Ask them what they require from you at this particular time. Be honest with each other and yourselves. If you just want to have lower vibration sex to enjoy, express and explore the human condition, then be honest with your mate. If you want to escape your physical reality and your current state of mind, then let that be known to your partner. Focus on each other's needs before, during and after sex, and in return, you will also be satisfied. Sex should have focus. Sex should have purpose. Sex should have intent.

Epilogue

As I approach the feeling of inevitability that every man experiences during sex right before he ejaculates, I enter the threshold between space and time, inside of time and space. My queen, Nekhebet, is waiting for me on the other side of the "Gateway." Without acknowledging me, she firmly grasps my left hand and whisks me away into the triple-black ethers of the unseen or spiritual realm. I find myself inside of a dark and damp, bottomless pit. I can barely make out the light that is hardly visible over my head. It seems miles away from my present condition. It is very cold, wet and muddy in my dark, isolated confinement. I realize that I have been transformed into one of the lowest creatures known on Earth. I am a worm. My colors are red and orange with yellow spots all over my body. My slimy body slowly creeps in and out of the moist soil. My only shelter from the Sun is dead leaves and discarded debris that has been left to decay and wither away. My journey to the top of the bottomless pit seems like it will take me a lifetime to complete.

As I finally wiggle my way out of this deep, dark hole in the ground, I find myself thoroughly exhausted, as I finally reach the top. All I want to do is rest and take a well-deserved nap, for my journey demanded every ounce of Inner G that I could muster.

What seems like a moment in time, I wake up from my slumber and realize that I have over slept, but for how long I do not know. I see Nekhebet towering over me. She tells me that I have been asleep for thirteen days. She grabs my left hand again and takes me to a tall cliff that sits among the clouds. Without warning, she jumps head-first off the towering cliff, while locking my hand in hers, eliminating all means for my escape from this suicidal plunge. Suddenly, she releases my hand in midair as we both free fall. I feel my heart jump immediately in my throat, as I choke on the rushing air that suffocates me. I am petrified by the fear of plunging to my death. Nekhebet tells me to focus on the reflecting pool of water that is rushing towards us from below. In the water's reflective surface, I can see my new image. While I was in hibernation as a worm, she had transformed me into a beautiful butterfly with turquoise, indigo and purple wings! I proceed to flap my newly discovered wings and soar towards the Sun in the far distance.

I see a crystal clear, pristine lake below me. It beckons me to partake of its sweet waters to quench my thirst. I land by its shores and get a glimpse of a colony of ants on my right side. I am able to see inside the deepest regions of the colony that lies beneath the ground. Through what seems to be miles and miles of underground tunnels, my journey finally ends up in the queen's chamber. She has thousands of ants serving her at her beck and call. She has wings from which I identified her as the royal queen. She uses her wings in order to create an environment that will oppress her colony in a lifetime of servitude. These wings have given her higher knowledge that the normal ants are not privy to because they lack the perspective to see life from above. The worker ants can only see and interpret life from the ground up, just like when I was a worm in the bottomless pit. These wings have given her perspective and consciousness that regular ants, which are stuck on the ground, have no way of knowing or understanding. With these wings, the queen can instantly see for miles in the distance. This same distance would take a worker ant a lifetime to discover. She does not share her knowledge with her colony, but uses it to keep them in perpetual servitude to her empire.

My tunnel vision pulls out from the queen's chamber. It reverses back out of the underground colony through the miles of tunnels, finally retreating to the opening to the world above ground. As I take off in flight to assume my journey to the Sun, I see a trail of ants that seem to be a mile long underneath me. On the right side of the trail, the ants were traveling away from the colony in search of food. Their mouths were empty. On the left side of the trail, the ants were returning to the colony, carrying food in their mouths to be stored for the queen and the system she created. The ants always stayed in formation and never dared to get out of the formation that they were conditioned to instinctively follow without thought. Far off in the distance, I see a single ant that was far away from the ant trail and the colony. He seems like he is lost and maybe injured. I wondered if he was kicked out of the colony or left on his own accord. I also wondered if he was worried about finding food, shelter and safety, since he left the comforts of the colony. There was something very peculiar about that single ant. Even though all the ants from the colony looked at him with disdain and pity, he seemed to have a smile on his face and self-assurance that he was better off making his own way, out of the confines of the colony. My vision fades with each flap of my wings as I ascend, and I observe the solitary ant crawling into a left-footed boot, far away from the colony. It is in this boot that he now calls his home.

I continue to set my flight plans on the Sun and let the four winds guide me to my final destination. As I fly over a grassy hill, I see a metropolis far off in the horizon. As I make my way closer to the city, I see the highways leading out of the city in a very familiar pattern. I come to realize that the same ant trail that I had observed when I flew over the ant colony resembles the human highways I see going in and out of the city. They are either going to the city to work for their bosses or leaving to go home after work.

I continue to fly to the highest skyscraper in the middle of downtown. I believe this is where I will find the ruler of the people, just like the queen ant had the biggest chamber in her colony. As I reach the top floor, I see a person through the window of the biggest office. I can't help but compare this most powerful and influential man to the queen ant back at the ant colony. I wonder if he possesses the same privileged knowledge as the queen ant. I wonder if he also uses this knowledge to keep his workers on the floors beneath them, enslaved and under his control as well. As I fly back down the side of the building, I peak through the windows of the skyscraper. It also looks just like the interior of the ant colony, only instead of going below ground it is built straight up in the sky above ground. All the workers are busy doing their specific jobs and they are all oblivious to the world around them. Just like the ants, they work when their boss tells them to work. They eat when their boss tells them to eat and they come and go whenever the boss instructs them to do so.

As I fly away from the building and the highways, away from the city, I see in the distance a man who does not live in the confines of the metropolis, just like the solitary ant I had witnessed. He is not worried about his shelter or where his next meal is coming from. People seem to shun, pity, and despise him when they walk by him. He does not participate in the activities of the people in the skyscraper. It actually seems like this man feels sorry for the people in the skyscraper and highways. He has the same sly smile on his face that I saw on the ant that did not participate in the ant colony. I also notice the shoes this man is wearing. He is only wearing a boot on his right foot. Just then, I realize his missing left boot is the same boot that the solitary ant uses to make his new home many miles away from his ant colony.

In an instant, Nekhebet swoops down from the cosmos and grabs my right hand. I instinctively know that it is time for me to return to the seen world. I awake on top of a beautiful Black woman, who had trusted me enough to give me access to her gateway to the unseen realm. My body is covered with a slight mist of perspiration that feels cool with each gentle movement from the inhaling and exhaling of our lungs. I wonder how long I have been unconscious as I look for signs around me that may give me a clue to this mystery. The woman on top of me awakes just after I come to. It seems like she had to wait for my return in order to claim her consciousness. She also has no idea how much time has passed since my departure. It feels like I have been awakened from a deep hibernation or slumber. It takes a minute for me to catch my bearings just as a newborn baby has to learn how to manipulate his newly acquired body. I am filled with answers to questions that I have not yet asked. I promise myself to remember everything Nekhebet has shown me and one day share this information with people who are searching for answers for the questions they cannot seem to pose. That time has finally come for me. She has given me this knowledge and understanding to usher in the new age of Black Power. Let the Black Sexual Revolution begin! I hope you have enjoyed this book as much as I have had the pleasure of acquiring its knowledge from within the infinite depths of the sacred Black woman, otherwise known as, the "Gateway." Travel well and far. One love, T.C.

Notes

CHAPTER ONE: LOSE YOUR MIND TO FIND THE TRUTH

1. Website: http://www.quotationspage.com/quote/26032.html Albert Einstein Attributed to German born physicist (1879-1955)
2. William Shakespeare, "Julius Caesar." Act 2: Scene 2.
3. Website: http://www.thefreedictionary.com /Conscience
4. Website: http://thinkexist.com/quotes. Harriet Tubman American escaped slave, Civil War Soldier and Abolitionist, 1820-1913
5. The Holy Bible King James Version: (Thomas Nelson Publishers, 1982), Hosea 1 —6. Pg. 1291

CHAPTER TWO: RETURN TO YOUR PAST IN ORDER TO MOVE FORWARD:

1. Count C.F. Volney, *"The Law of Nature."* (New York, Twentieth Century Pub. 1890) pg. 3
2. James C. Prichard's, *"The Natural History of Man."* London: Hippolyte Balliere, 1845.
3. **Oyibo, Gabriel A.** Grand unified theorem representing the unified field theory or the theory of everything. Int. J. Math. Game Theory Algebra **9** Online at http://www.geocities.com/igala1/new_page_6.htm
4. Gerald Massey, *"Egypt, Light of the World."* (London 1907) Pg. 251
5. www.elevatedloc.com/.../Sphinx.jpg (picture.)

6.   http://www.rainbowcrystal.com/egypt/E-86maat.jpg(picture)

7.   http://forum.prisonplanet.com/index.php?topic=184101.80 photo of scales of Maat.

8.   http://www.nubeing.com/unblind2/42.htm 42 Principles of Maat.

CHAPTER THREE: THE BIBLE: THE BLUEPRINT OF UNIVERSAL LAW & HIGHER CONSCIOUSNESS:

1.   Dr. Phil Valentine, *"The Metaphysics of the Bible."* DVD. Date unknown.

2.   Dean Dudley, *"History of the Council of Nice."* A & B Dist Inc. (July 1992.)

3.   http://www.daghettotymz.com/current/herujesus/heruvsjesus.htm. Chart Jesus vs. Heru.

4.   http://www.thefreedictionary.com/symbol

5.   http://www.thefreedictionary.com/convention

6.   http://carm.org/what-biblical-numerology

CHAPTER FOUR: THE KHEMISTERY OF MELANIN

1.   Frances Cress Welsing, *"The Isis Papers."* C W Publishing (Dec. 2004).

2.   Sun Tsu, *"The Art of War."* Shambhala 1st. Edition (Oct 26 1988.)

3.   http://www.citizendia.org/Ancient_Egyptian_burial_customs. Photo of Anpu.

4.   http://www.crystalinks.com/egyptafterlife.html. Photo of Book of the Dead.

CHAPTER FIVE: WAS BLIND BUT NOW I SEE

1. Photo : *http://humanityhealing.net/2010/09/pineal-gland-the-transcendental-gateway/*

2. Photo :*http://humanityhealing.net/2010/09/pineal-gland-the-transcendental-gateway*

3. McMullen, T., 1979, **Philosophy of science and the pineal gland**, *Philosophy* 54, pp. 380-384.

4. Website: *http://divinecosmos.com/index.php/videos/access-your-higher-self*

5. Image*: http://www.tldm.org/news4/markofthebeast.htm*

6. Image of Goliath*:*
   http://www.virtualchurch.org/vchurch/gallery/vcgoliat.gif

7. Image of David:
   http://www.virtualchurch.org/vchurch/gallery/david.gif

8. Image of Christmas Tree*: http://siobhanwilcox.wordpress.com/*

9. Image of Pope:
   http://www.flickr.com/photos/31451773@N04/3118007704/in/photostream/

10. Image of Stanford University mascot
    http://www.thesportsbank.net/college-bball/99-in-99-84-stanford-cardinal/

11. Image of Marduk *http://www.secrets-of-longevity-in-humans.com/pine-pollen-powder.html*

12. Image of Pine Cone
    http://www.hiddenmeanings.com/singleeyepineal.htm

13. Image of Angel & Devil
    http://www.thousandtyone.com/blog/TheWarTheAngelTheDevilAndTheProgrammer.aspx

14. Image of Dionysus

    http://www.flickr.com/photos/31451773@N04/3117181353/lightbox/

15. Kerast definition *By zorroz — Posted on March 9th, 2008 Home :: Zorroz's Blog http://memes.org*

16. *By zorroz — Posted on March 9th, 2008 Home :: Zorroz's Blog http://memes.org*

CHAPTER SIX: MAN VS. MANKIND

1. Napoleon quote

   http://www.brainyquote.com/quotes/quotes/n/napoleonbo161968.html

2. *By Dirk Van Tuerenhout, Houston Museum of Natural Science, AP file*

3. Definition of Man :*http://www.merriam-webster.com/dictionary/man*

4. Churchill quote*: http://www.quotedb.com/quotes/1772*

5. Taj Tarik Bey: **DVD** *"The Metaphysics of Astrology."* **date unknown.**

6. Definition of Mankind:

7. Earth is 12,000 years old:

8. Definition of Adam:

9. Commom ancestors —*Natl Geographic, From Lucy to Language by Donald Johanson & Blake Edgar.*

10. Illustration: — *J. Pritchard Univ. of Chicago see illustration.*

11. Neil Armstrong quote: *http://history.nasa.gov/alsj/a11/a11.step.html*

12. JFK quote: *http://quoteworld.org/quotes/7623*

13. *"In the name of Elijah Muhammad: Louis Farrakhan and the Nation of Islam."* Duke University Press 1996. Author: Mattias Gardell; page 59.

14. *"The Isis (Yssis) Papers: the keys to the colors."* Frances Cress Welsing. Third World Press 1991.

15. Definition of Jacob: —- *http://www.christian-resources-today.com/bible-study-online-14a.html*

16. Definition of Esau: —- *http://www.christian-resources-today.com/bible-study-online-14a.html*

17. Definition of Psychopath: —*"Without Conscience."* Dr. Robert D. Hare. The Guilford Press; 1 edition (January 8, 1999)

CHAPTER SEVEN: SEEN & UNSEEN SEXUAL INNER G.

1. Freemason symbol: *http://masoniccenter.blogspot.com/*

2. Galileo quote: *Opere Il Saggiatore p. 171."* Great Italian astronomer, mathematician, & physicist.

3. Geometry definition: *http://www.answers.com/topic/geometry*

4. *http://www.answers.com/topic/gnostic*

5. Wavelength image: *http://cnx.org/content/m11118/latest/*

6. King Tut image: *http://mstecker.com/pages/egyptnn_fp.htm*

7. Shiva image: *http://www.flickr.com/photos/arjuna/206975273/*

8. Snake track image: *http://www.jockeysridgestatepark.com/images/animals/lg/s-snaketrack.jpg*

9. *The frequency information was taken from Taini Technologies http://www.heavenscentoils.net/frequency_of_essential_oils.htm]*

10. Battery image: *http://cnx.org/content/m20196/latest/*

11. Solution define: *http://dictionary.reference.com*

12. The Kybalion: *http://en.wikipedia.org/wiki/Kybalion*

13. Davinci image: *http://brandnewwoo.blogspot.com/2010/01/olympics-2010-free-admission-to.html*

14. Law of Reflection: *http://strongphysics.wikispaces.com/ch29_esjp*

15. Atomic Shells image: *http://www.tulane.edu/~sanelson/eens211/crystal_chemistry.htm*

16. Valence definition:

CHAPTER EIGHT: THE BIGGEST SEXUAL ORGAN IS BETWEEN YOUR EARS NOT YOUR LEGS

1. Brain: http*://www.bibleufo.com/humanbody.htm*

2. *http://www.testcafe.com/lbrb/*

3. President Obama image:
   http://www.guardian.co.uk/world/oliverburkemanblog/2009/jan/20/obama-inauguration-barackobama

4. Baphomet image: **http***://sspx.agenda.tripod.com/id84.html*

5. Right definition*: http://www.merriam-webster.com/dictionary/right*

6. DVD Dr. Jewel Pookrum. *"Seven Circuits of the Brain."* Date: unknown

7. Brain image:
   http://www.daviddarling.info/encyclopedia/P/pineal_gland.html

8. Crucifixion image:
   http://www.wpclipart.com/religion_mythology/new_testament/illustrations_1/crucifixion_of_Jesus_Christ.png.html

9. Jekyll and Hyde image:
   http://aldersgatecycle.wordpress.com/tag/steampunk-culture/

10. Circle of Willis:
    Uston C. Dr. Thomas Willis' famous eponym: the circle of Willis. J Hist Neurosc i. 2005 Mar; 14(1):16–21

11. Circle of Willis:
    http://www.wikidoc.org/index.php/Circle_of_Willis

12. Pavlov's Dog: *http://en.wikipedia.org/wiki/Ivan_Pavlov*

CHAPTER NINE: AS ABOVE, SO BELOW

1. Nut and Geb image: ***http://www.cesras.org/Szen/NutGebSchu.html***
2. Astrology Wheel image:
   http://www.readersandrootworkers.org/index.php?title=Category:Astrology
3. Astrology image: ***http://www.hps.cam.ac.uk/starry/astrology.html***

CHAPTER TEN: CHAKRAS: LEVELS OF SEXUAL CONSCIOUSNESS

1. Caduceus image: ***http://www.energyenhancement.org/Prices.htm***
2. Chakra image:
   http://www.energyenhancement.org/meditation_energy_enhancement_br1.htm

CHAPTER ELEVEN: SCIENCE OF THE HEART

1. Baby image: ***www.superstock.com***
2. Murmur define: **www.thefreedictionary.com/murmur**
3. "The Prophet." Author: Kahlil Gibran
   Pages: 128
   Publisher: Knopf (September 12, 1923)

CHAPTER TWELVE: THE ORGASM: THE GATEWAY TO HEAVEN

1. Crystallized water: ***"Apa: Water the Great Mystery."*** Documentary. Date unknown.
2. Sephedet image:
   http://www.stainedglassmagic.com/sun_catchers_star_david.html
3. Pyramid image: ***http://famouswonders.com/great-pyramids-of-giza/***
4. Tetrahedron image: ***http://starseeds.net/forum/topics/star-tetrahedron-and-other***

5. Pythagoras theory:

   http://hiddenlighthouse.wordpress.com/category/pythagoreanism/

6. Star Tetrahedron: .—**http://www.***Academy of Sacred Geometry.com*

7. Missionary definition: *www.thefreedictionary.com/missionary*

8. Geb and Tefnut image: *http://4brightminds.info/creation.htm*

9. Hindu gods image:

   http://www.flickr.com/photos/alicepopkorn/4779303699/

10. Bruce Lee quote:

    http://www.completemartialarts.com/information/styles/chinese/jeet kunedo.htm

11. Lilith: The Bible of ben-Sira:

    http://www.lilithgallery.com/library/lilith/The-Bible-of-ben-Sira.html

12. Clitoris definition: *dictionary.reference.com/browse/clitoris*

13. Atom definition: *http://hubpages.com/hub/vacuumofspace*

14. X Chromosome image: *http://www.istockphoto.com/stock-photo-985366-xx-red-female-chromosomes.php*

15. Gateway image: unknown

16. Memory definition:

    http://hiddenlighthouse.wordpress.com/2010/05/23/star-tetrahedron-the-star-of-david/

17. Genomics definition: *http://en.wikipedia.org/wiki/Omega*

18. Ankh image: *http://urikalish.blogspot.com/*

19. Omega and alpha image:

    http://christopherjharris.blogspot.com/2010/11/christian-symbols-part-2.html

20. Ohm's Law: *Robert A. Millikan and E. S. Bishop (1917). Elements of Electricity.* American Technical Society. p. 54.

21. Current,Voltage, Resistance and Power: Consoliver, Earl L., and Mitchell, Grover I. (1920). ***Automotive ignition systems***. McGraw-Hill. p. 4.

22. Ohm's Law: **http://www.the12volt.com/ohm/ohmslaw.asp**

CHAPTER THIRTEEN: THE FINAL SOLUTION

1. Willie Lynch Letter: ***Author: N/A***
    ISBN: 0948390530
    Binding: Paperback
    Pages: 30
    Publisher: Lushena Books, Inc.

2. Kemetic trinity:
    http://www.daghettotymz.com/current/rasjew/rasjew.html

3. Ausar resurrecton image:
    http://itsanoptionok.blogspot.com/2010/01/in-ies-and-out-ies.html

4. Ausar Metu Neter image:
    http://www.mesacc.edu/~tomshoemaker/spring11/rel291/images/Min_Egypt.jpg

5. Washington Monument image:
    http://www.trekearth.com/gallery/North_America/United_States/South/District_of_Columbia/Washington_DC/photo638063.htm

BLACK LOVE TOPICS & ISSUES

1. Oxytocin:
    http://answers.yahoo.com/question/index?qid=20100430102929AAaWVPp Lee HJ, Macbeth